AF469251

Peter Heard's

PAINTINGS OF A WEST COUNTRY LIFE

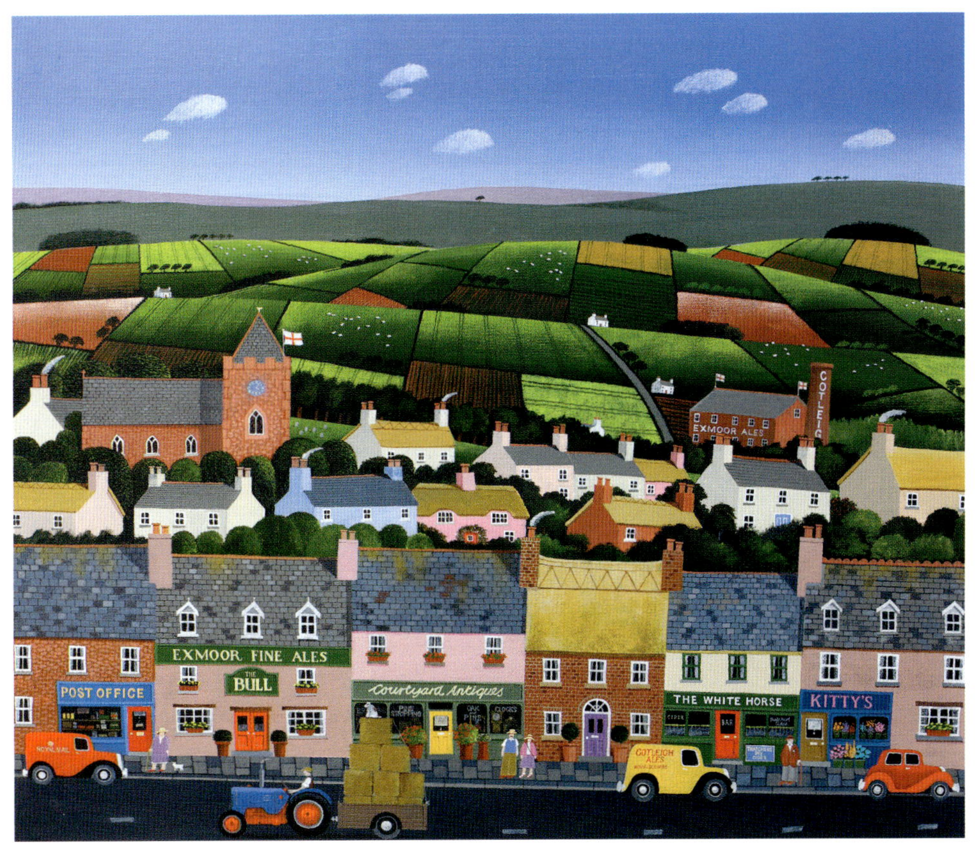

Words by Michael Woods

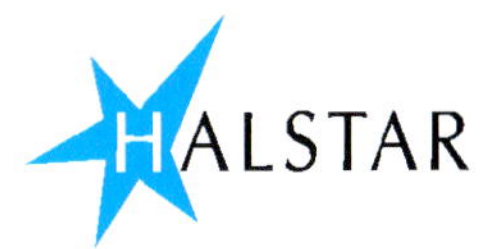

First published in Great Britain in 2012

British Library Cataloguing-in-Publication Data
A CIP record for this title is available from the British Library

ISBN 978 1 906690 37 3

HALSTAR
Halsgrove House,
Ryelands Business Park,
Bagley Road, Wellington, Somerset TA21 9PZ
Tel: 01823 653777 Fax: 01823 216796
email: sales@halsgrove.com

Part of the Halsgrove group of companies
Information on all Halsgrove titles is available at: www.halsgrove.com

Printed in China by Everbest Printing Co Ltd

For Mary who took me West...

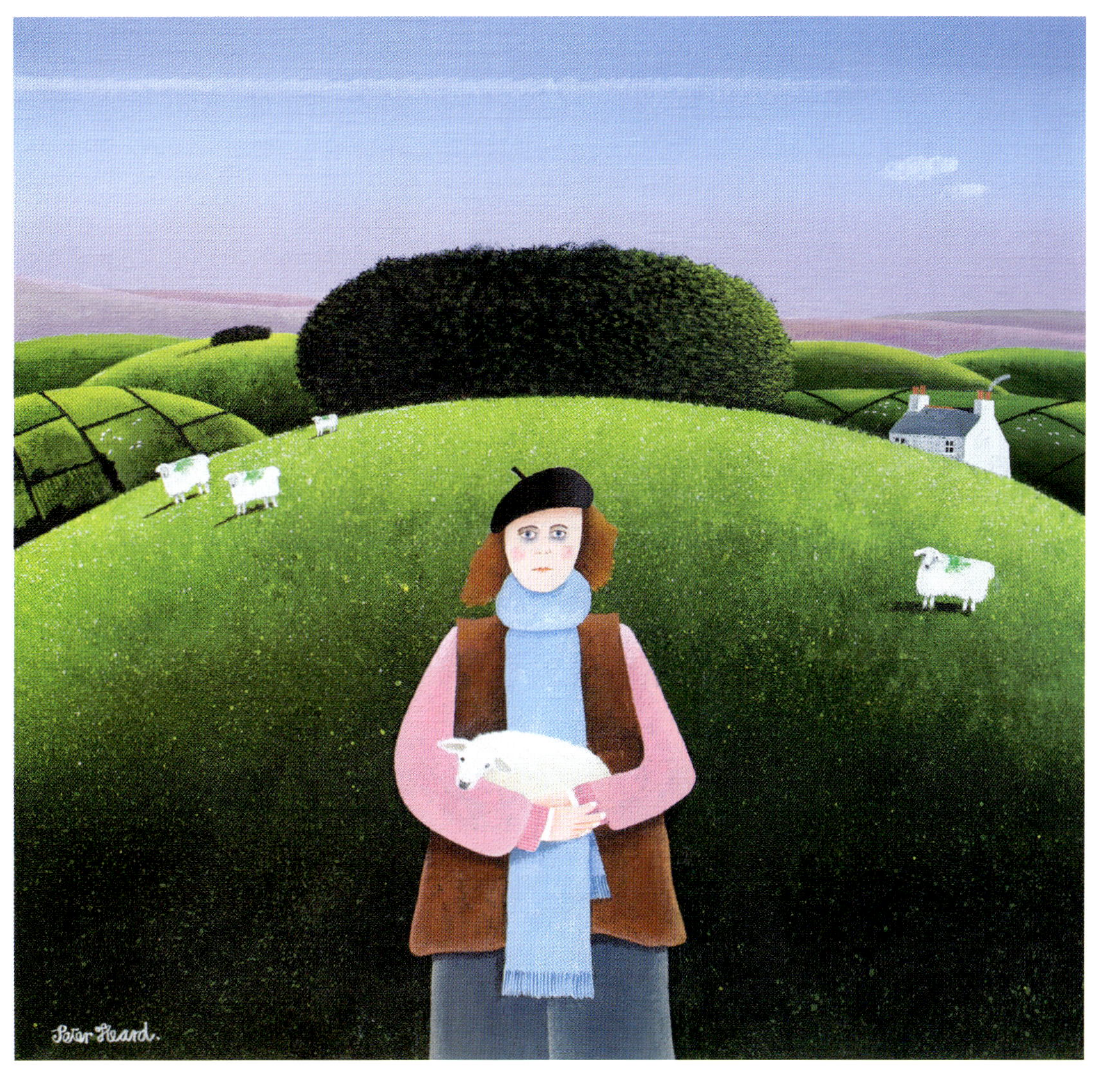

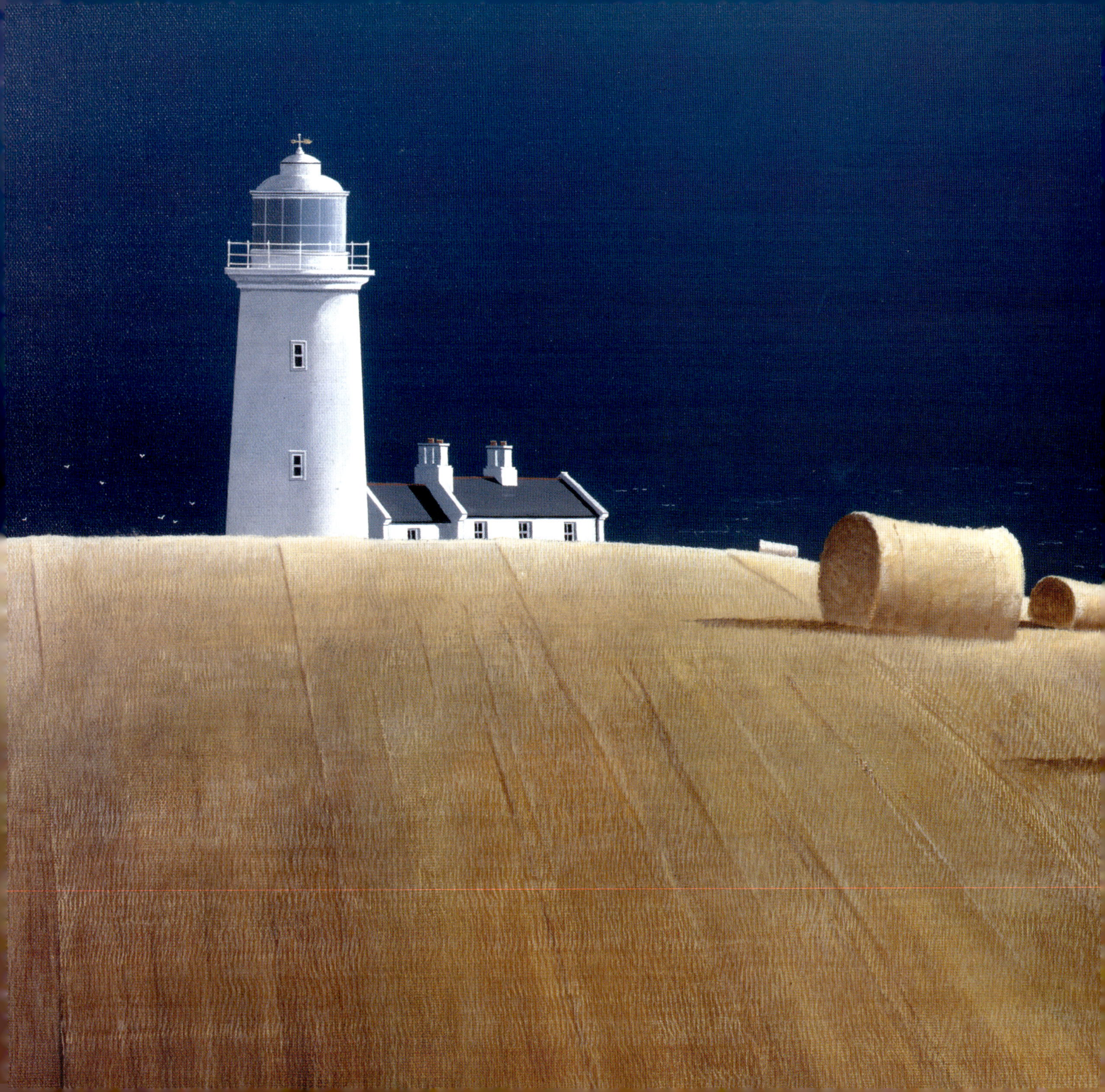

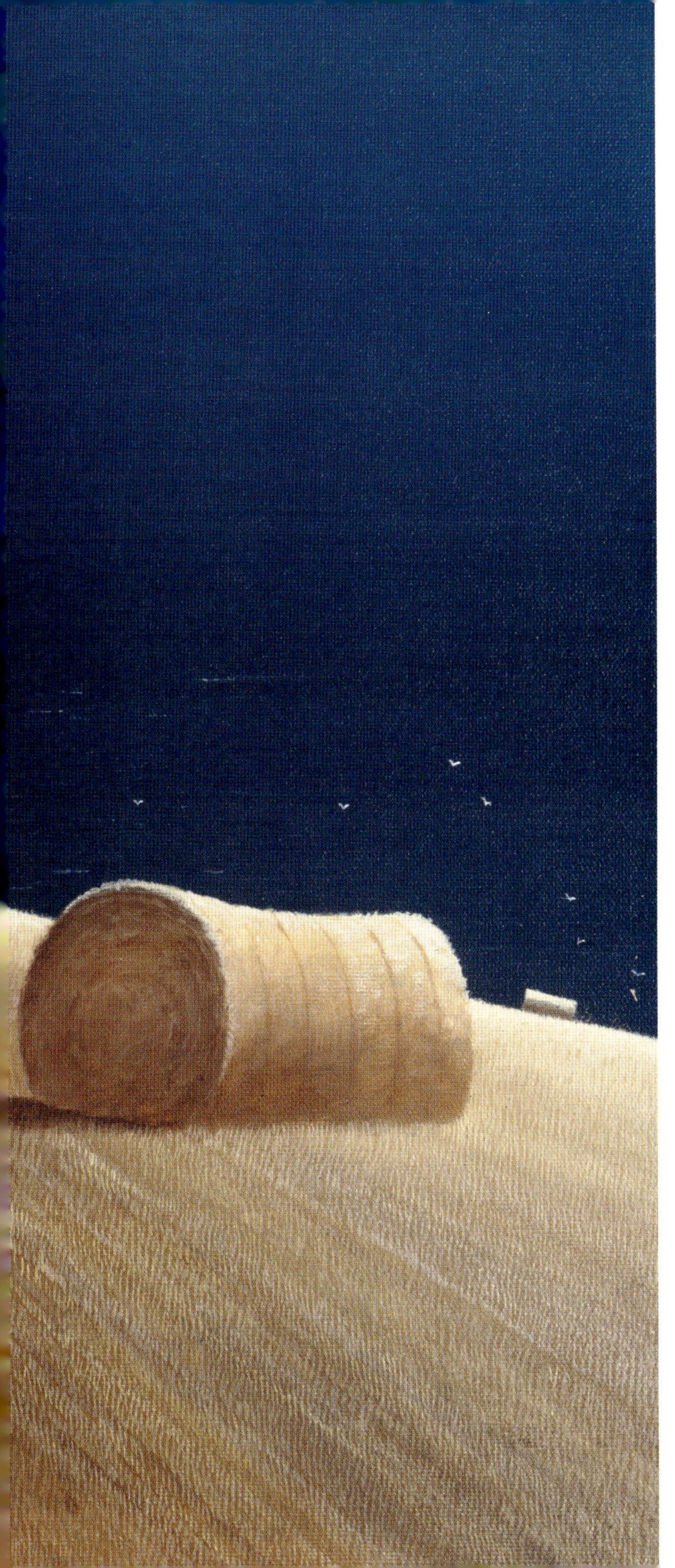

Contents

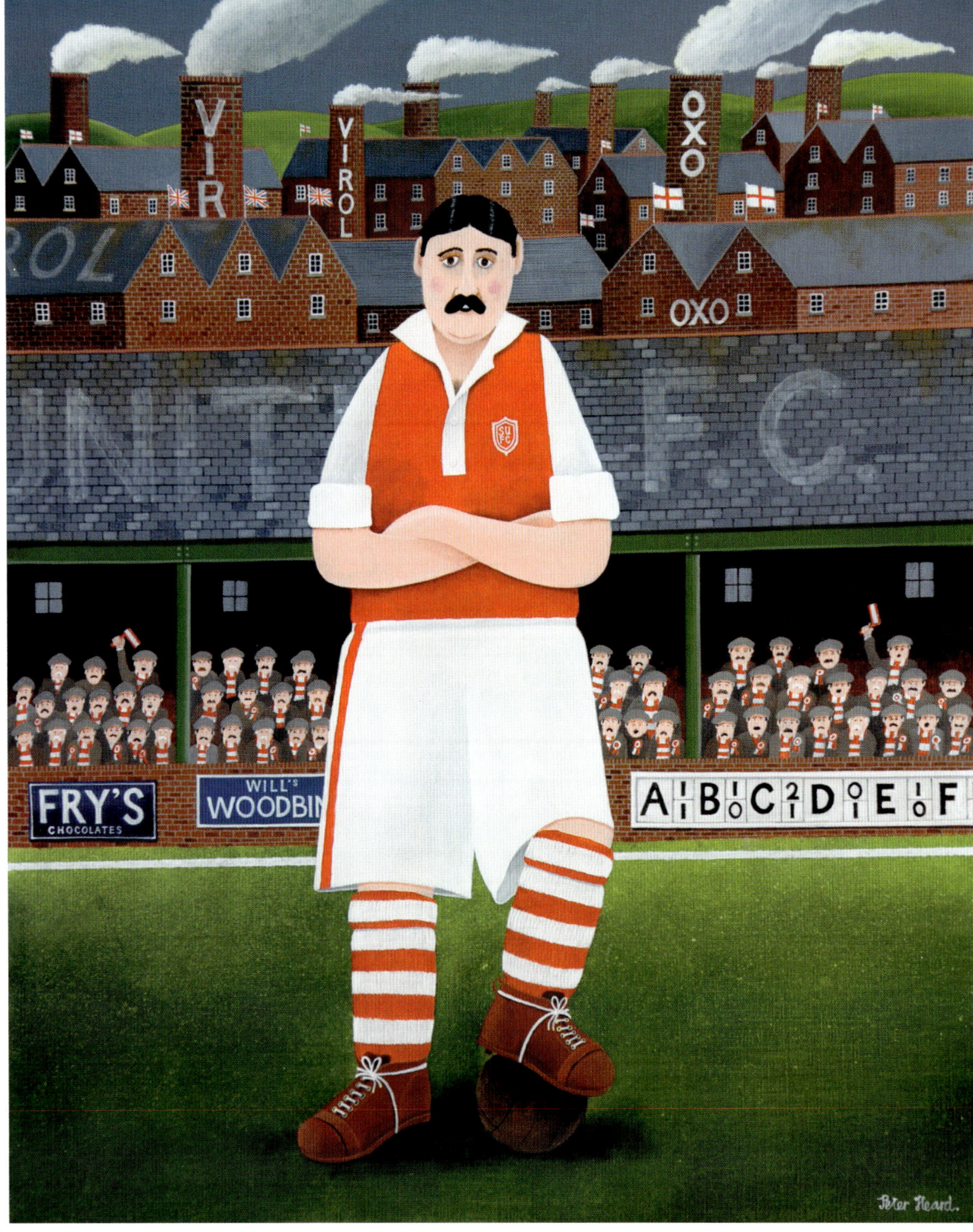

The Brylcreem Boy
Acrylic on Linen
50 x 60 cm

Preface

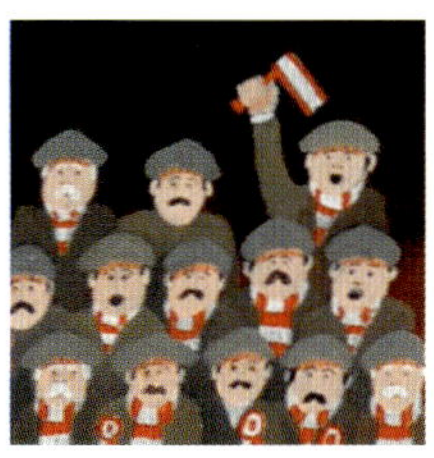

Picture the scene – a tiny scrap of an island a few hundred metres off the coast of Tolon in the Greek Peloponnese. In August. With the temperature touching 30 degrees. A band of about 20 holidaymakers are drinking wine, chatting and watching a whole lamb roast on a spit over a bed of charcoal. One of them was Peter Heard, on holiday with his family. And I was the after-barbecue entertainment, part-time guitar player and married to the rep who had organised this afternoon of fun for her clients. Thinking back, it was the songs and guitar playing that first attracted Peter and we started talking. And, after the boat returned to Tolon, we continued the discourse in the bar of the Dolphin Hotel. It was a meeting of kindred spirits and the start of a friendship that has stayed strong for nearly 30 years. My wife and I fell a little bit in love with Peter – and later we were to fall in love with his paintings. At the time Peter was working as a civil engineer and painting whenever he could. He had just had a successful show at the Portal Gallery in London with a series of paintings titled Dear Old England. The characters in these pieces are etched in the memory – the footballer, the cricketer, the vicar – evoking a gentler time. With their strange hands, funny shoulders and unsmiling faces. The paintings are intricate, detailed – and often have a touch of humour about them.

Time passed. I returned to my real-life job as a journalist. Peter and I saw each other rarely. We were busy having children, he was going through a marriage break-up. Production of national newspapers in Manchester stopped in the late '80s and I had to go to work in London. Peter was living in South Woodford with Mary and that gave me the opportunity to visit, share a meal and several bottles of wine and talk and talk and talk. Football, music, painting, books – it all fused into one. But it never got boring and the conversation never dried up. Peter started changing direction with his paintings, away from his people-dominated earlier work. He was inspired by what he calls a life-changing visit to America's East Coast and the "simply unbelievable" giant lighthouses of North Carolina's Outer Banks. He began a collection of paintings of lighthouses – "a magnificent obsession". There are now more than 100 of them. Many look very simple – a lighthouse set against a landscape. But the buildings reflect Peter's attention to detail and his fascination with structure and engineering.

In 1996, Peter retired and, with time to concentrate purely on his painting, became more prolific. The lighthouses started to give way to uncluttered landscapes, more of a minimalist approach and a move into abstraction. Like a songwriter who has mastered the three-minute pop song, it seems so simple. But the artist simply makes it appear simple. And that is the craft.

Then ten years later, Peter and Mary decided to leave London. They chose to live in Somerset, not an area that either of them was familiar with. As Peter says: "My London world had not prepared me for life in an agricultural village, nestling in a valley between the Quantock Hills and Exmoor." And with the move came a further shift in focus. He was struck by the colours of the fields, of the stone and of the changing light in the sky. A London boy suddenly confronted with the beauty of nature.

A note in his journal soon after arriving in Somerset reads: "Already influenced by the land, the red fields are amazing as are the newly shorn beech hedges bordering the lanes – clearly a

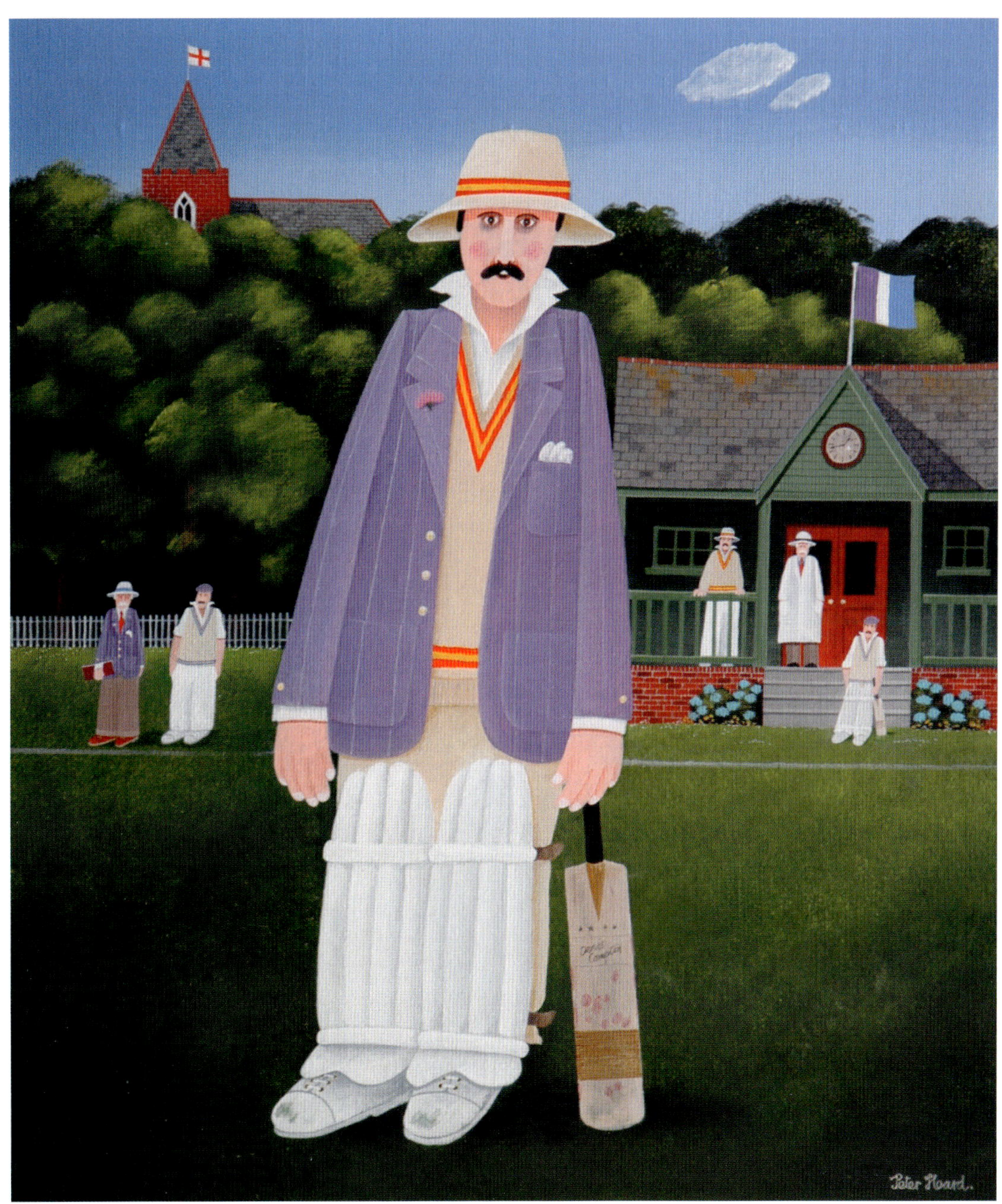

Padded Up
Acrylic on Linen
50 x 60 cm

group of paintings will appear – I look forward to seeing what happens.” First there were more landscapes. Then as he delved into the culture and history of rural Somerset he saw the chance to combine his later paintings with the emphasis of his earlier work. He discovered a culture of fêtes, hunting and shooting, open gardens, vintage tractors – and the West Somerset steam railway. Peter researched farming books and found old Victorian photographs of people harvesting and haymakers posing with their scythes. So he put people in his paintings again, set against the Somerset landscape. They still don’t smile but like the Dear Old England collection they bring a smile to your face.

So what do you get with a Peter Heard painting and especially his West Country Life collection? The paintings work on two levels – from a distance they are attractive and pleasing on the eye and they draw people in. Then close up the craft and the skill become evident. The meticulous attention to detail – everything has to be just perfect in Peter’s world – the well-defined edges, the way the light falls. There is no room for what Peter calls the “happy accident”. Everything is controlled in a way that creates a painting that is both realistic and naïve at the same time. They are paintings that you can look at again and again and always find something new to look at. And that is why you know you would just love to have a Peter Heard painting on the wall. Enjoy this collection.

Michael Woods

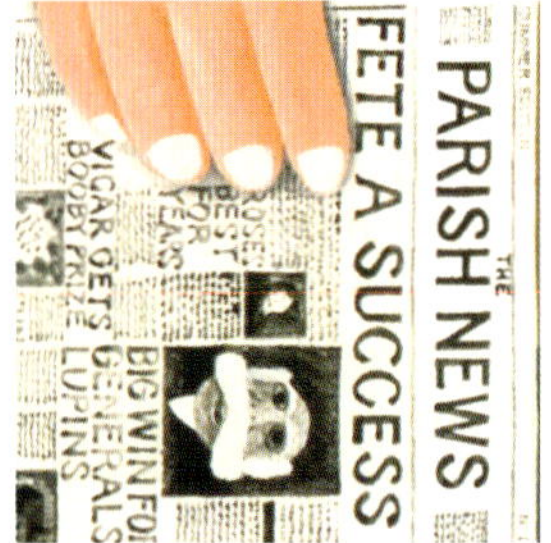

Vicar
Acrylic on Linen
40 x 40 cm

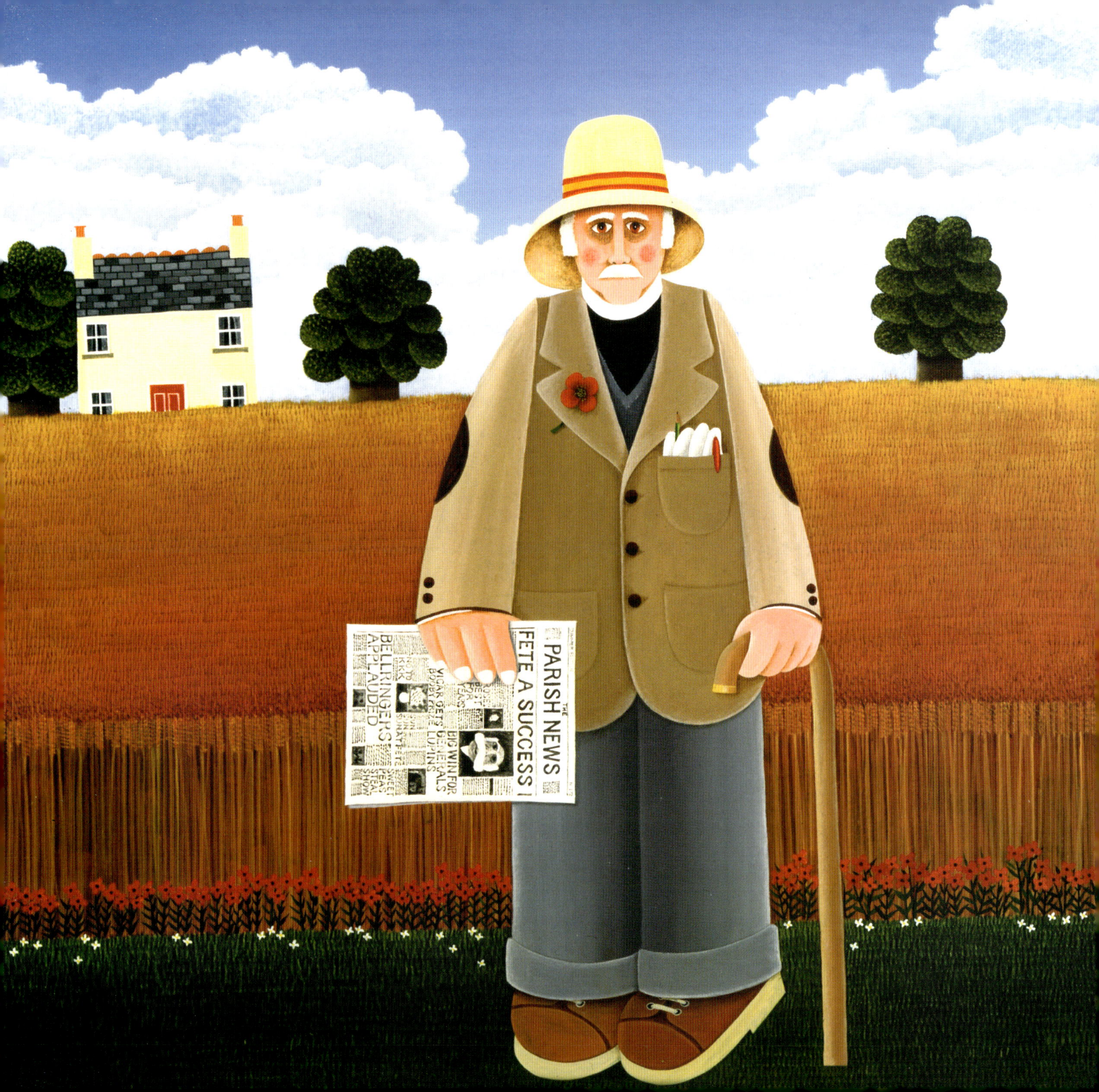
THE PARISH NEWS
FETE A SUCCESS!
BIG WIN FOR GENERALS LUPINS
VICAR GETS BOOBY PRIZE
SWEET PEAS STEAL SHOW
BELLRINGERS APPLAUDED

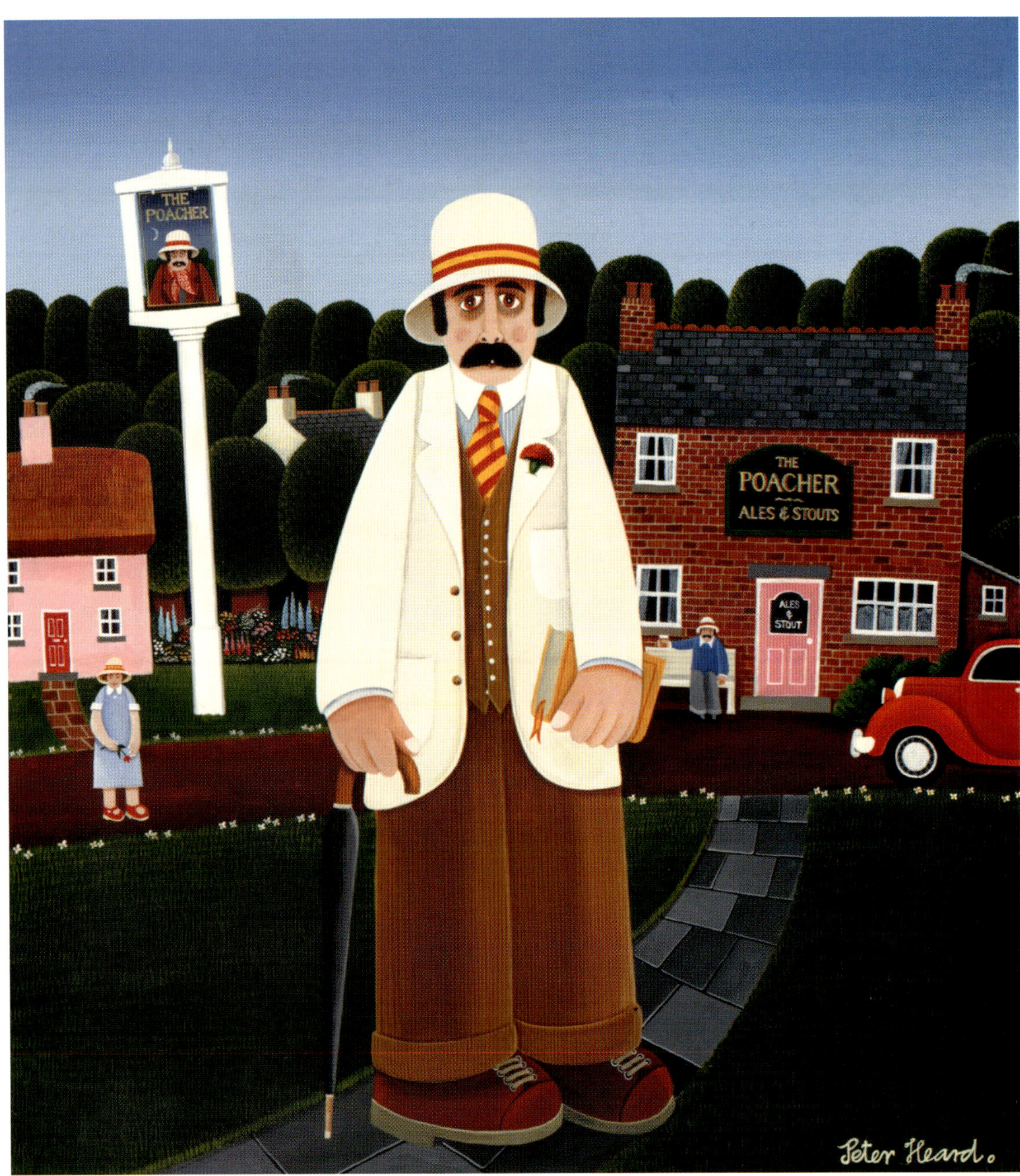

Off to the Pub
Acrylic on Linen
50 x 60 cm

What is Naïve Art?

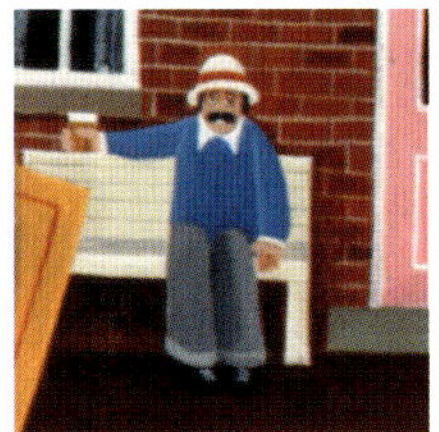

Art books tend to describe painters like me as "naïve realists". The realist element is the observation and recording of the world around us and is easy to grasp as a concept. The "naïve" is more elusive and more difficult to pin down. Here is my attempt at a definition. The genre has historically been difficult to title, never mind define. Naïve, childlike, innocent and folk are all terms which have been used, with "primitive art" often being an umbrella description. The more research I have undertaken and the more books read and artists studied the harder it has often seemed to distill the essence and magic of this wonderful artistic movement. It seems that naïve artists really fall into two categories. They are either "unconscious" or "conscious" naïves. They paint in their untaught, idiosyncratic and often obsessional way either naturally or by design.

The "unconscious" school, working far from the formal tenets of art, include, for example, L.S.Lowry, Alfred Wallis and Henri Rousseau – who is considered to be among the historical greats of art. It includes truly primitive cave painting, Aboriginal dot paintings, the art of psychiatric patients and children's art. Folk art is part of this category, with quilts, samplers, fairground art and canal boat art all created unconsciously by people a world away from art schools, museums and fashionable galleries.

The great folk portrait paintings of early America were generally the work of itinerant artists known as Limners, from the French to illuminate. They spent hard colonial winters at home painting a range of bodies on to canvas. Come spring, they filled their covered wagons with these and would travel the land and, in the age before photography, add any face for a dollar. Mrs Rockefeller could have afforded any painting in the world but in the early twentieth century chose to buy naïve art. Her family derided her but such paintings are now considered almost priceless and hang in her own gallery and in great American museums.

While researching I have found some wonderful descriptions and quotations that capture, for me, something of the special delights of the genre. “The true naïve artist works as if he was the first person alive whereas the trained artist cannot ignore the art of predecessors or contemporaries.” “They create without the barrier of tradition which perhaps gives immediacy and surprise. An observer confronted by a Picasso may remark that they could do that but confronted by true innocent art they are silenced by uncorrupted imagery which is impossible to imitate.” “True naïves find their own pathways and paint in an unfettered self-taught manner. They are born free, have no message and generate the excitement of sheer existence.”

Artists such as these are pretty well impossible to find today as it is so very difficult to be unaware of the society in which we now live, or of the history of art. Therefore a parallel strand exists of artists like me who embrace the genre but work in a deliberately designed naïvety.

These artists are described as “conscious” naïves. They are educated and live in today’s sophisticated world with all its influences. They paint this world around them, the realism bit, and use an abundance of imagery and art reproduction that our Limner friend would have found miraculous.

They probably set out on their journey by seeing the work of their naïve peers, as I do think that most artists develop their way by the inspiration of others. Innovators are very rare.
We strive to achieve self-expression, as the Limner did, with no formal art training, which I feel can be an advantage. Being self-taught I can do what I like, I can use lack of proportion, perspective, composition and tone in a manner that would be frowned upon in art school. Does this give our paintings a special quality? One place to judge is London's Portal Gallery, which has always been a world leader in showing naïve works. How will you know that the exhibition is "naïve"? Maybe by the smiles on the faces of the people looking at our paintings and, with paintings of the late great Beryl Cook, by outright laughter. The gallery was hugely instrumental in the development of my career as well as hers and I thank them.

Of course, a border between the naïve world and "proper" art has been policed by art critics for many years. Is this important? Not if one thinks of the Salon des Refuses it isn't. The genre for me has been and is a world of wonder and the more I see and learn about it the more entranced I become. I have always hoped that at its best our work is colourful, harmonious, sometimes humorous and always entertaining which perhaps explains some of its enduring appeal.

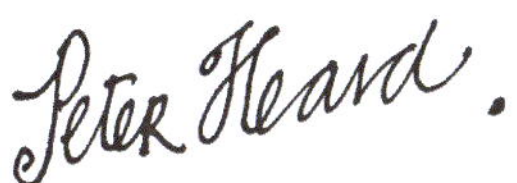

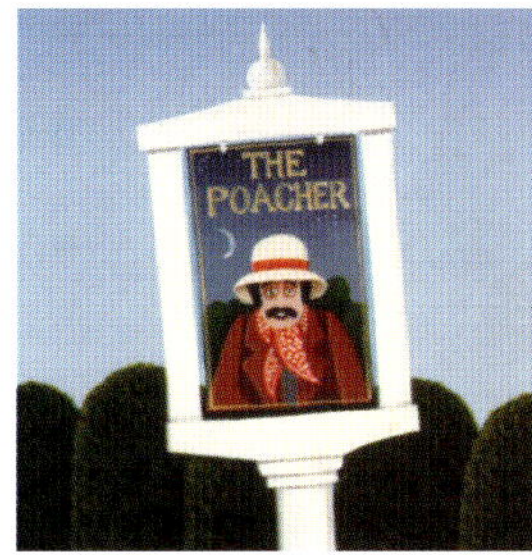

Day Tripping

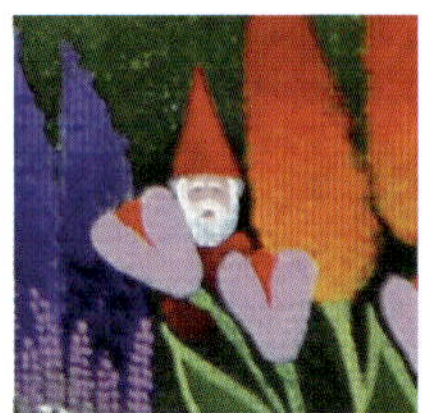

As a child Saturdays in summer were special – if the sun was shining it meant we were going somewhere. A day trip. Usually to the seaside but sometimes to a huge park or country estate. And sometimes by train, sometimes by bus and, perhaps, sometimes by car. And we always took a picnic. Times have changed and it is not just Saturdays that are made for day tripping. Here Peter has captured the essence of those special days out, from the shoreline and its lighthouses to the grand old estate with its greenery.

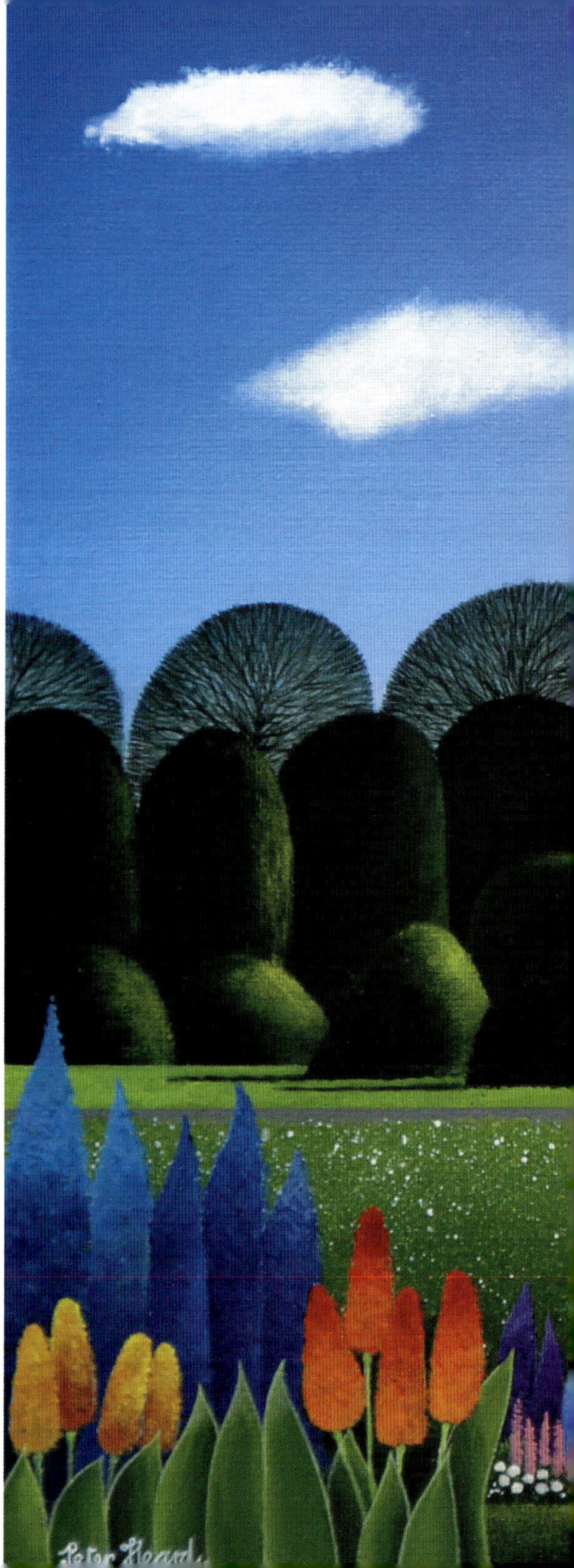

National Trusting
Acrylic on Linen
60 x 50cm

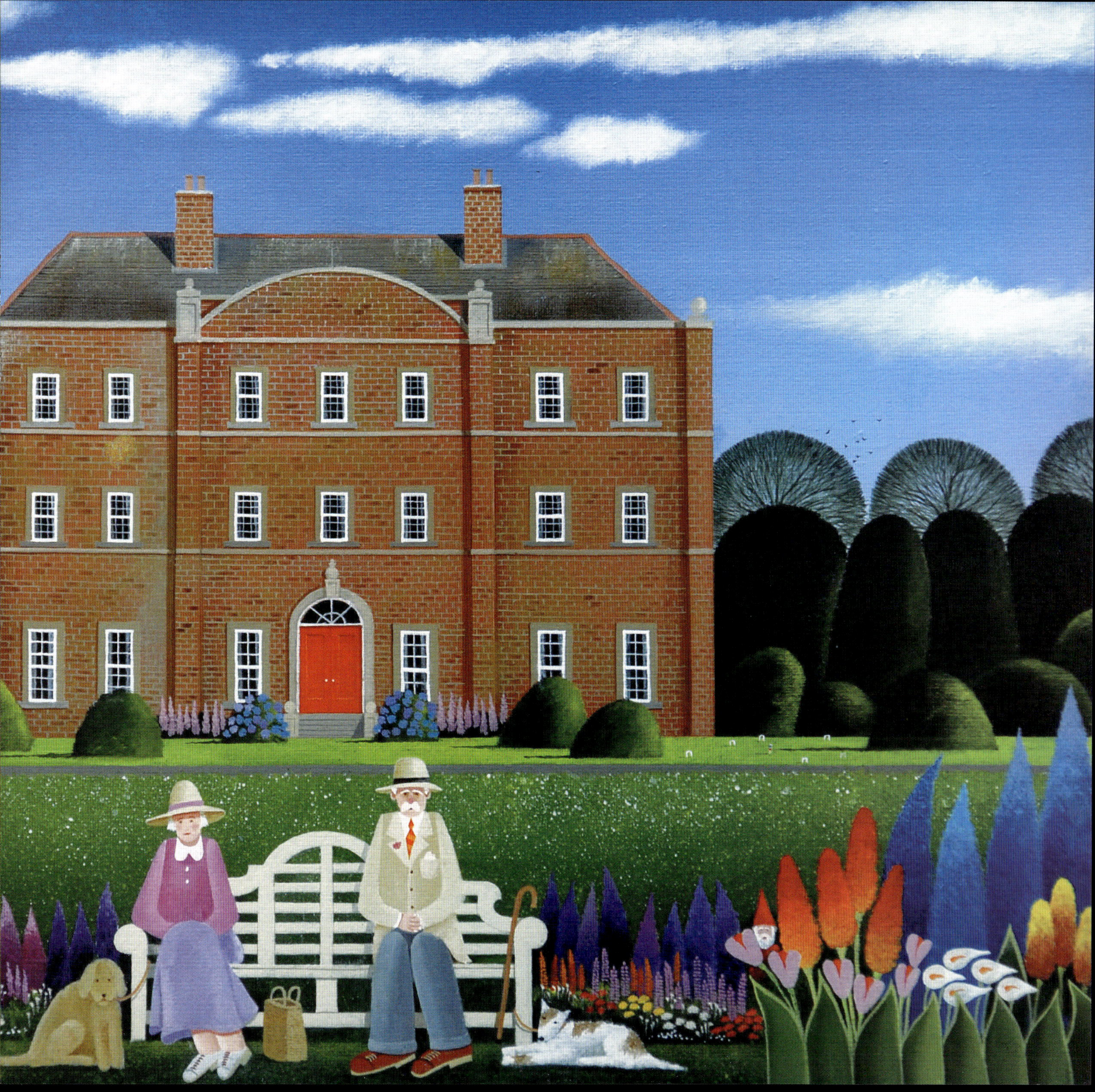

THE QUANTOCK BELLE

For young boys and old boys steam trains have a particular fascination. The West Somerset Railway was a branch line of the old Great Western Railway. It runs for 20 miles from Bishops Lydeard to Minehead on a nostalgic journey through 10 stations with views of the Quantock Hills, Exmoor, the Bristol Channel. Almost exactly as it was in the days before Dr Beeching. Peter, who can hear the steam engines from his garden, has set the train against a landscape that has fascinated him during his time in the West Country. When he first arrived in Somerset he could not believe the contrasting colours of the fields or the way they are terraced on the hillsides – like a wall of fields.

Iron oxide from the erosion of the sandstone stains everything, including sheep who tend to end up pink. There are rape fields, corn fields, freshly ploughed fields, green fields, harvested corn fields, corn fields with tractor lines. And you may notice the contrast between the speed of the train and the stillness of the fields. You won't see all the fields like this all at once or so perfectly formed – that is artistic licence!

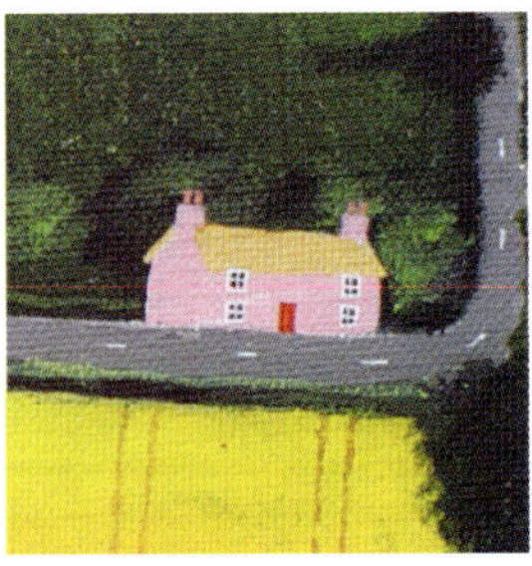

The Quantock Belle
Acrylic on Linen
60 x 50 cm

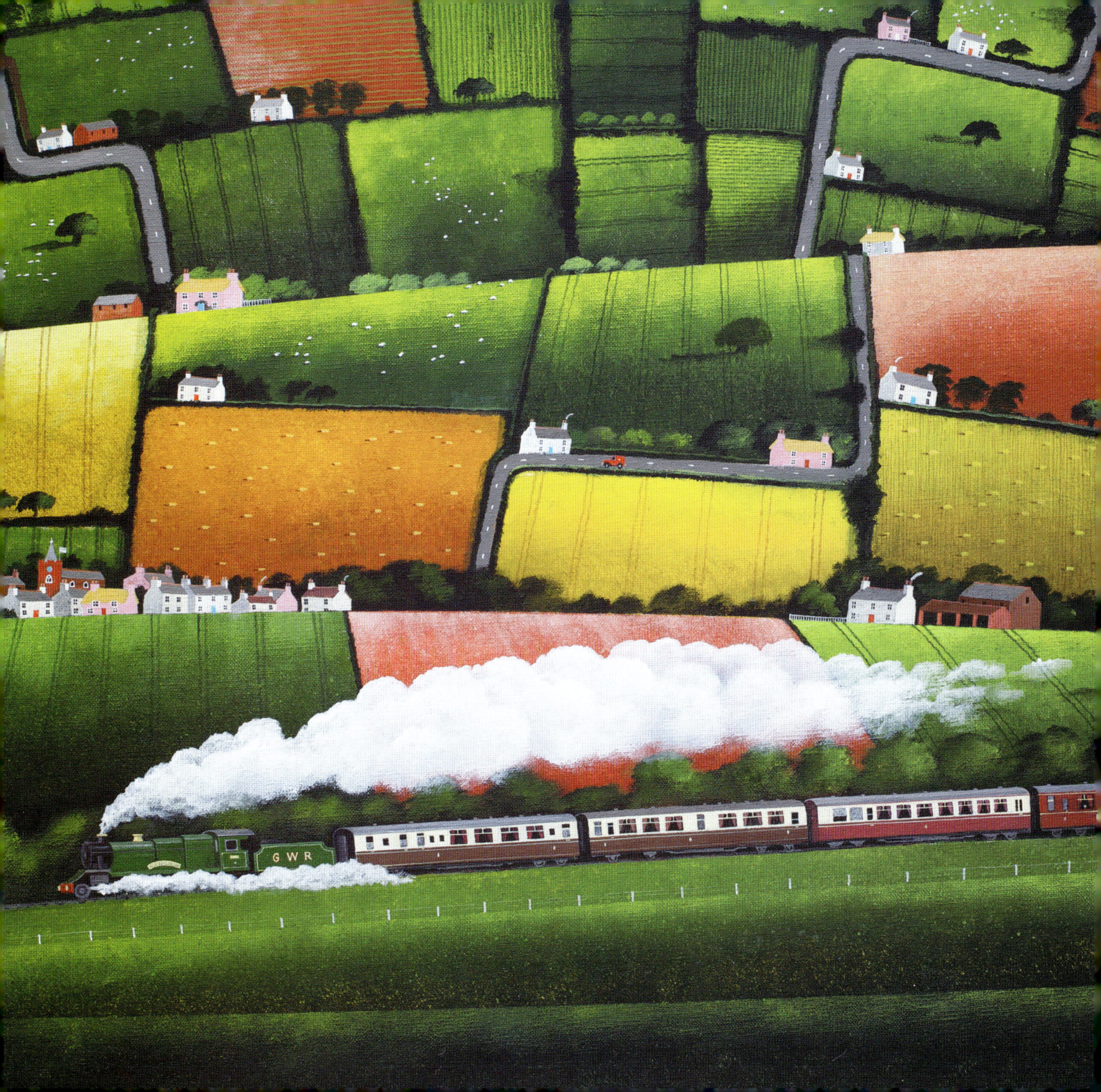
GWR

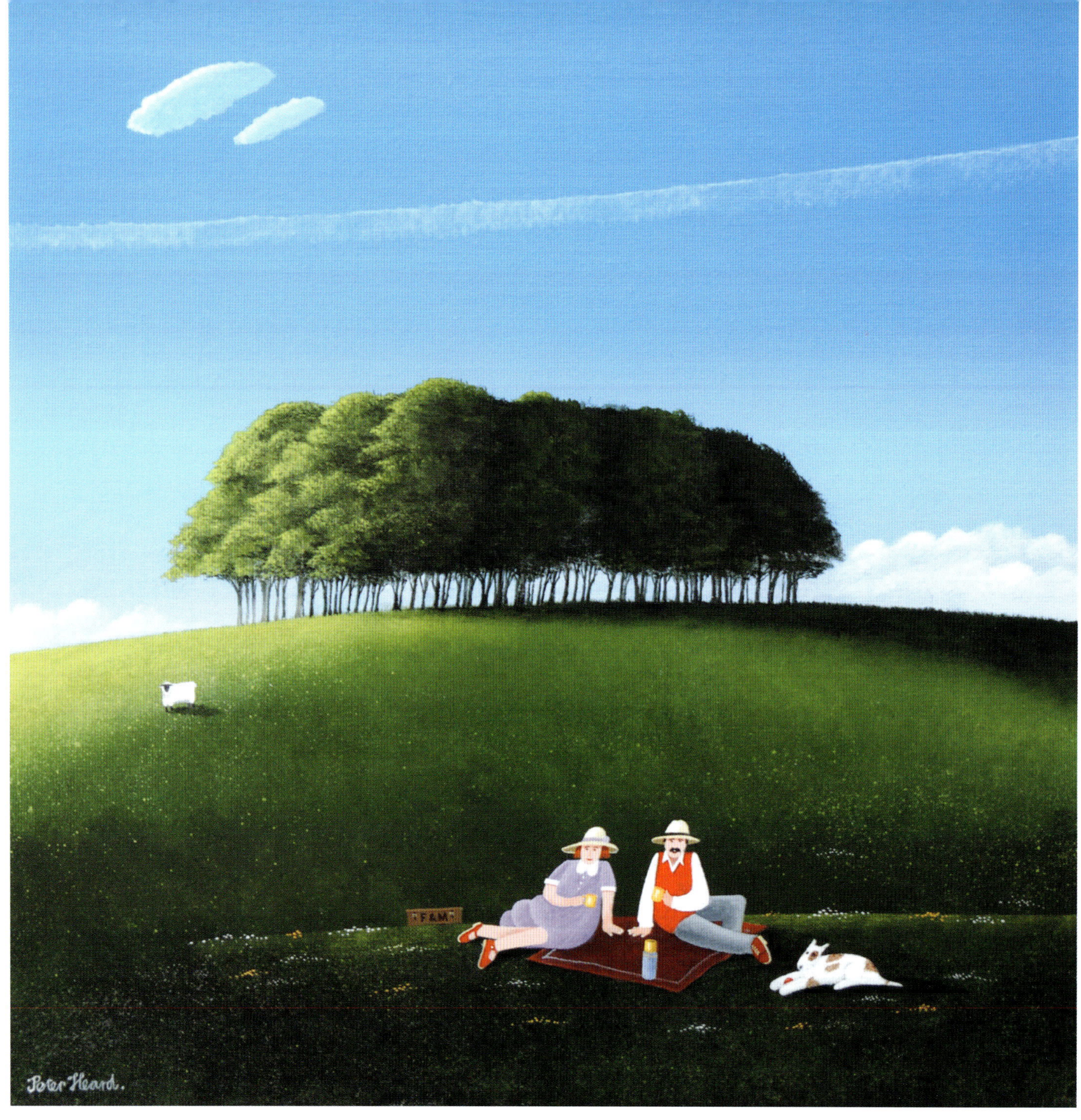
F&M
Peter Heard.

PICNIC AT FRIENDBERRY

This picture is all about the stand of trees and the way the light plays on the land. And there are the stylised elements that make up the composition of a Peter Heard painting – the fluffy white clouds, the vapour trail, the sheep and the total symmetry and harmony of the couple having their picnic. Even their dog is sitting just so. Peter photographed these trees in late afternoon light and was taken with their shadows, shape and their lacy trunks. All that remained was to build a painting. And Mr and Mrs Somerset having a summer picnic, with a Fortnum and Mason hamper, seemed a natural. The West Country landscape seems to abound with tree groups on the tops of hills! There is also a certain Englishness about spreading your travel rug in a field and having lunch, complete with a thermos flask of tea, and keeping your shoes off the rug!

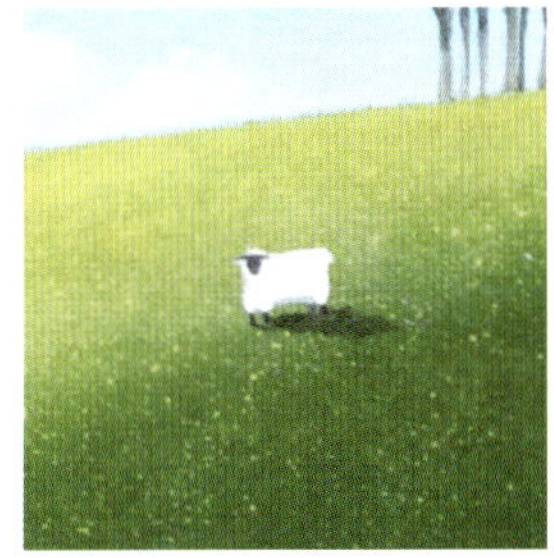

Picnic at Friendberry
Acrylic on Linen
50 x 50 cm

TRUST MEMBERS

The National Trust for Places of Historic Interest or Natural Beauty was formed in 1895 by three people. It now has almost four million members. The focus on country houses and gardens began in the middle of the last century when it realised the owners of these properties could no longer afford to maintain them. Many were donated to the Trust in lieu of death duties. The Trust now has more than 200 houses and Mr and Mrs Somerset are visiting one of them. They are taking their lunch beneath a sheltered arch of topiary, which is based on the gardens at Powis Castle in Welshpool. In 2005 the Trust moved to a new head office in Swindon, Wiltshire, called Heelis, which is the married name of writer Beatrix Potter, who was one of the Trust's major benefactors.

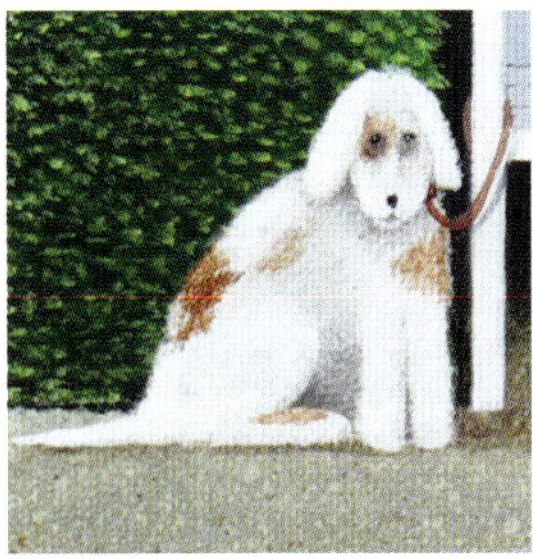

Trust Members
Acrylic on Linen
36 x 36 cm

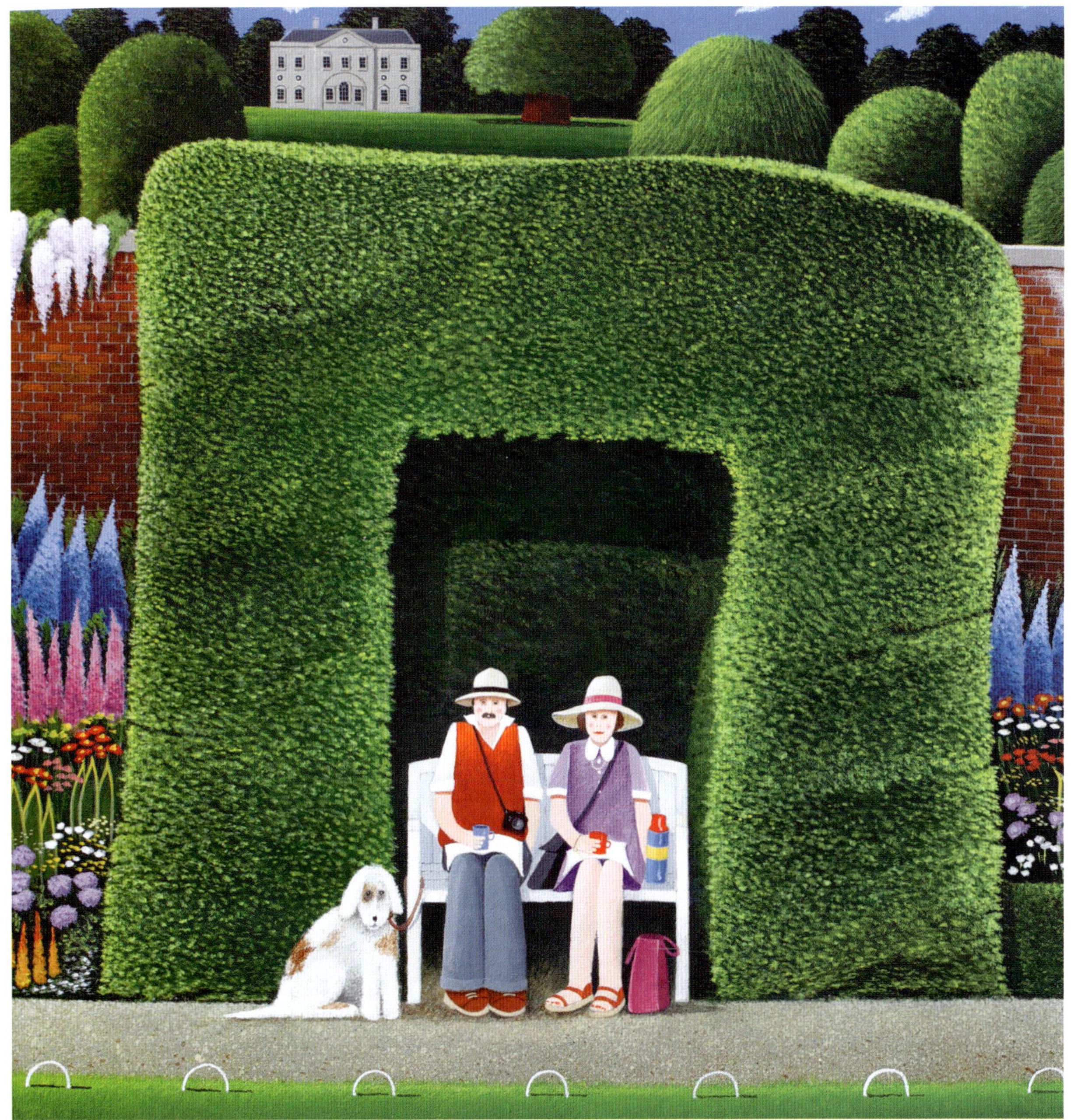

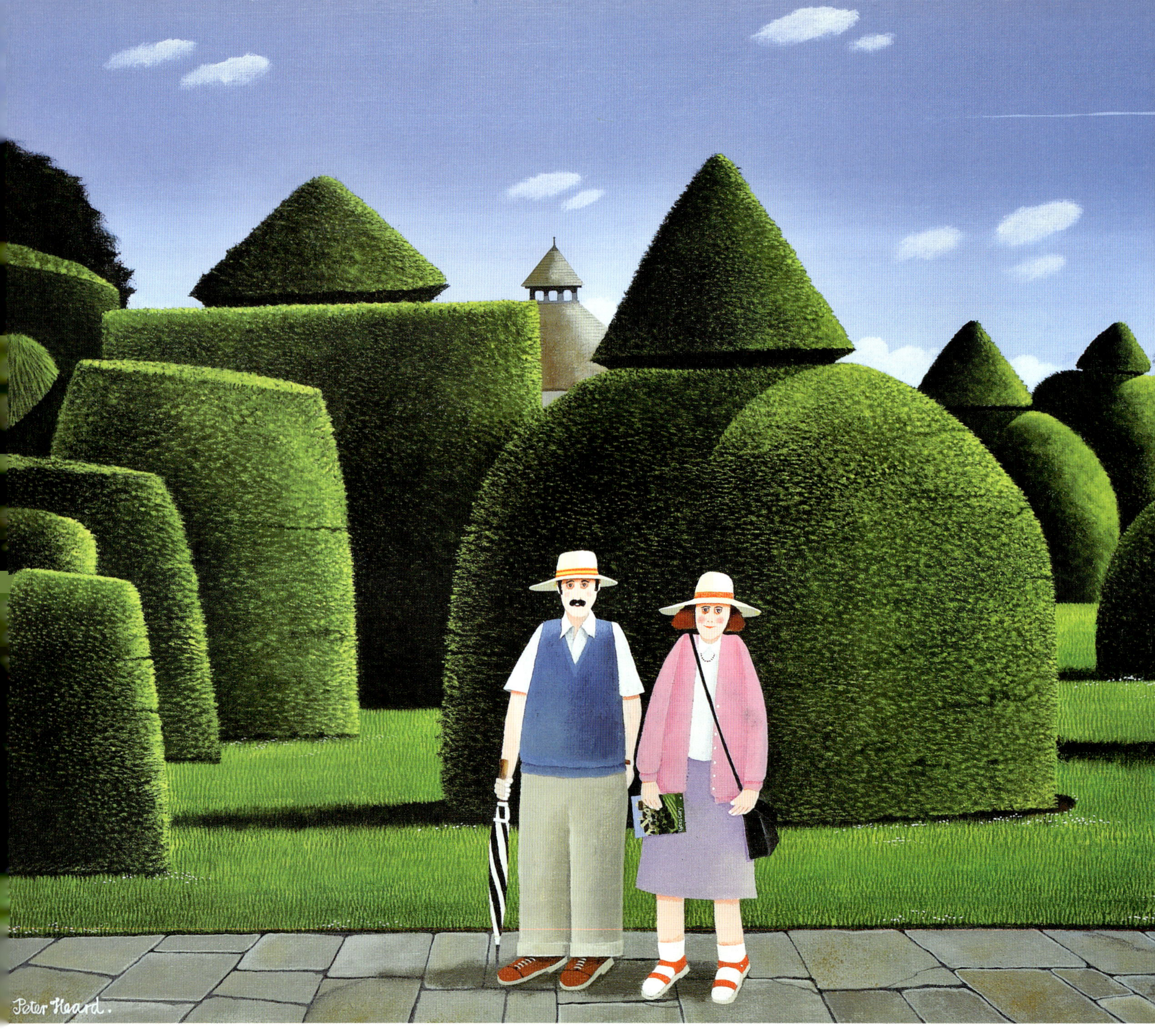
Peter Heard.

THE TWELVE APOSTLES OF LYTES CARY

Topiary has interested Peter for years and appears regularly in his work. It is first mentioned in Roman times during the reign of Julius Caesar who invaded Britain in 55BC. Topiary is the art of creating sculptures by clipping evergreen trees and shrubs – such as box, bay laurel, myrtle, holly and privet. Sometimes topiary is of a geometric shape, sometimes in the form of birds and animals. Here Mr and Mrs Somerset are visiting the National Trust house at Lytes Cary Manor and the Apostles Garden there. The hamstone pathway is flanked by lawn and two rows of six topiary yews representing the 12 apostles. In the background is a pigeonnier, a particularly French institution. While strange in the Lytes Cary garden, it echoes the shape of the Apostles and works well in the painting.

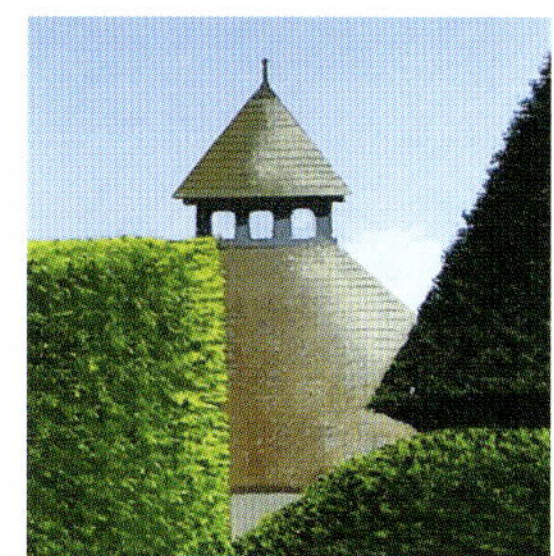

The Twelve Apostles of Lytes Cary
Acrylic on Linen
60 x 50 cm

RUSH HOUR

The secret of this painting is the creation of motion from what appears to be total stillness and calm – hence Rush Hour. Yes, the boats are moving but not much else appears to be happening… until you look closer. There's the woman with her dog on the harbour front waving and welcoming the fishermen safely home, the man waiting for the pub to open, the postie on his rounds, the cars going up and down the hills, the tractor working away in the field at the very top of the painting. And the flags and chimney smoke wafting in what must be a stiff breeze. You can look at this painting and see something new each time. And then there is the meticulous skill in creating the detail of the fishing village complete with its imposing lighthouse. This is a very West Country fishing village!

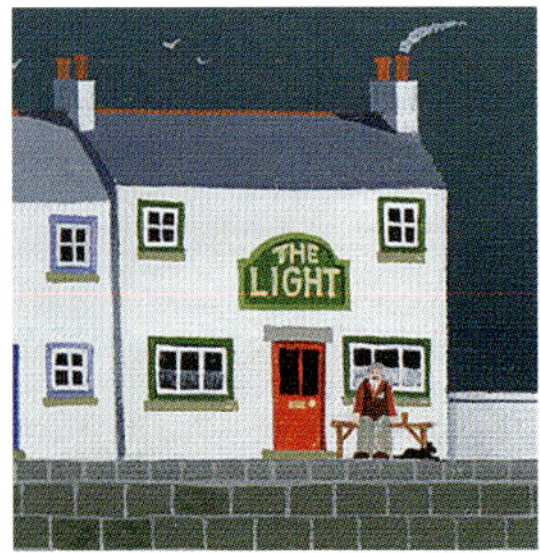

Rush Hour
Acrylic on Linen
70 x 60 cm

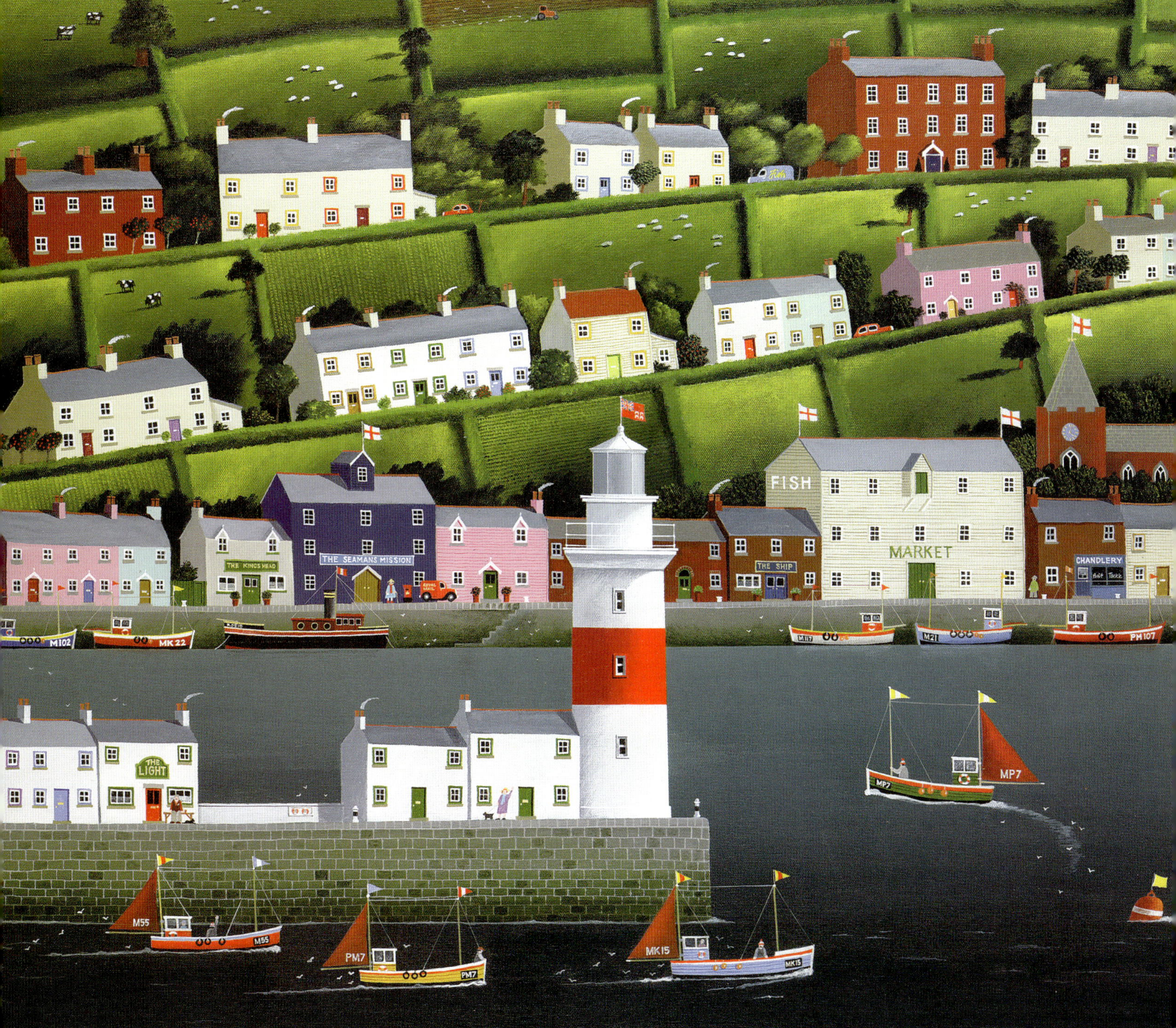
FISH
MARKET
THE SEAMANS MISSION
THE KINGS HEAD
THE SHIP
CHANDLERY
THE LIGHT
M102
MK22
PH107
MP7
M55
PM7
MK15

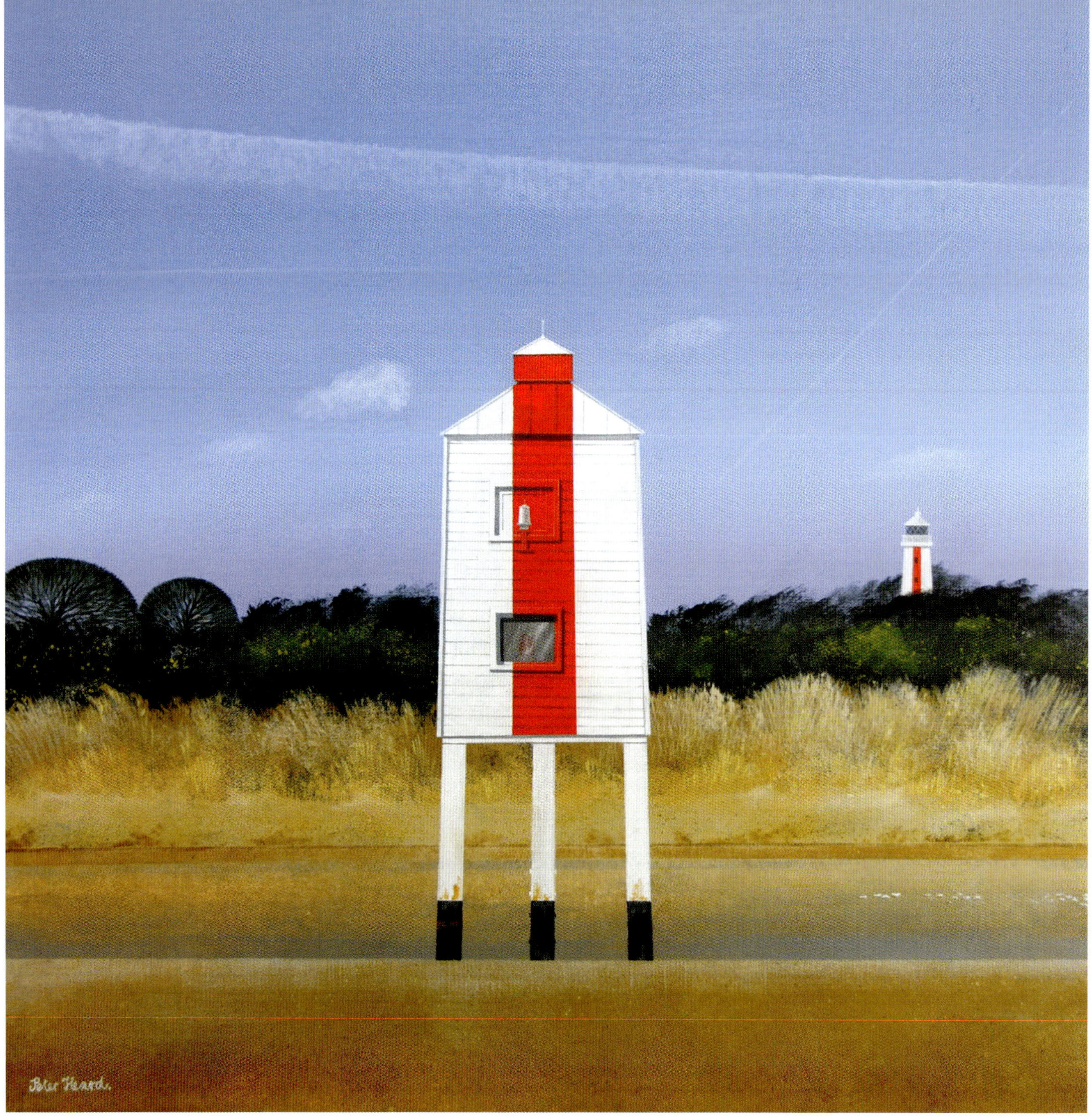
Peter Heard.

LIGHTHOUSE AT BURNHAM ON SEA

Now we come to Peter's "magnificent obsession" – lighthouses. If you are familiar with Peter's work, you will know that he has produced more than 100 paintings of lighthouses, a collection in themselves. Many of Peter's lighthouse paintings were inspired by the magnificent structures in the Carolinas on America's east coast. While not on the same scale the lighthouse at Burnham is particularly interesting. In the background is the Pillar Lighthouse, built in 1830. It is 100ft high and originally had a paraffin-fired light. It has a spiral staircase that visitors would climb to see the views of the South Wales, Somerset and Devon coasts. But it was soon found that the vantage point chosen for the lighthouse was too low to take into account the massive rise and fall of the tides in the Bristol Channel. So in 1832 the Lighthouse On Legs was built on the beach. The Pillar Lighthouse went out of service in 1993 and is now a private house.

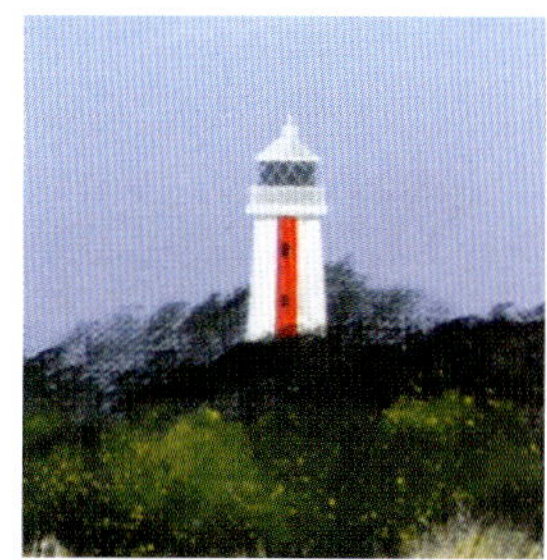

Lighthouse at
Burnham on Sea
Acrylic on Linen
50 x 50 cm

PORTLAND BILL

There has been a lighthouse at Portland Bill since 1716 to protect shipping in one of the most treacherous stretches of the English Channel. Even earlier than that, from 1620, there was a beacon on the site. The first lighthouse, the Old Higher Lighthouse, was about half a mile from the Bill point. It was the first lighthouse to use Argand lamps, or oil burners, named after the Frenchman who invented them. The lighthouse stayed in use until 1906 when the present red and white Portland Bill was built. The lighthouse was then sold and became a private house. Doctor Marie Stopes, the pioneer of birth control, owned it from 1923 until 1958.

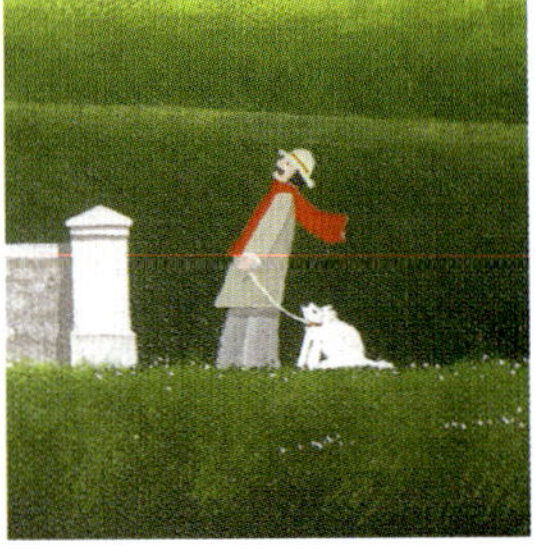

Portland Bill
Acrylic on Linen
90 x 75 cm

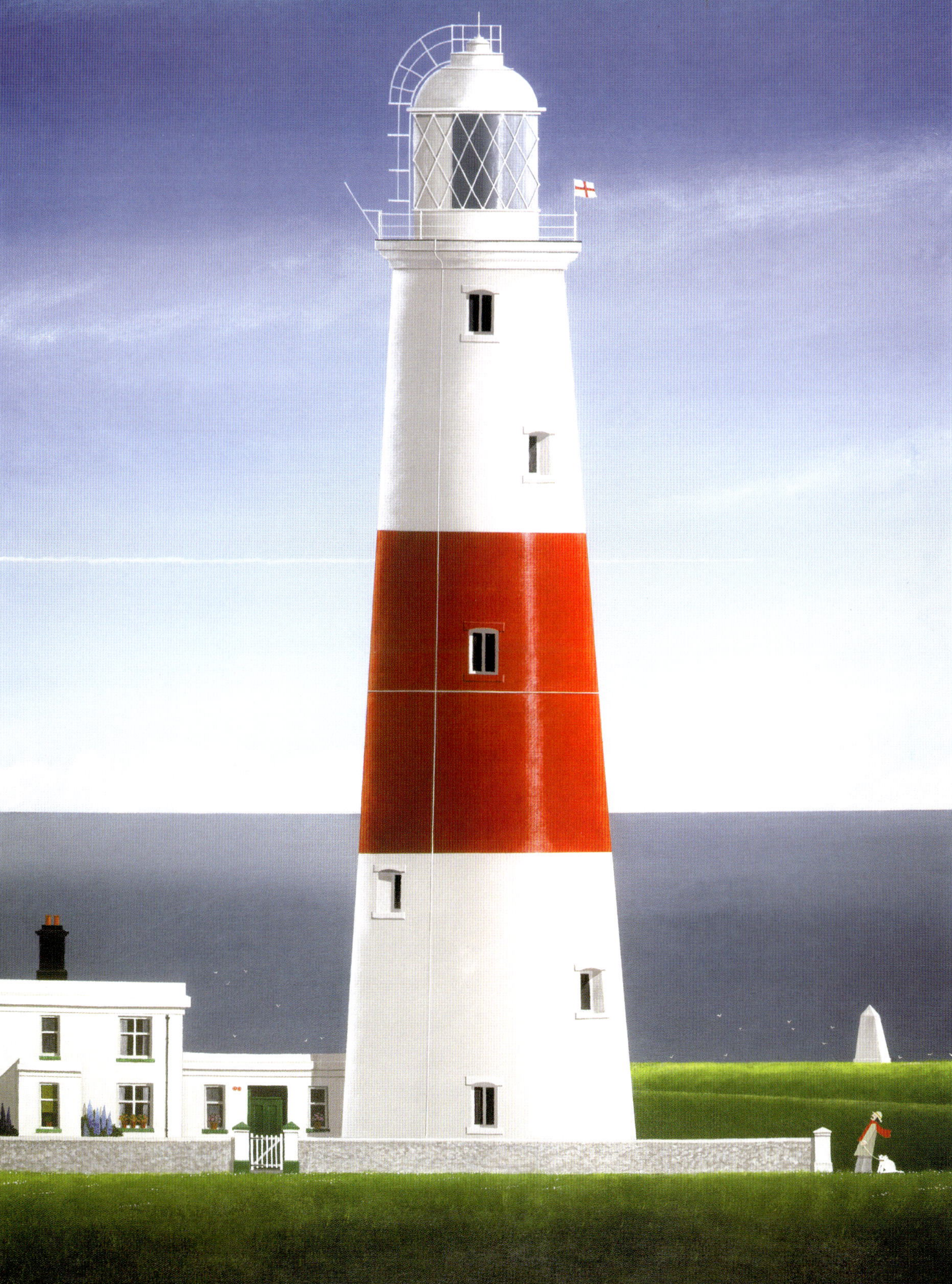

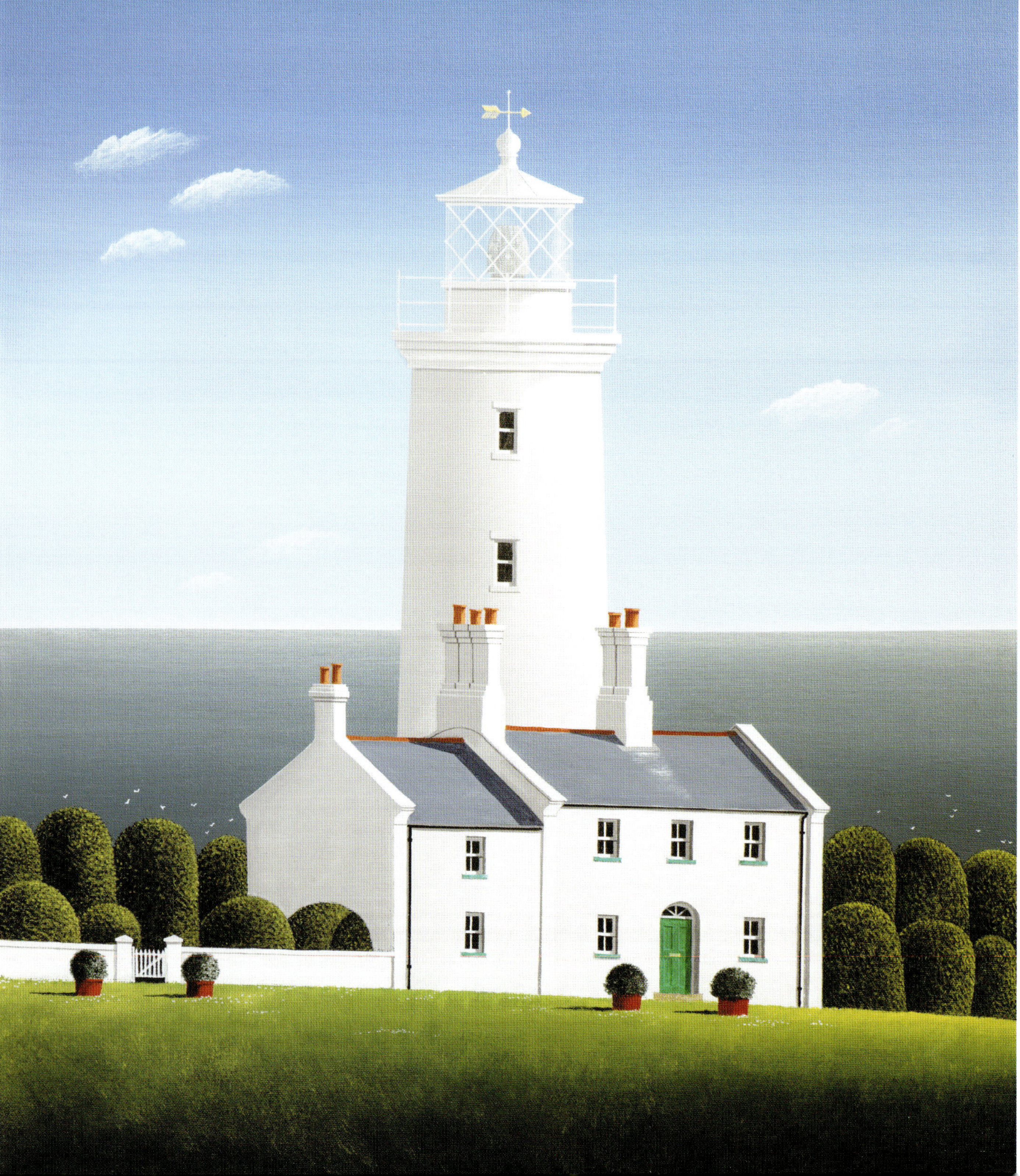

LOWER PORTLAND

The second lighthouse – the Lower Lighthouse – was built in 1789. It was turned into a bird observatory in 1961 by Sir Peter Scott. The present Portland Bill is now fully automatic but guided tours can be arranged. Portland itself is not really an island. It is separated from mainland Dorset by a causeway from Chesil Beach. Thomas Hardy called the people who lived on Portland "slingers" because they used to throw stones at visitors.

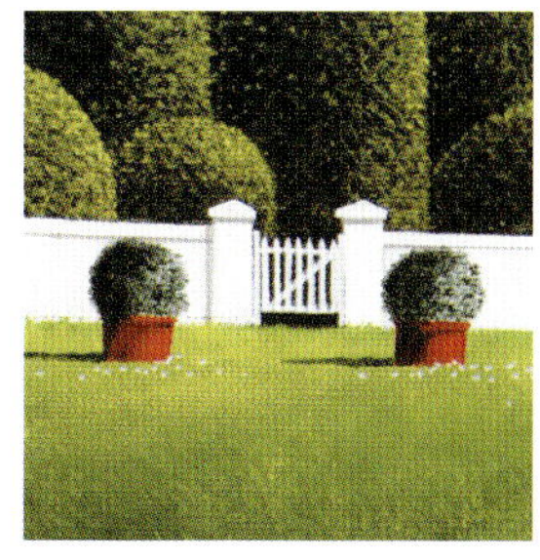

Lower Portland
Acrylic on Linen
50 x 60 cm

A LIGHTHOUSE CALLED PENDEEN

Sitting low on a dark cliff, halfway between Land's End and St Ives, is the classic white tower of Pendeen Lighthouse. It was built in 1900 to warn ships of the dangerous rocks of Pendeen Watch. The tower is only 17 metres high but, of course, is much higher than this above sea level. Lighthouses are for the night but are also daymarks for sailors. England's lights are painted white, sometimes banded in black or red so they are visible in daytime. Icelandic lighthouses are orange so they stand out against the snow and Canada's red for the same reason.

The low position of the lighthouse relative to the rising land behind it affords a perfect and unusual viewpoint for photographers. This painting is based on a photograph Peter took one perfect summer day – as always with a future painting in mind. There used to be three keepers and their families looking after Pendeen but automation took over in 1995. The keepers' cottages are now holiday lets and are a perfect and evocative base from which to explore the West Country...

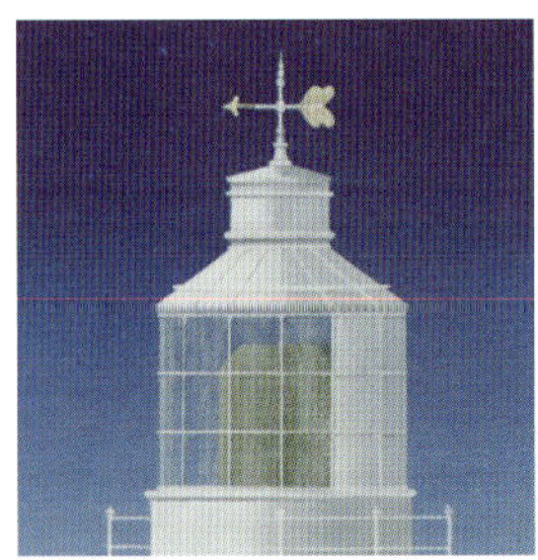

A Lighthouse Called Pendeen
Acrylic on Linen
50 x50 cm

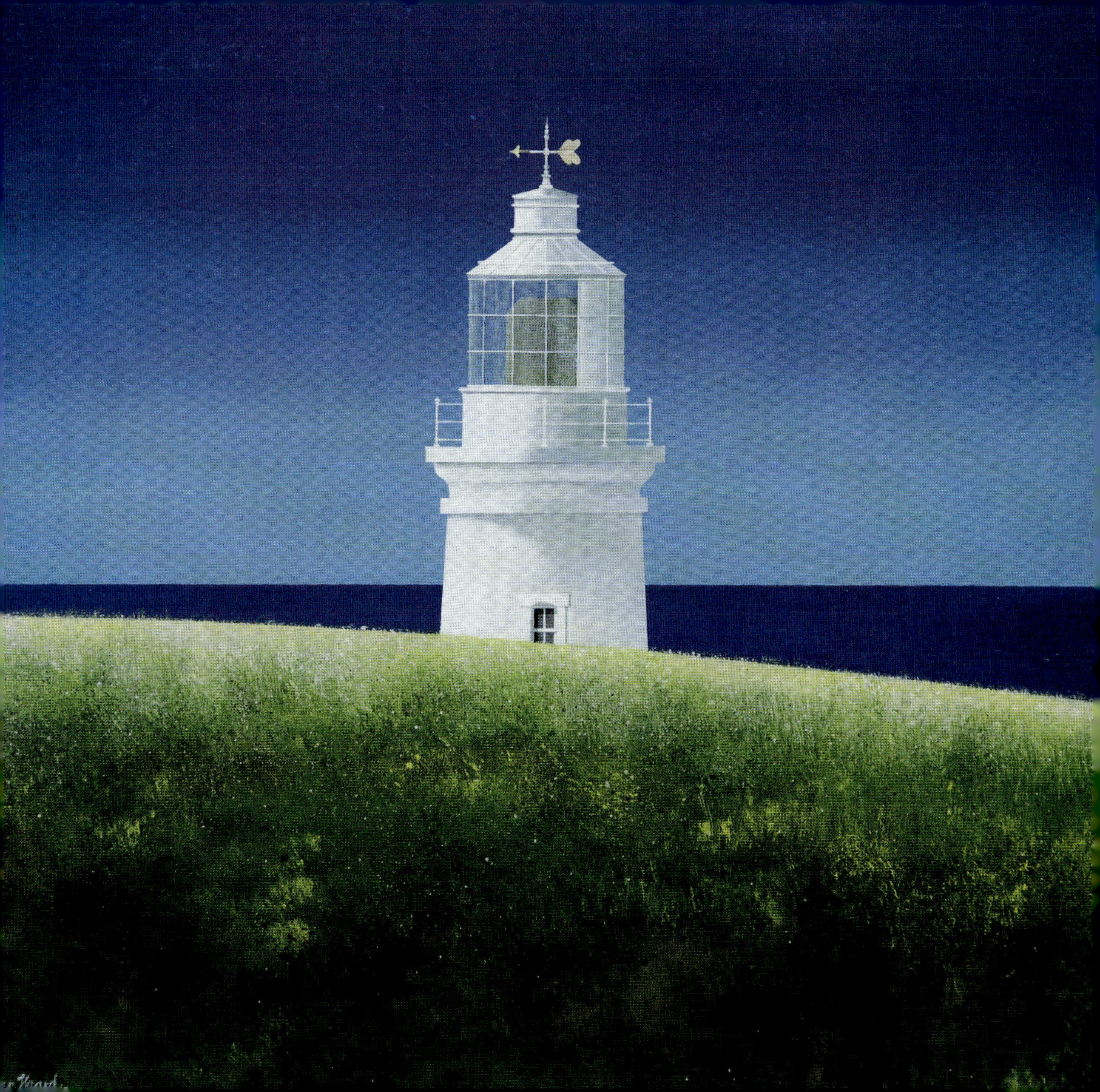

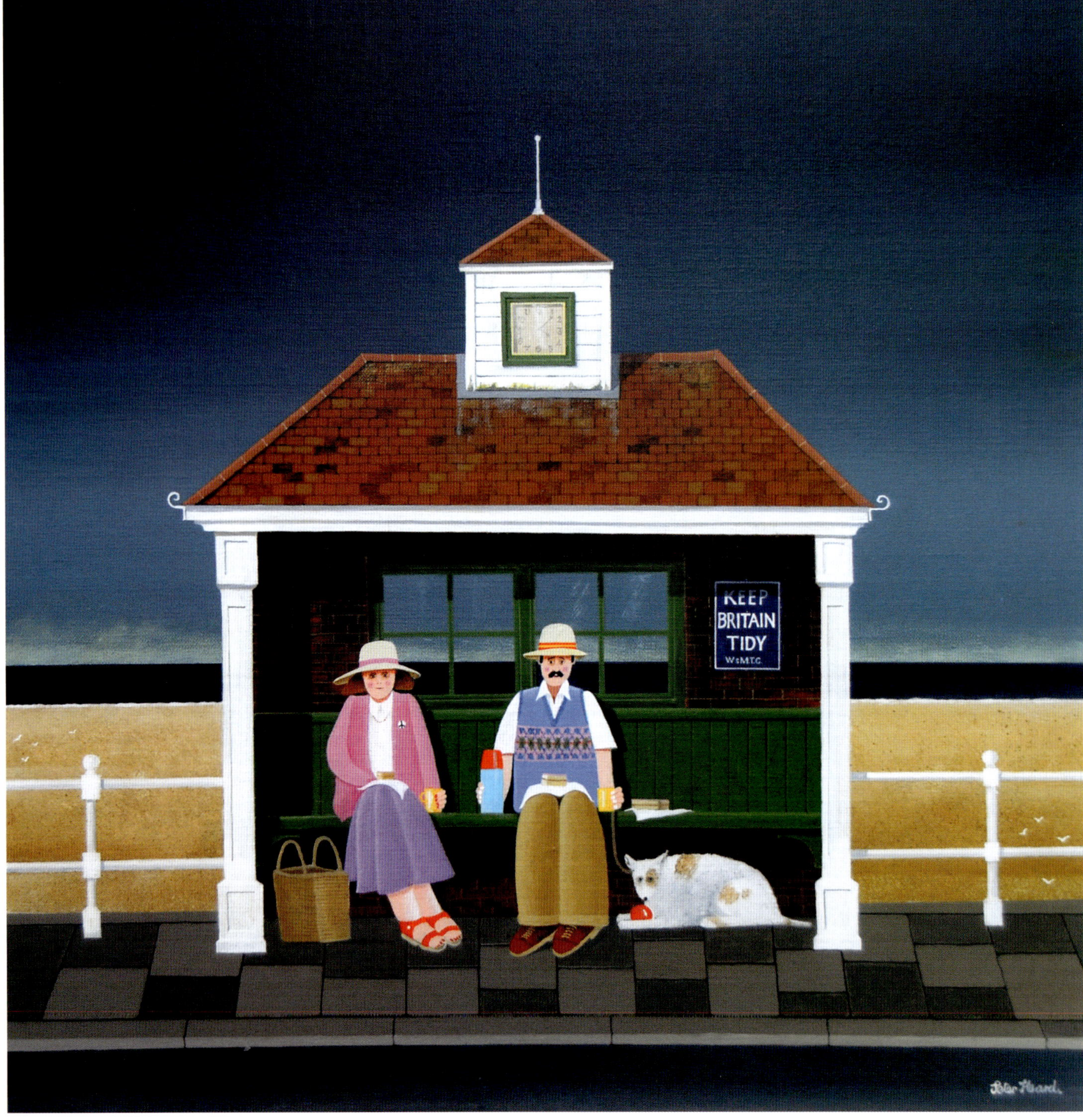
KEEP
BRITAIN
TIDY
WsMTC

SEASIDE TRIP TO WESTON

This painting evokes Peter's earlier Portal Gallery work, especially the "Dear Old England" phase. Mr and Mrs Somerset are on a day trip to Weston-super-Mare. They have their flask of tea or coffee and sandwiches neatly cut on paper napkins. He is wearing his MCC hat and she has a CND badge. A very Sixties, keep Britain tidy, theme. Like many English seaside resorts, Weston had its heyday before the age of the cheap package holiday. The Grand Pier, which opened in 1904, had a 2,000-seat theatre! The pavilion on the pier was destroyed by fire in 2008. But a £34milion scheme to rebuild it has just been completed. So perhaps Peter's painting is not the past but the future.

Seaside Trip to Weston
Acrylic on Linen
50 x 50 cm

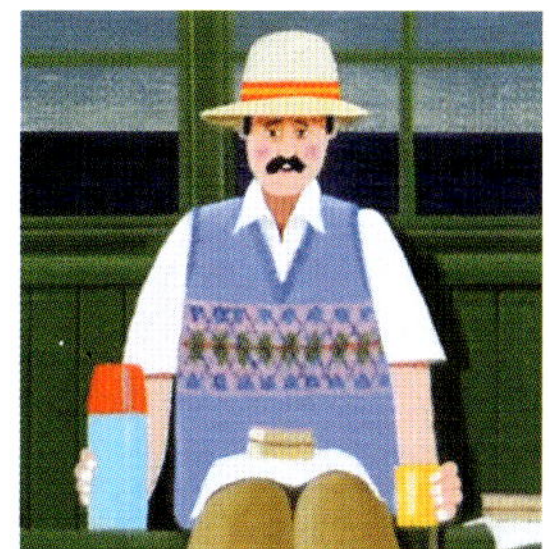

GLASTONBURY TOR

The mythology surrounding the Tor is immense – basically you can find a theory or explanation that fits what you want to believe about it. The Tor has been associated with the name Avalon, which was a legendary island of the ancient Britons surrounded by marshland. In the twelfth century, monks from Glastonbury Abbey claim to have found the buried remains of King Arthur and Queen Guinevere there. When Celtic mythology became a focus of interest, the Tor became associated with Gwyn ap Nudd, who was first Lord of the Underworld and later King of the Fairies. The Tor was seen as an entrance to Avalon, the land of the fairies. Here Peter is simply adding to the speculation with his strange moon hanging spaceship-like above the Tor. Aliens or what?

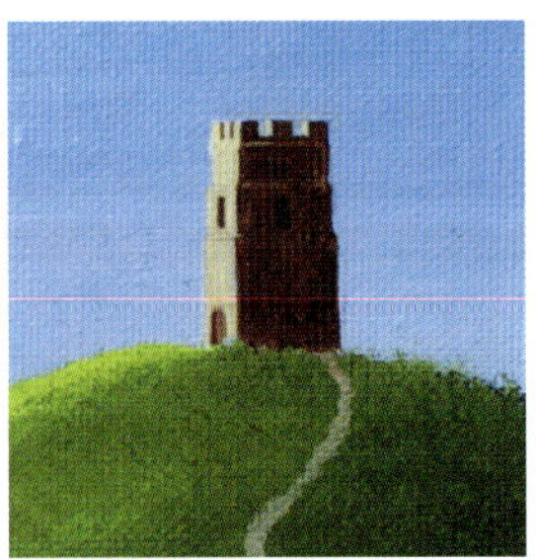

Glastonbury Tor
Acrylic on Linen
50 x 50 cm

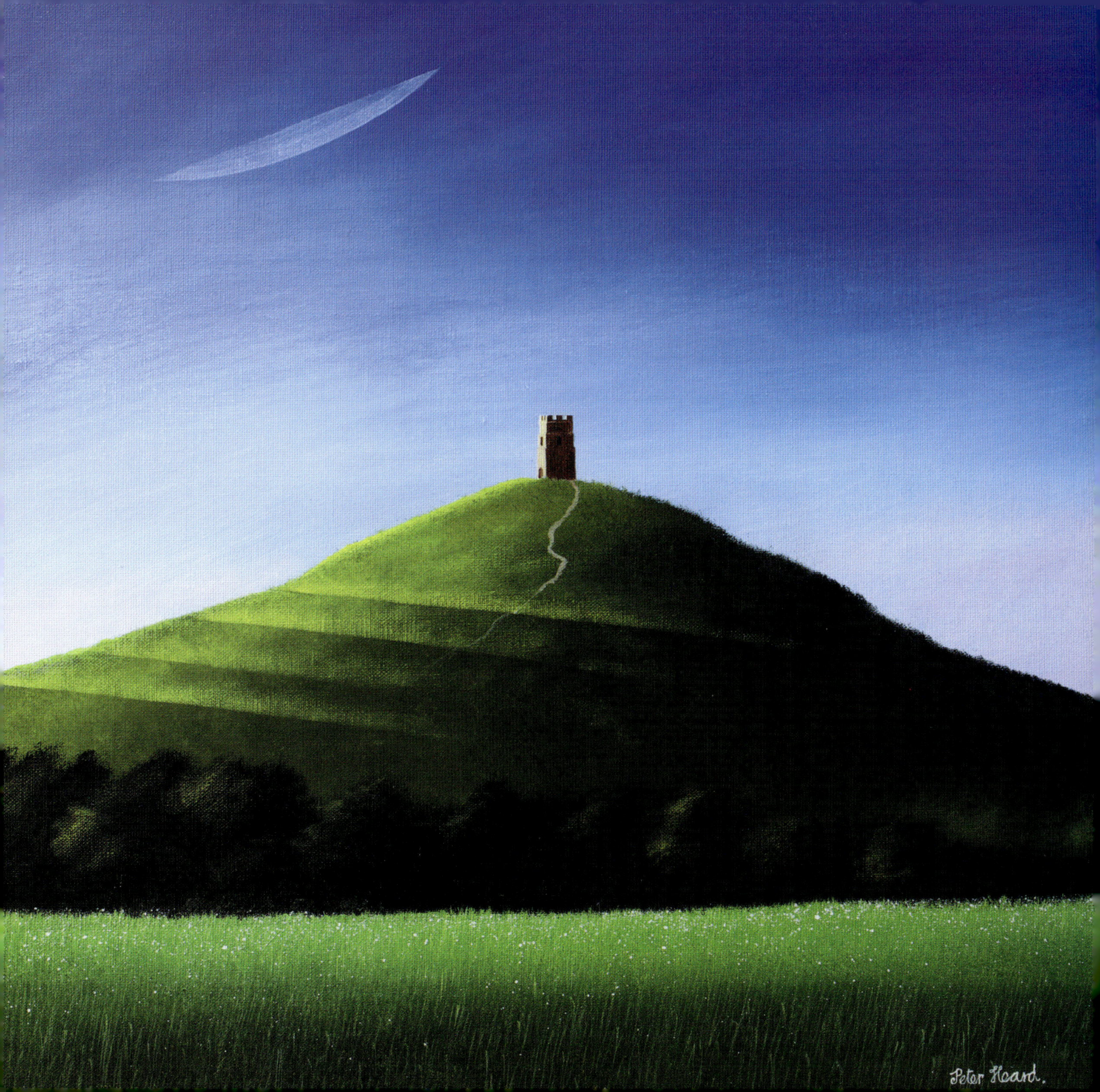
Peter Heard.

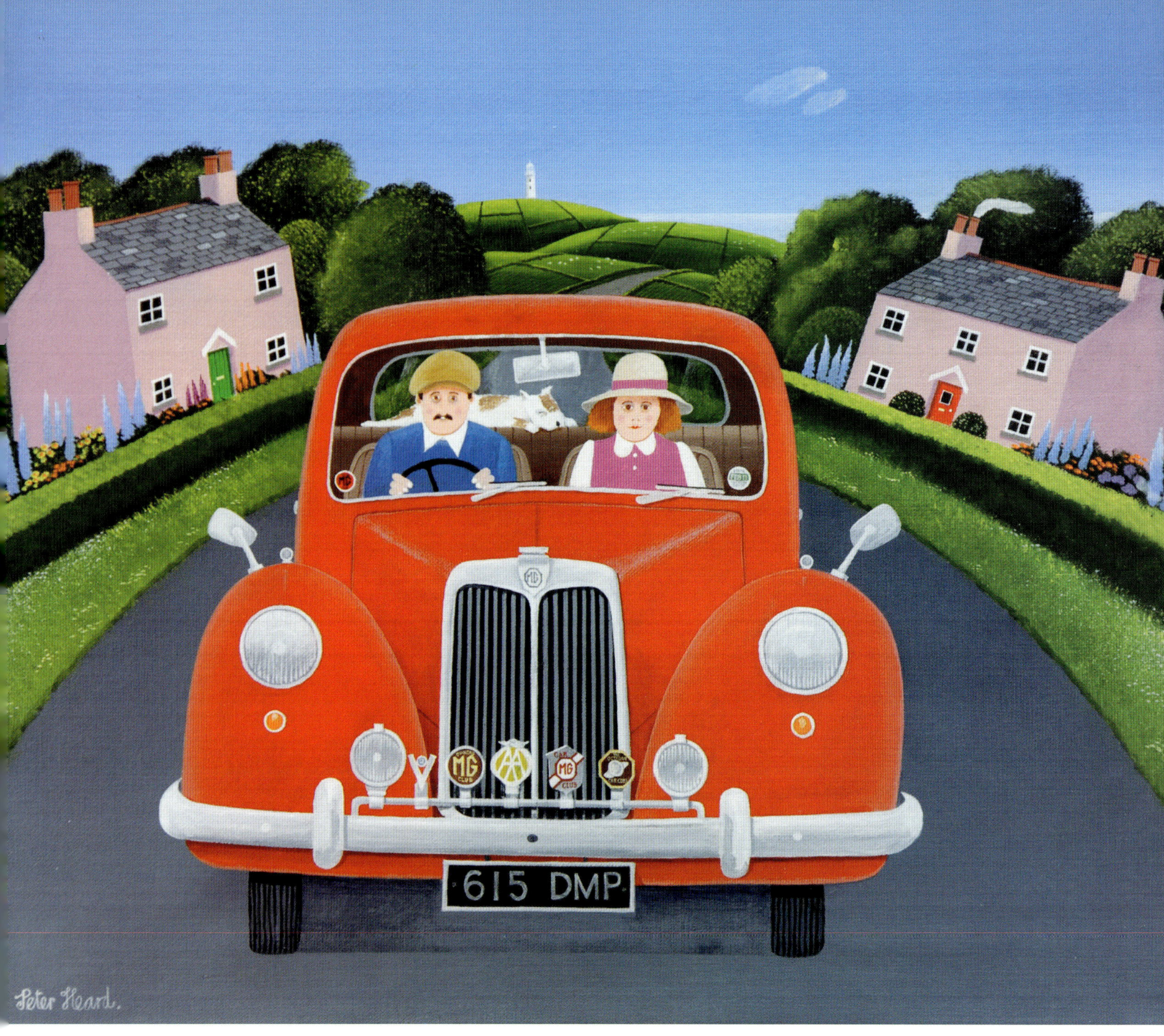
615 DMP
Peter Heard.

CLASSIC CAR RALLY

Peter had always wanted to own a "classic" car but it was not possible while living on the crowded streets of London. Moving to the West Country gave him the perfect opportunity and he is now the proud owner of a white MGA roadster. Not only that but Peter discovered there are lots of vintage motors lurking in garages in villages all over Somerset. They are lovingly cared for and polished and brought out on sunny days. Then over drinks and banter at The White Horse pub in Stogumber a Classic Car club was formed for days out and petrolhead chats. The country lanes and open moors are the natural habitat for these old cars. They evoke an era when the roads were quieter and cars went at a more sedate speed – even though their brakes still leave a lot to be desired! For the more daring there are actually rallies across Exmoor and the real enthusiast might wish to visit the Exmoor Classic Car Collection in Porlock which is in a time-warp garage in the high street. This painting also recalls the days of metal badges, for the AA and other car organisations – days when the AA patrolman on his motorbike used to salute when you drove past!

Classic Car Rally
Acrylic on Linen
60 x 50 cm

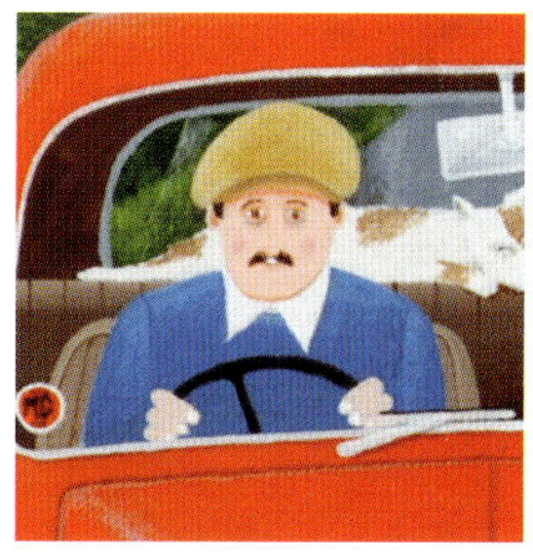

BATHING BELLE

At first glance this seems a simple, fun picture illustrating the innocence of the naïve genre. Our daring bathing belle is on a day trip to the seaside where she must venture into the sea for a swim while her friend can only manage a paddle with her clothes on. But on closer analysis the painting is a perfect example of the "conscious" naïve artist at the height of his skills. It contains a narrative and is a balanced, detailed composition that shows the power of the golden rule of thirds . The water line and the chimney line divide the picture into horizontal thirds while the bathing belle is positioned centrally. This age-old graphic device creates an instant sense of balance and harmony, which the viewer may not be conscious of. On this platform Peter has layered strong vibrant colour. Could her bathing suit be anything but red and white stripes? And see how easy it is for the naïve artist to paint waves!

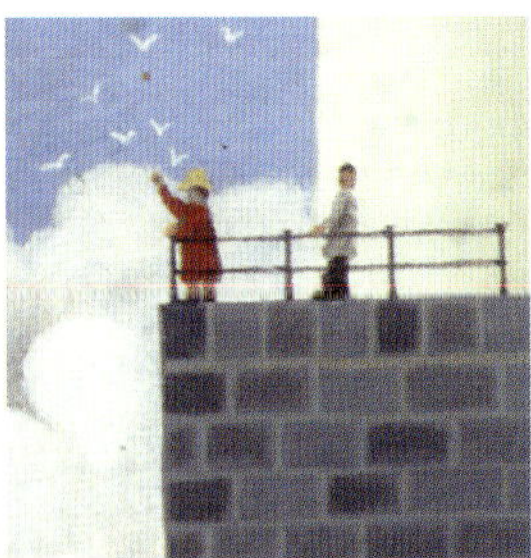

Bathing Belle
Acrylic on Linen
50 x 60 cm

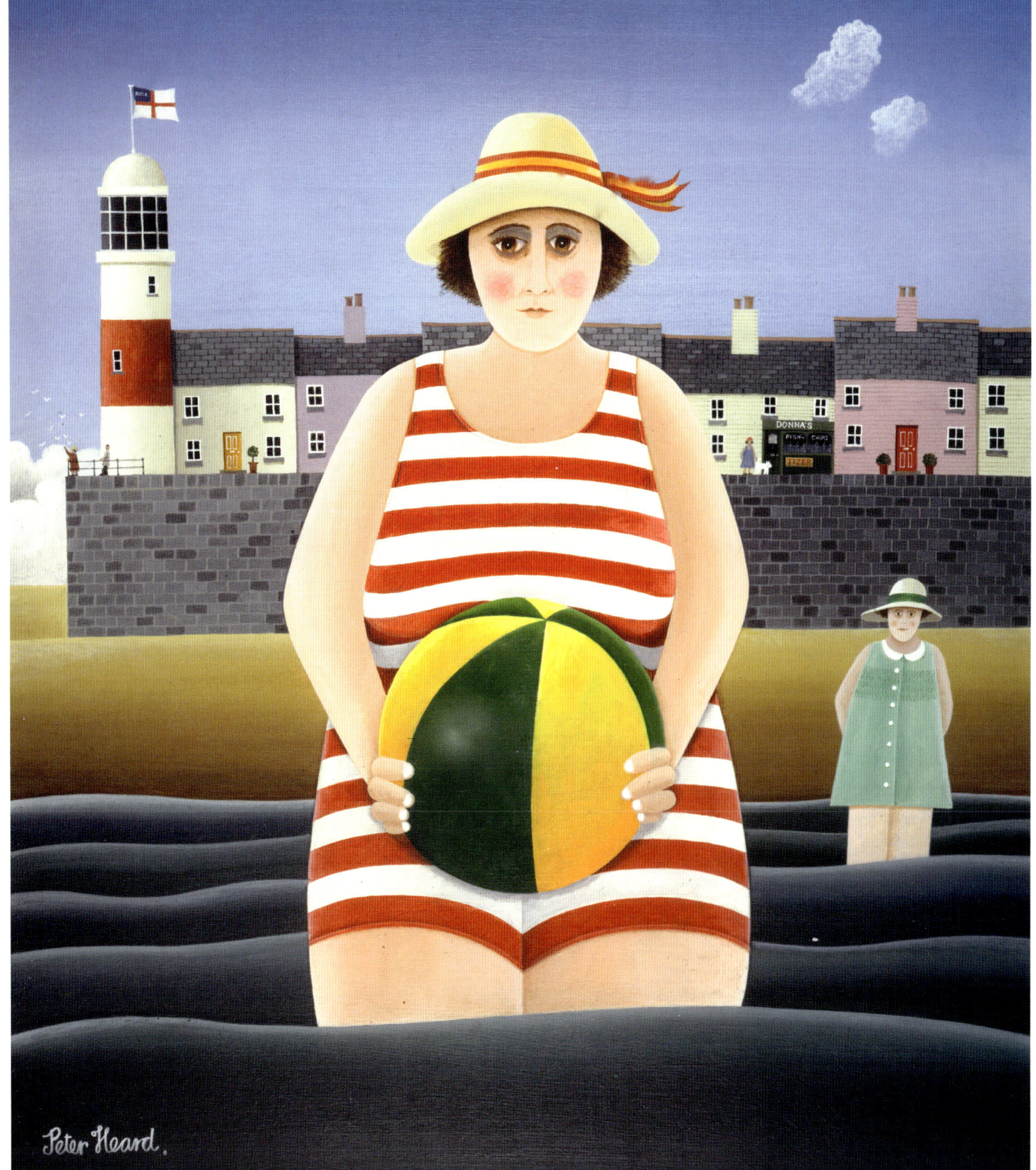
DONNA'S
Peter Heard.

The Graphic Landscape

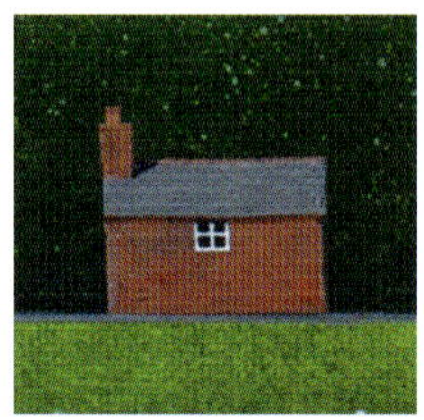

Peter's modus operandi is to see a field, a hill or a copse, become fascinated by it and then take a photograph. From that snapshot he creates his stylised painting of the land and the landscape. He is interested in the terraces of fields, the contrasting colours of cultivated and uncultivated meadow, the changing sky. As part of this the Turnaround Tree has become a particular symbol – Peter has photographed it more than 1,000 times from his studio window in the changing seasons of the year.

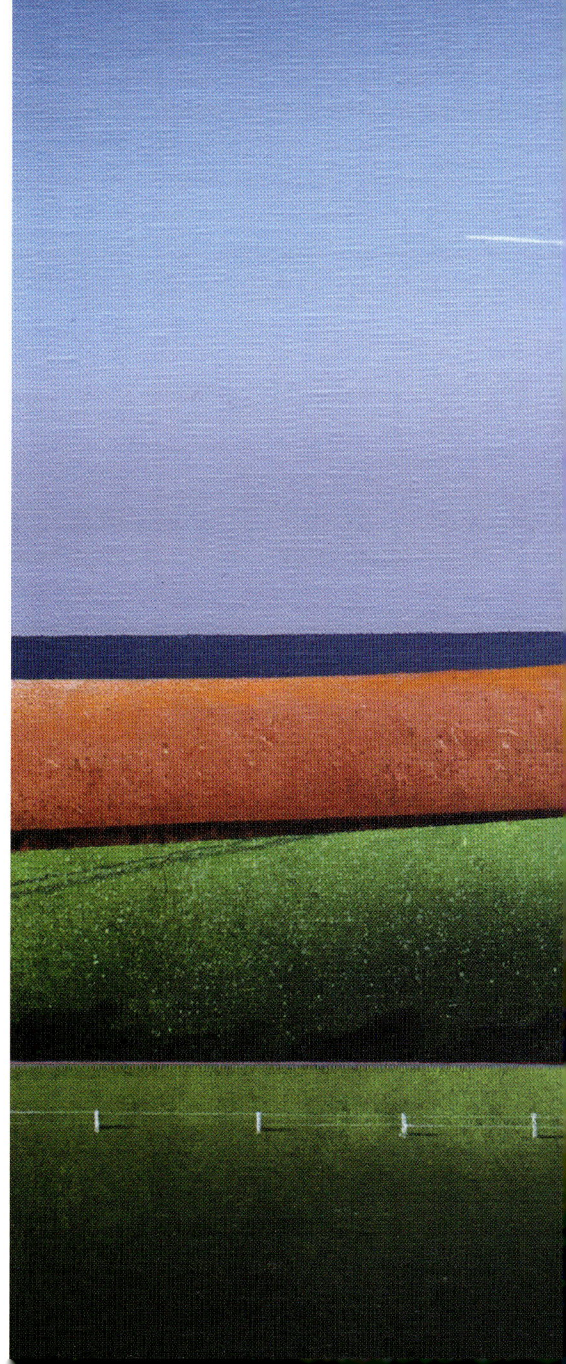

Railway Hut by Dunster
Acrylic on Linen
60 x 50 cm

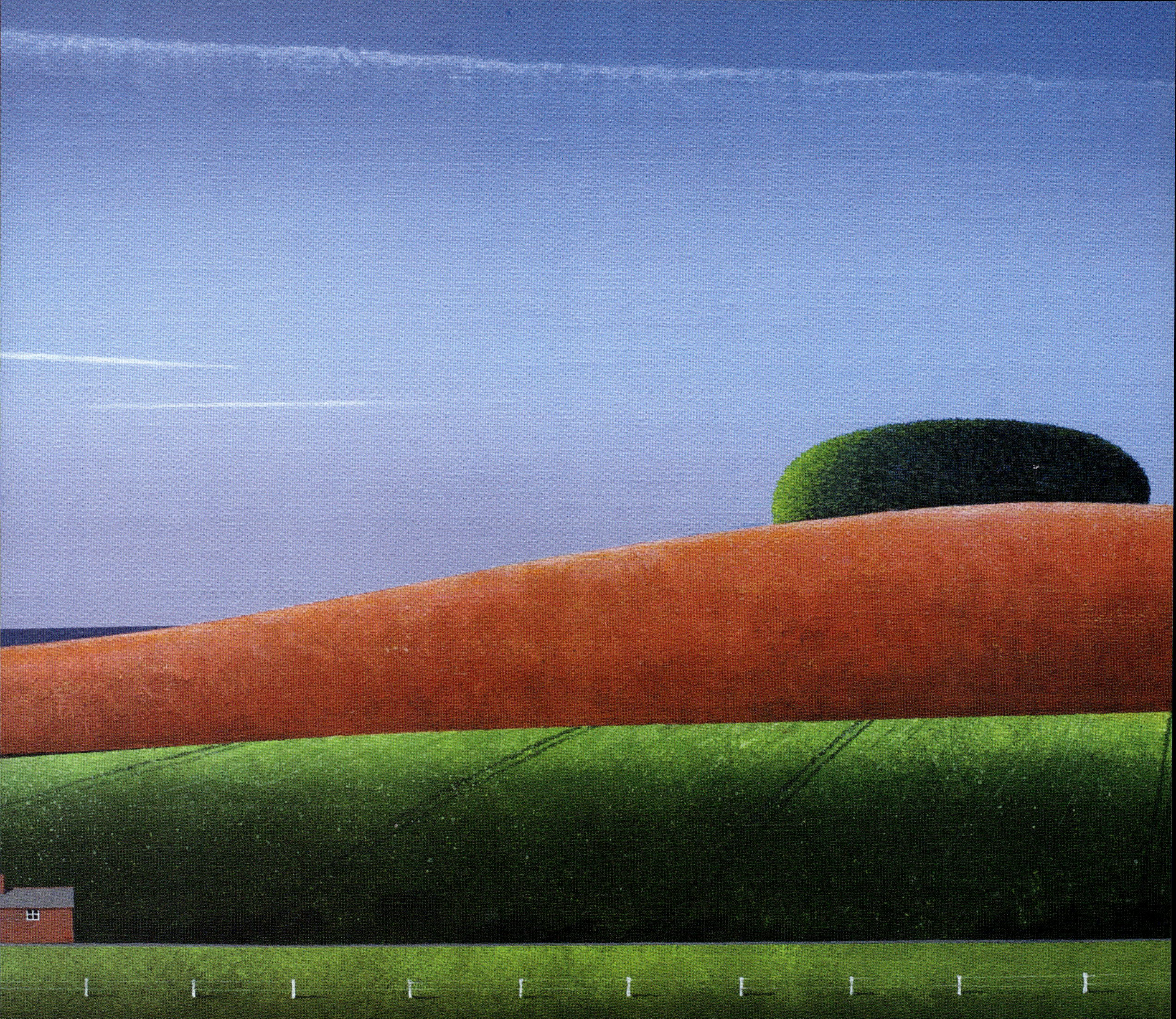

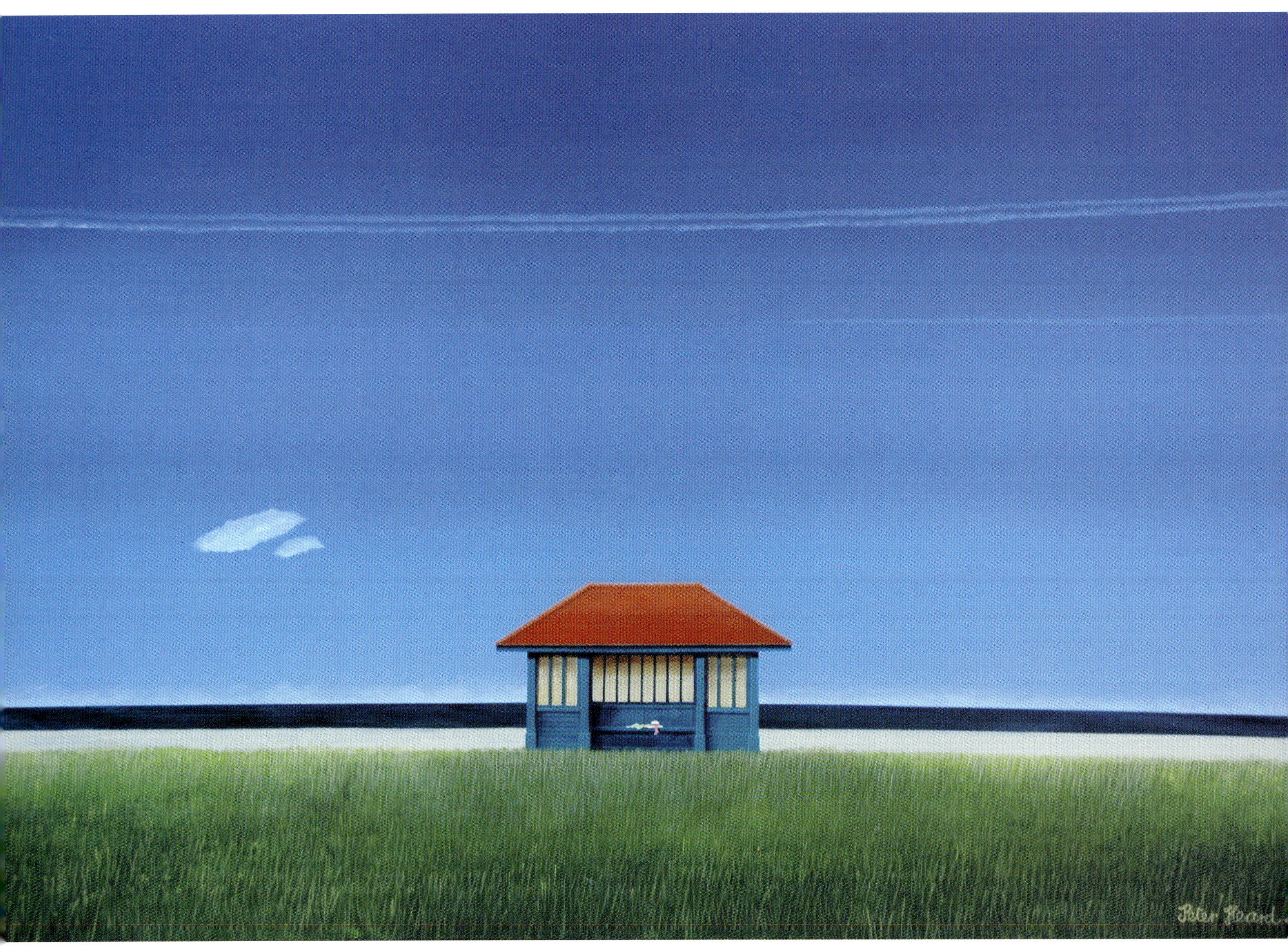
Peter Heard

GONE FOR A DIP

Peter has a theory that as painters get older they move inexorably towards abstraction. They divest themselves of extraneous detail perhaps in an unconscious search for pure shape, colour and harmony. They pare things back. This painting is perhaps an example of Peter's move in this direction. From a distance it could be read as an abstract composition of proportion and colour. On closer inspection however, there appears a narrative plus some trademark details in the seaside shelter and the straw hat. Where has she gone ?

Gone for a DIp
Acrylic on Linen
50 x 75 cm

PINK COTTAGE BY KILVE

This is a painting of pure simplicity. Balance and colour – is the green background a dark threatening sky or a wall of forest? The image breaks the golden rule of thirds in painting in that it is virtually split in half. The colours blend so well, the pink-walled cottage, the reddish-brown roof and the golden field with hints of red flowers in the foreground. The earliest pink pigments used in limewash were from Devon red ochre, vermillion from sulphur and quicksilver, and madder from the root of the madder plant. The pinks were used historically because they please and satisfy the eye. The farmers did not know that the traditional pink limewash blends well with yellow corn or red ploughed earth because it has a similar chroma. This cottage in Kilve illustrates this well. Good colour combinations provide tranquillity and a timeless sense of harmony that no alteration could improve. Luckily it is also a great colour for using in landscapes!

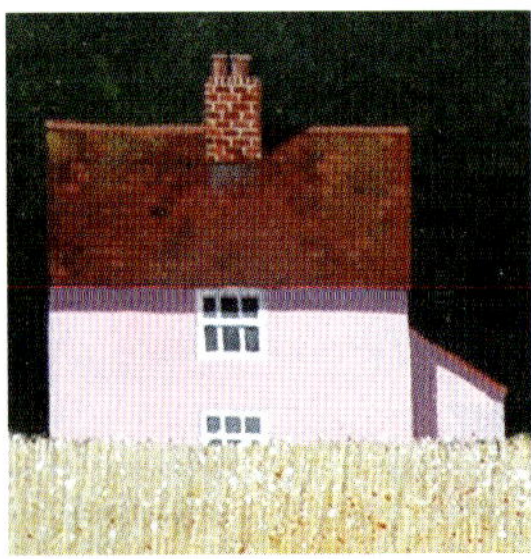

Pink Cottage by Kilve
Acrylic on Linen
40 x 40 cm

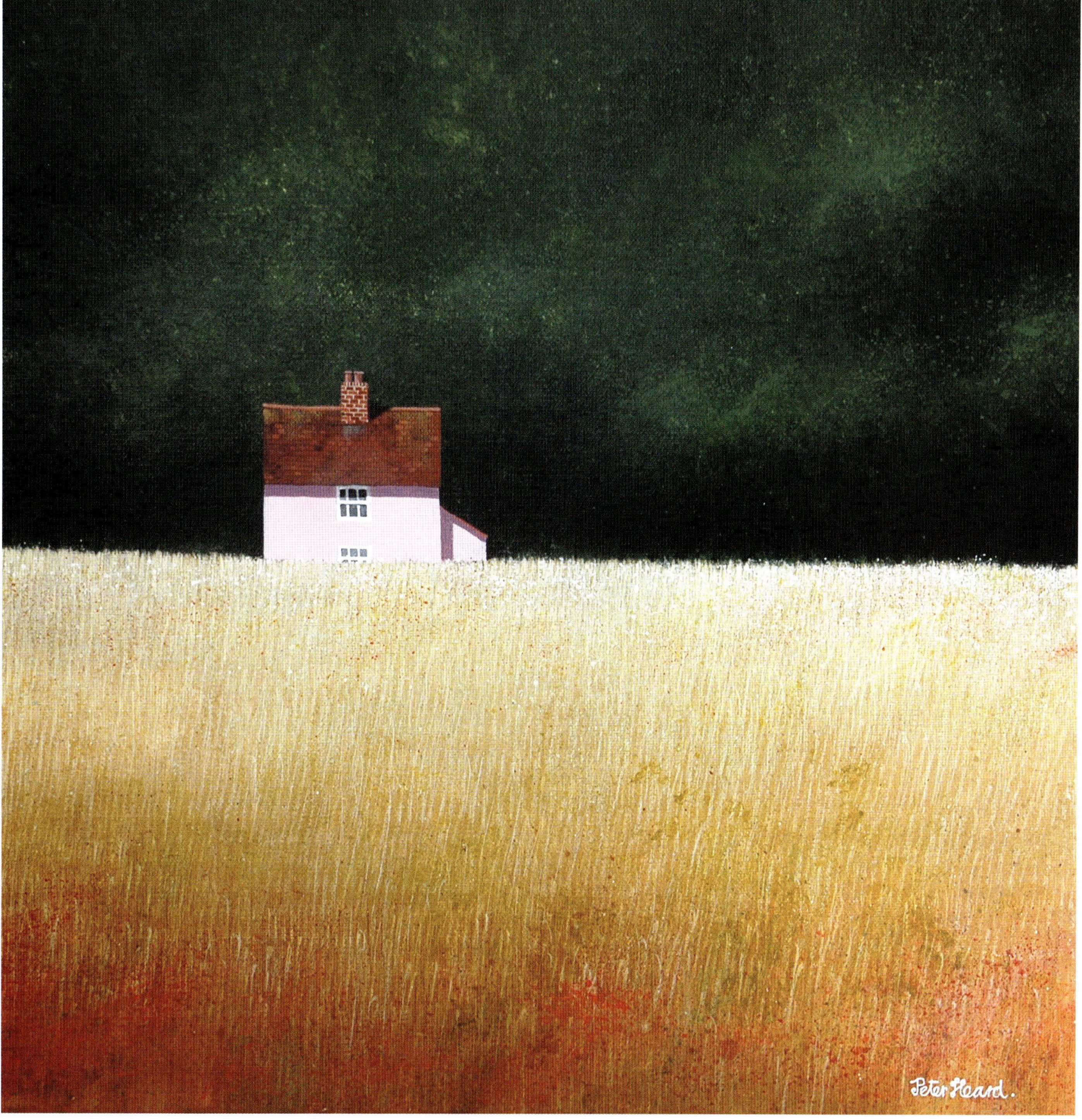
Peter Heard.

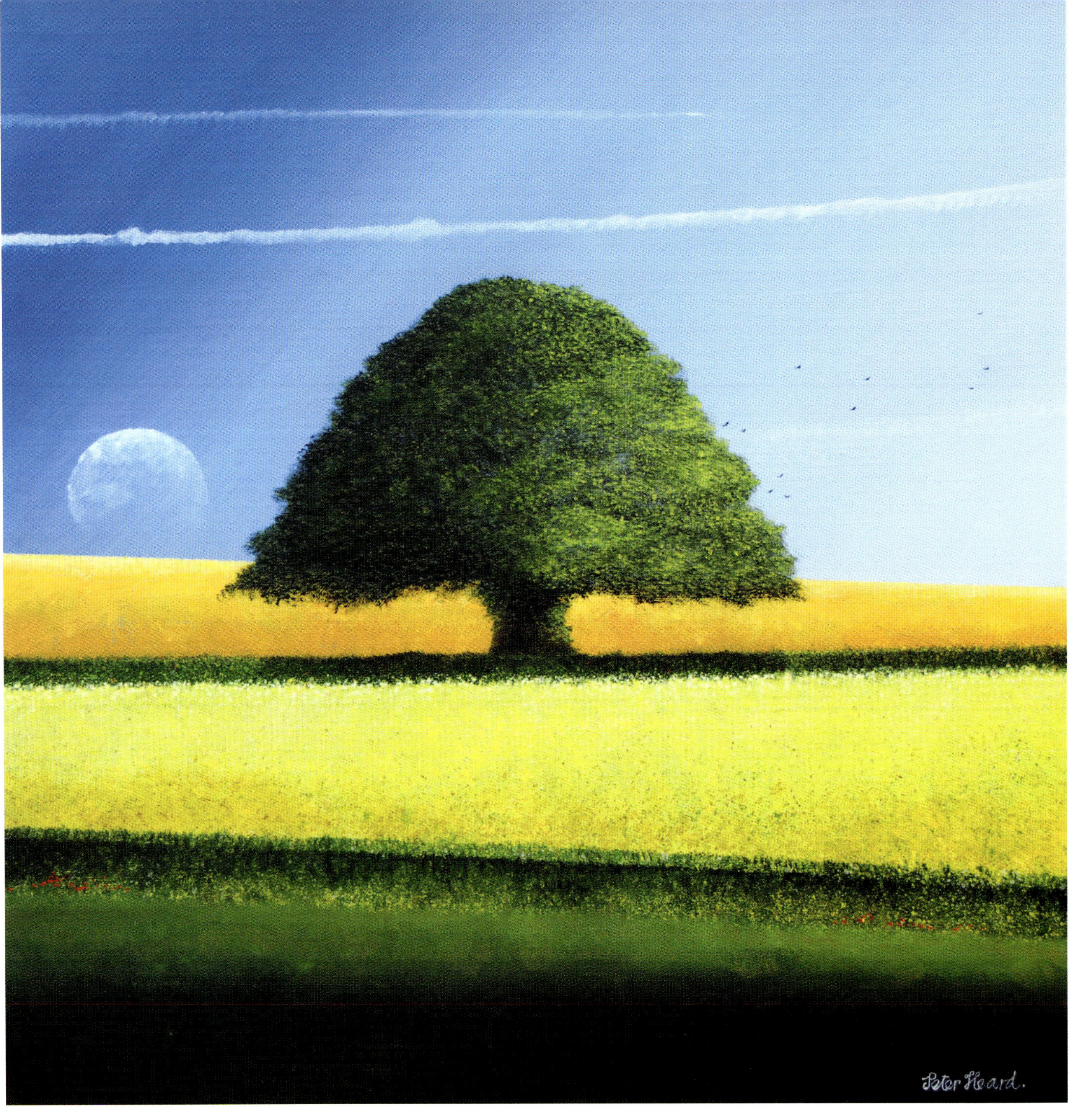
Peter Heard.

THE TURNAROUND TREE

This is the oak tree that so fascinates Peter. Here it is in full leaf. It is on a hillside above Stogumber and is called the Turnaround Tree because it is a suitable distance from the village and people can walk their dogs to it, turn around and return home. The oak tree is a symbol of strength and endurance and is the national tree of England and several other countries. "Hearts of oak are our ships" is a line from the official march of the Royal Navy. Besides being a fascinating tree in its own right, alone and defiant on the hillside, it is also an emblem of Englishness. And it has become emblematic to Peter in his rural life.

The Turnaround Tree
Acrylic on Linen
50 x 50 cm

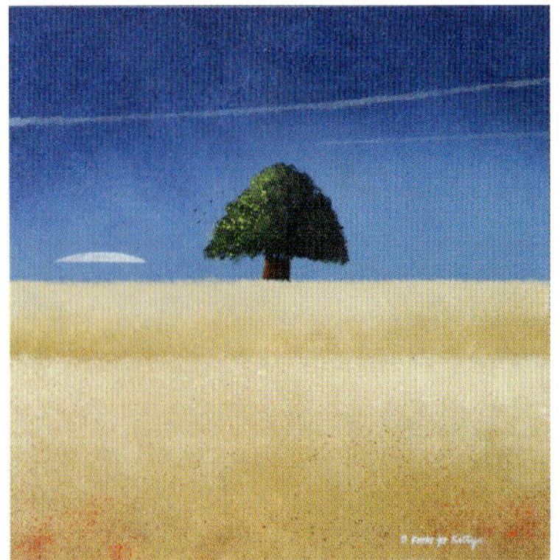
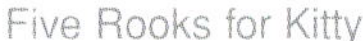
Five Rooks for Kitty

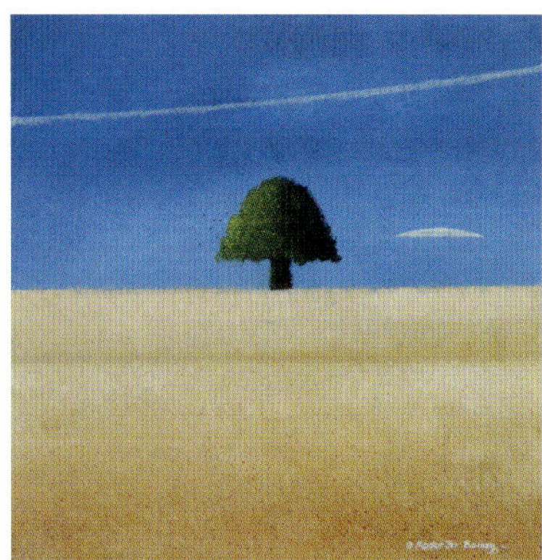
Nine Rooks for Barney

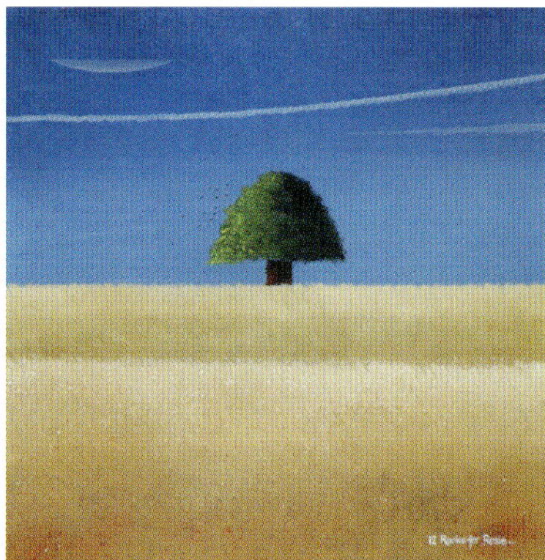
Twelve Rooks for Rosie

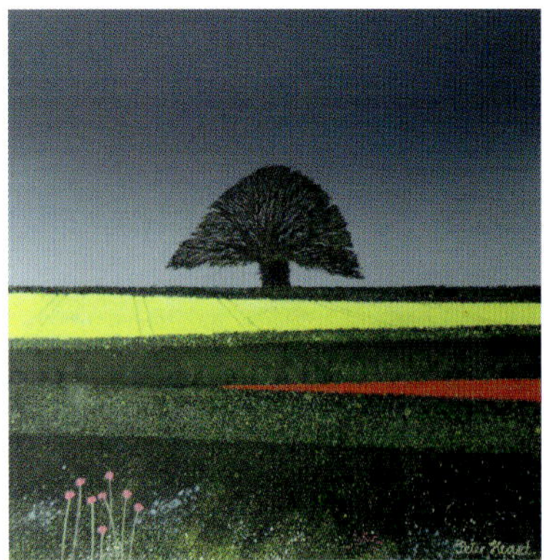
Spring

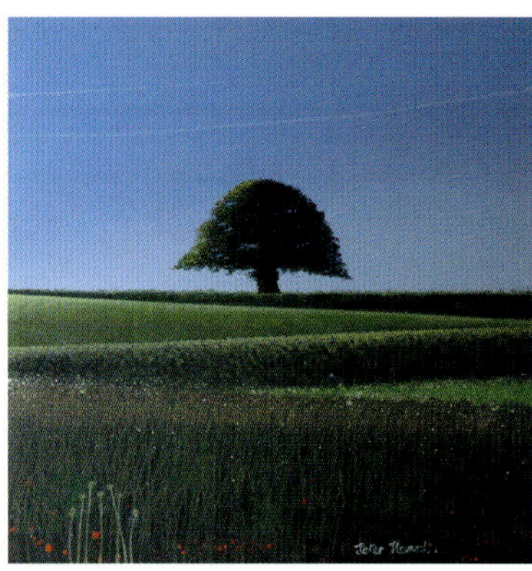
Summer

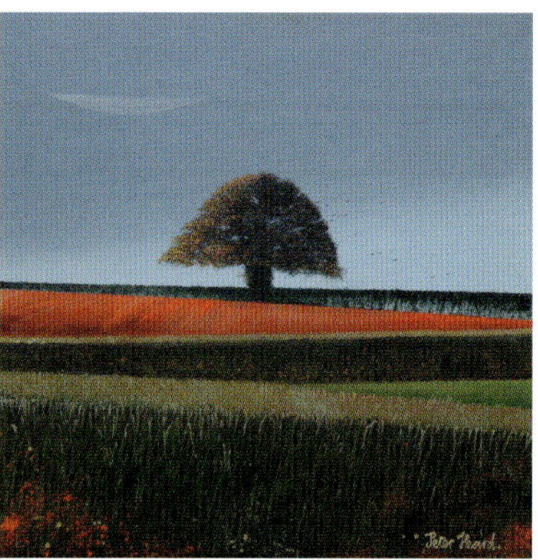
Autumn

Turnaround Tree 2
Acrylic on Linen
50 x 50 cm

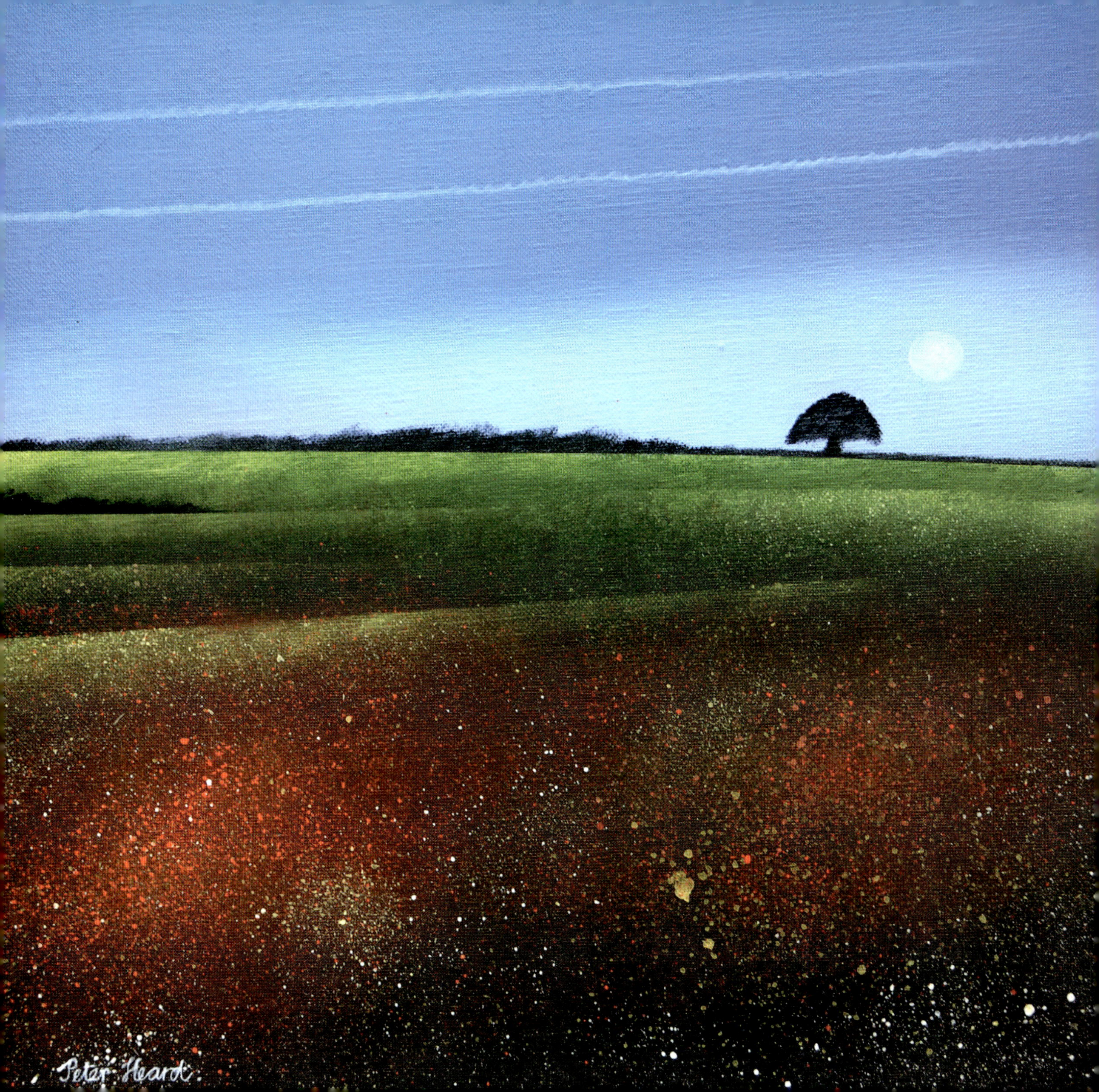
Peter Heard

FIELDS BY VEXFORD

Well, a Peter Heard painting with no blue sky or gentle fluffy clouds! This is a landscape painting that is more a graphic design. It has a lot of Peter's elements – the copse, the defined hillside, the remote and whitewashed farmhouse, the fields in various stages of harvesting. But the sky? It looks as though a storm is about to be unleashed or it already has been and the land is recovering. Really, this is Peter playing with the light on the fields. As he says, sometimes less is more.

Fields by Vexford
Acrylic on Linen
40 x 40 cm

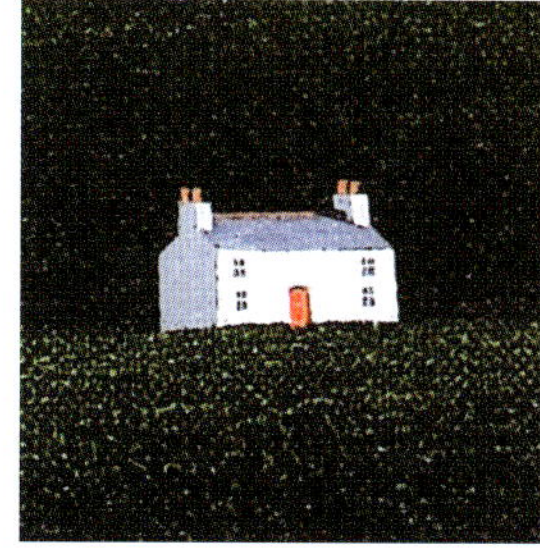

Hill by Crowcombe

Peter often uses a copse in his landscapes. This one sits high above the village of Crowcombe. A copse is a small lowland woodland, planted and used by farmers as cover. The name comes from coppice. Coppicing is a traditional method of woodland management. Young tree stems are repeatedly cut down to near ground level. In subsequent years, many new shoots will emerge and, after a number of years, the coppiced tree, or stool, is ready to be harvested and the cycle begins again. Coppiced stems are characteristically curved at the base.

The curve may allow the identification of coppice timber in archaeological sites – timber in the Sweet Track in the Somerset Levels (built in 3806 BC) has been identified as coppiced lime. In this painting the land is layered down from the copse with slivers of new ploughed red fields providing a graphic counterpoint to the greens.

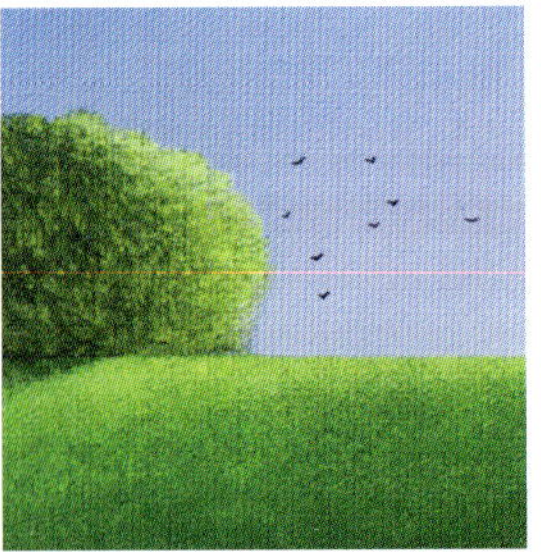

Hill by Crowcombe
Acrylic on Linen
40 x 40 cm

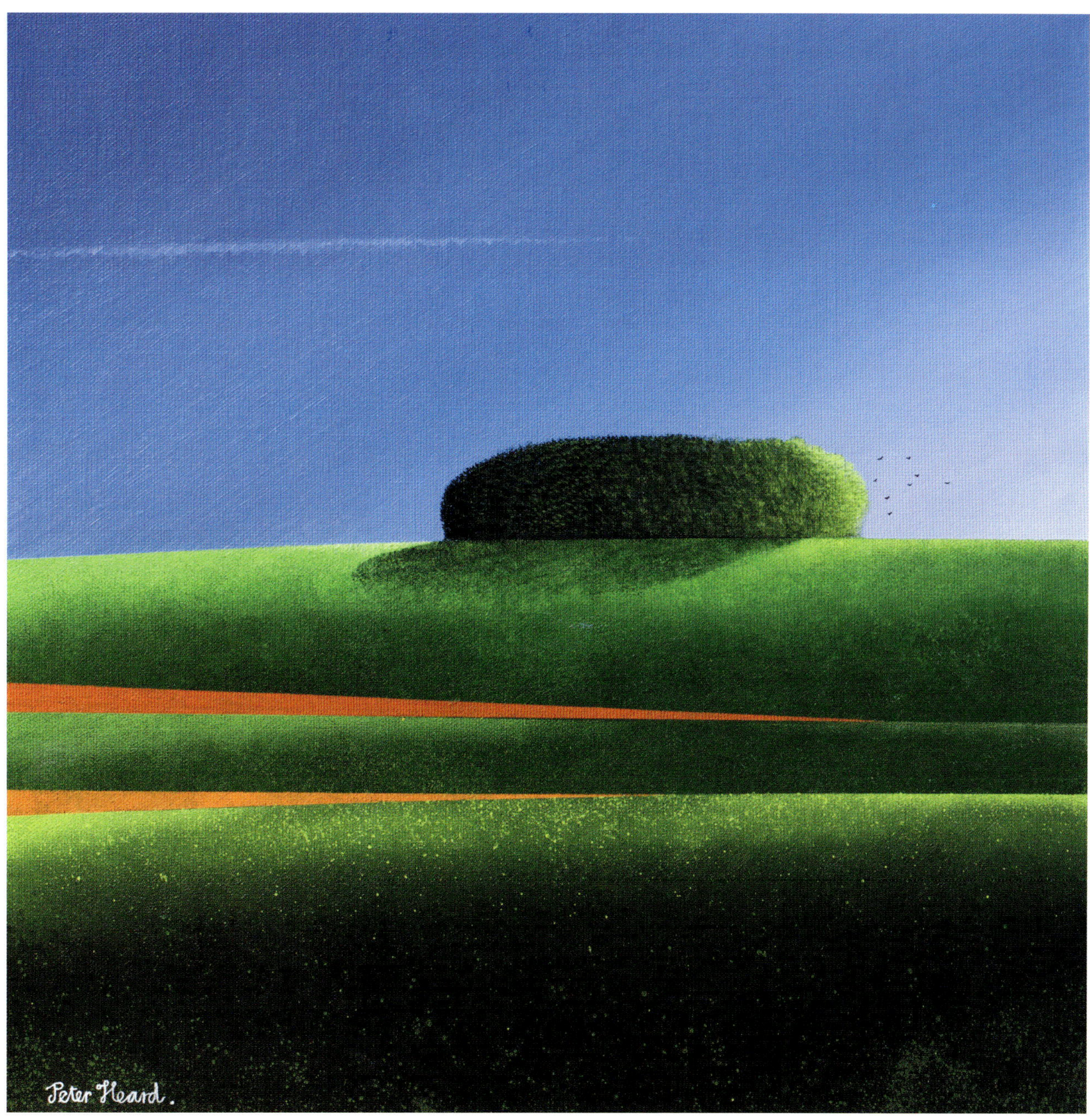
Peter Heard.

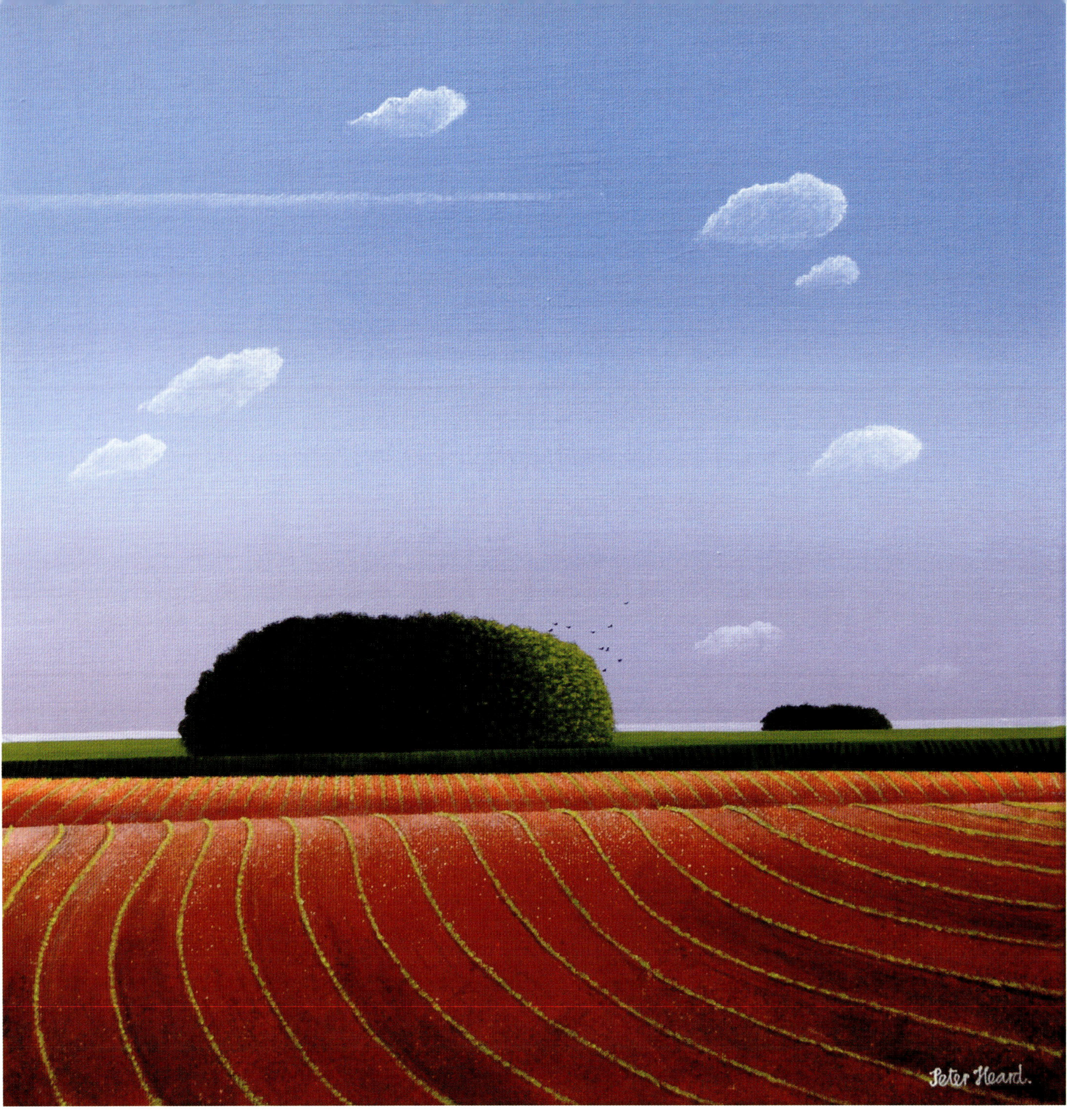
Peter Heard.

NEW CROP BY FRIENDSHIP JUNCTION

Peter saw this field by Friendship Junction near to where he lives. The old Somerset County Council black and white cast iron fingerpost road signs are wonderful. They are relics of the early days of motoring at the beginning of the twentieth century. A Local Heritage Initiative funded programme has seen 30 fingerposts repaired and maintained within the Quantock Hills Area of Outstanding Natural Beauty. They have had a triangular collar added with the historic name of the junction. And they have been painted in raven grey, a colour unique to posts in the Quantocks. This field near to Friendship Junction was newly planted and the first shoots were producing these bright green lines on the red earth. Peter field watches and photographs, which makes for graphic landscapes.

New Crop by Friendship Junction
Acrylic on Linen
40 x 40 cm

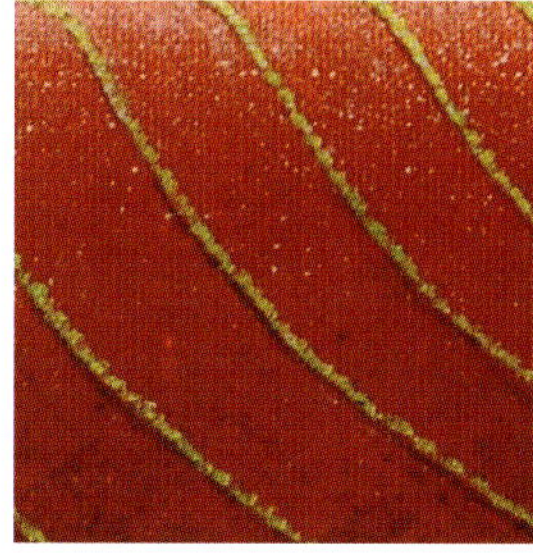

TOWARDS COVER

Copses and trees are referred to as "cover" by locals. Presumably they were planted to provide shelter for pheasants and other game before they were blasted out of the air come the killing time. Lots of them harbour rookeries. There is a rookery in the churchyard in Stogumber. When the wind is up their tails, they indulge in flock games and the jackdaws join in. The noise is amazing. Jackdaws are very sociable birds. When Peter first came to Somerset they would feed on his lawn. He thought the jackdaws were baby rooks – silly London boy! Pairs of rooks often play wonderful aerial games with a buzzard. There are plenty of buzzards in Somerset. They sit on the telegraph poles coming down the hill into Stogumber and will fly to the next pole as you drive along – great to watch in Peter's MGA Roadster! He and Mary were told not to let their kittens into the garden until they were bigger as the buzzards would have them for dinner. In this painting all is stillness apart from the motion of the rook returning home – towards cover. The alliums in the foreground are a graphic device to add balance and colour.

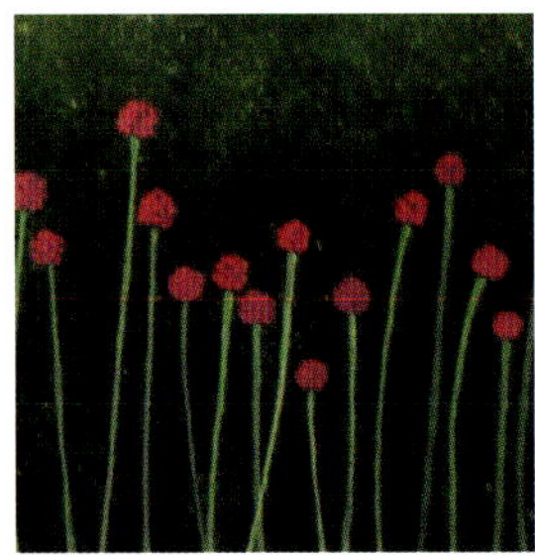

Towards Cover
Acrylic on Linen
50 x 50 cm

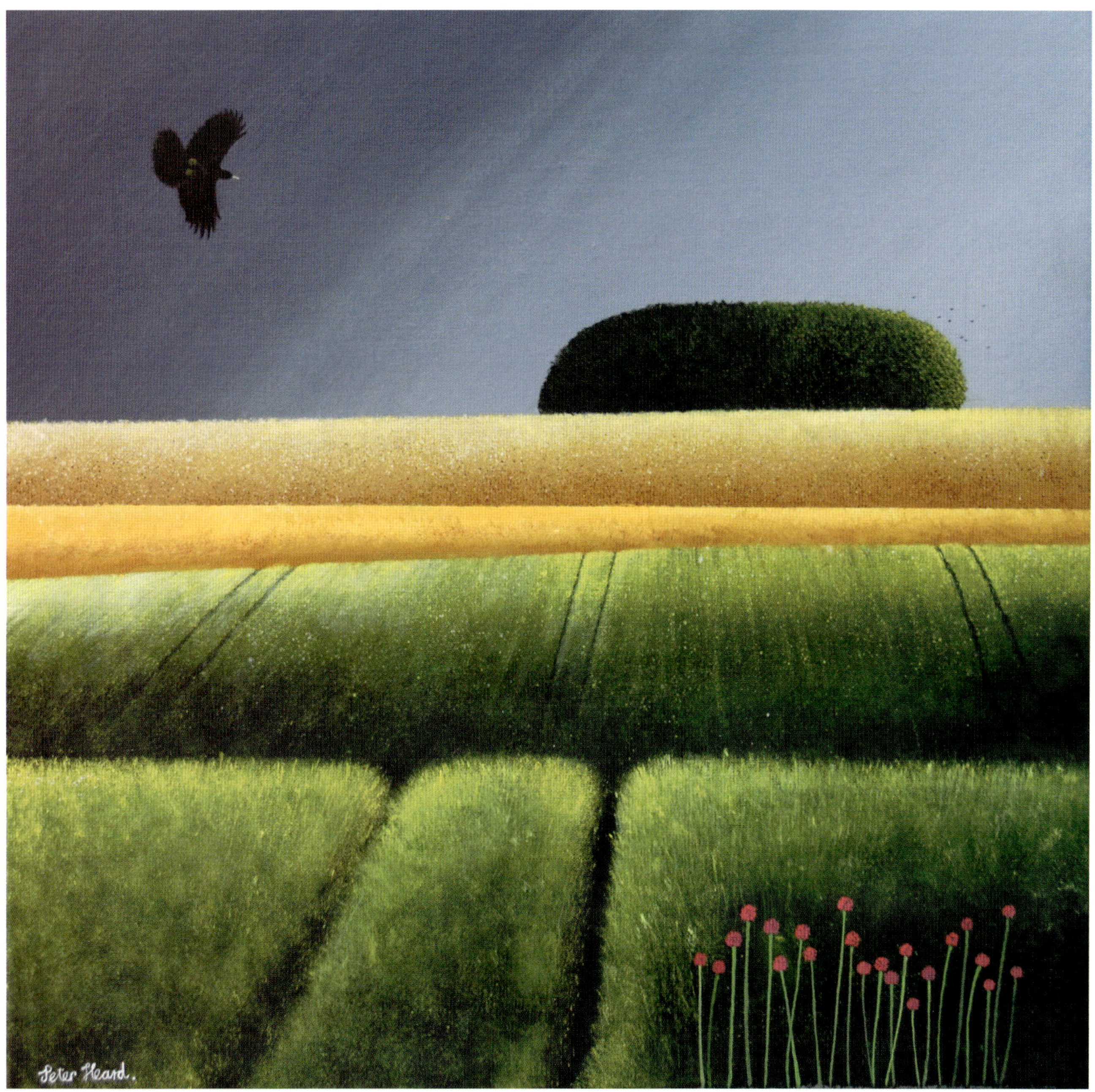
Peter Heard.

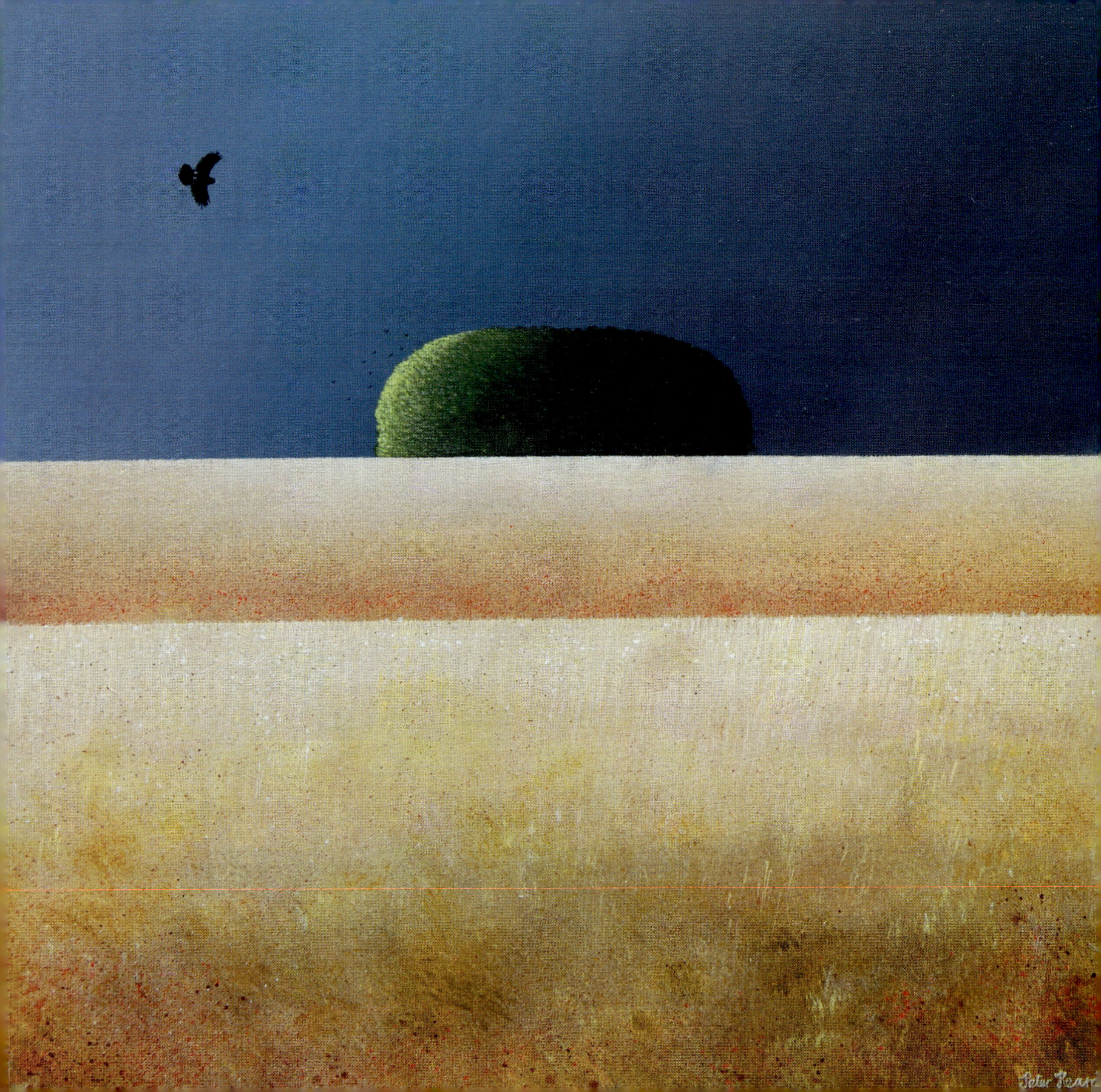

TOWARDS COVER 2

The title suggests this is a move on from Towards Cover – Peter knows that when he is working on any painting ideas for future work spring to mind. In this picture the imagery has become emptier, sparser and devoid of the green foreground of the original work. It is as if he has used a telephoto lens to zoom in on the copse and cornfields. It might seem to be a case of "less is more" but there is plenty going on!

Texture, spatter and an impressionist approach ensure the golden corn remains interesting. And the majesty of the black crow on the wing is something to behold. Once again it shows how Peter's paintings work on two levels – from across the room and up close and personal...

Towards Cover 2
Acrylic on Linen
50 x 50 cm

RED FIELD BY DEAD WOMAN'S DITCH

Legend has it the ditch on Quantock Common near Over Stowey got its name from the discovery there of the body of the wife of charcoal burner John Walford. She was murdered in 1789 and her husband was convicted of the killing. He was hanged at a spot that became known as Walford's Gibbet. His remains were put in a cage and left hanging from the gibbet for a whole year. It's a great story but probably not true. Somerset County Council records show that Dead Woman's Ditch was named on a map of 1782 – seven years before Walford! In fact the ditch is said to have been part of the Bronze Age fortifications of Dowsborough Hill Fort as early as 2700BC. It offers commanding views of the Bristol Channel and across the moorlands to warn of attack.

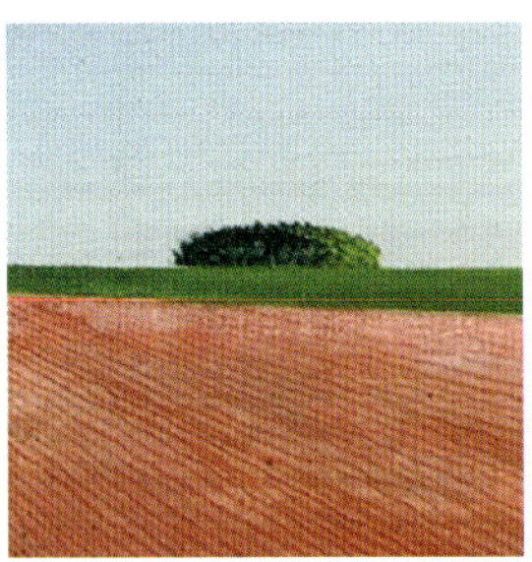

Red Field by Dead Woman's Ditch
Acrylic on Linen
40 x 40 cm

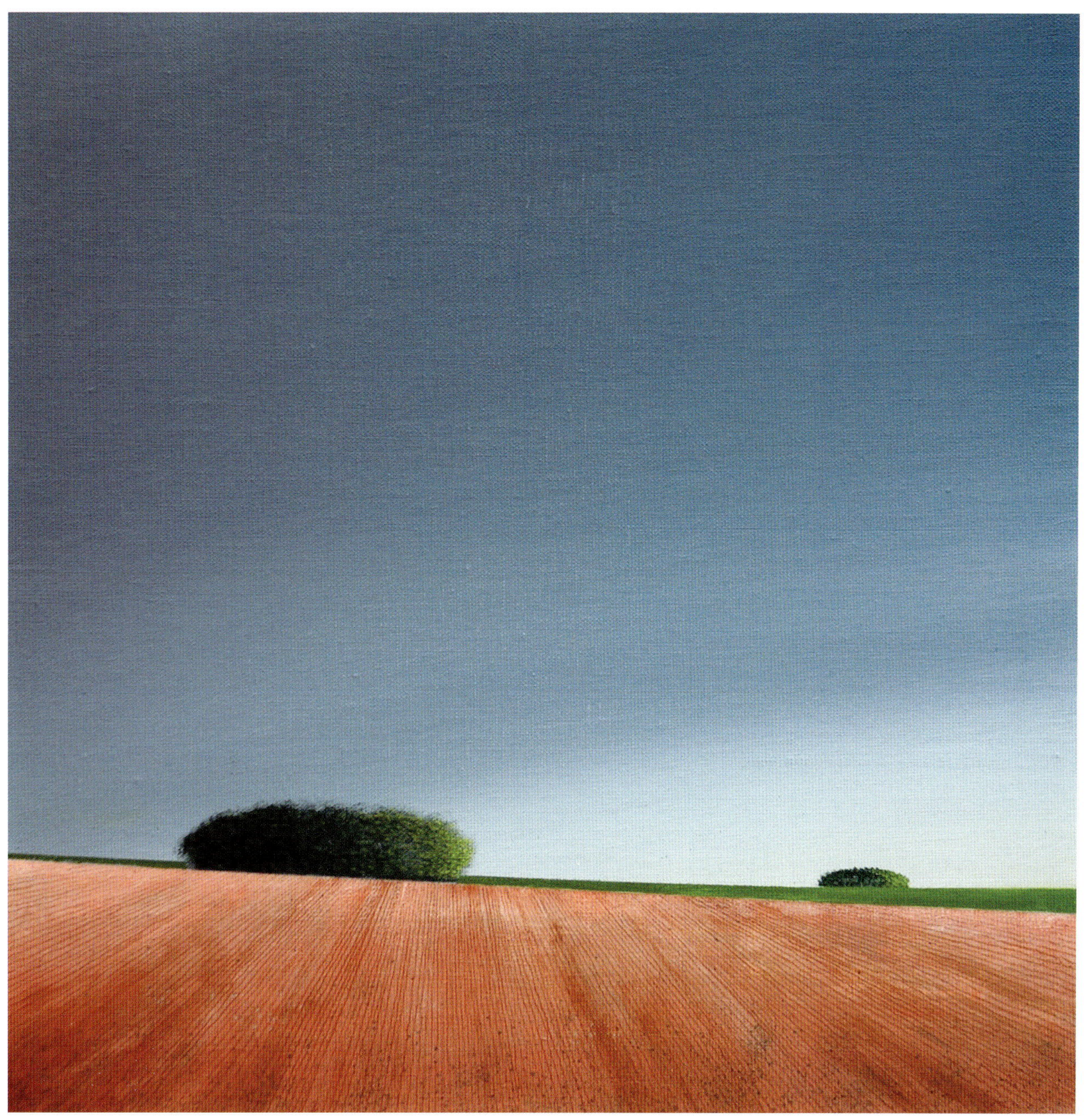

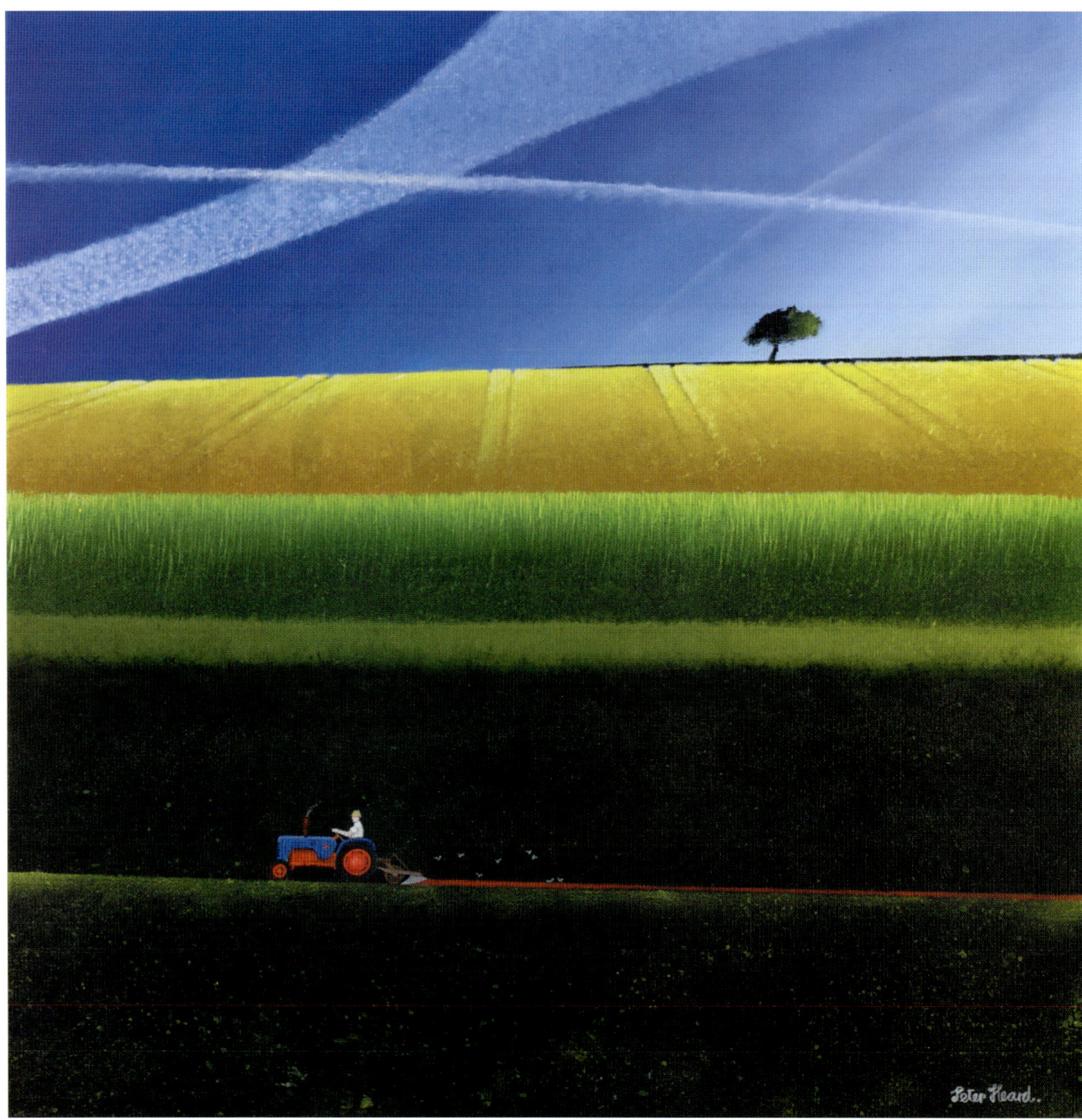
Peter Heard..

STUDIO FIELDS

Here is the Turnaround Tree above Stogumber as Peter sees it from the window of his studio, with the tiered lines of fields in various stages of growth and cultivation. The painting is humanised by the tractor ploughing and creating an extra thin red line in the field. The village was referred to as Waverdine Stoke in the Domesday Book. But after the Norman conquest the de Gomer family came to the area and it was called Stoke de Gomer. Over the years this merged into the present Stogumber. In the nineteenth century the village had 1,500 people a huge amount compared to the present 600. This was because it was a collecting point for wool before it was transported to the port at Watchet. It also had a brewery, three public houses and, rumour has it, a brothel to slake the thirsts of the iron ore miners in the Brendon Hills. The local ale made with water from a mineral spring in the village was advertised as “good for the clergy and others with weak lungs”.

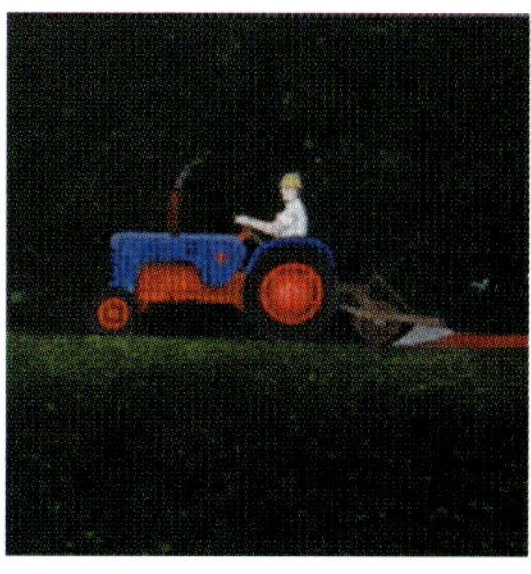

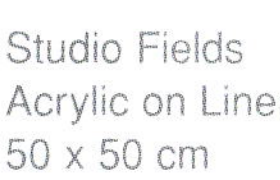

Studio Fields
Acrylic on Linen
50 x 50 cm

YELLOW BY VELLOW

Springtime brings an explosion of new growth in the fields. Corn is growing in this painting. A pagan symbol connected with the harvest is the corn dolly. It was believed that the spirit of the corn lived in the crop and the harvest made it homeless. So a corn dolly was made from the last sheaf of the harvest where the spirit could live during the winter. Next spring the dolly was ploughed into the earth as the first furrow was dug – and was there to look after the next harvest. Dolly may be a corruption of the word idol. Here the dolly is in a wall of fields in which corn is growing. And the cottage in the distance shows that this is not just a pretty landscape to look at. The earth is being worked and people are living on the land.

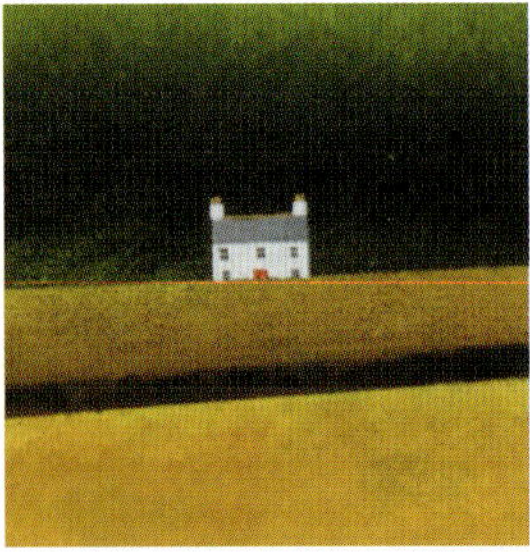

Yellow by Vellow
Acrylic on Linen
60 x 60 cm

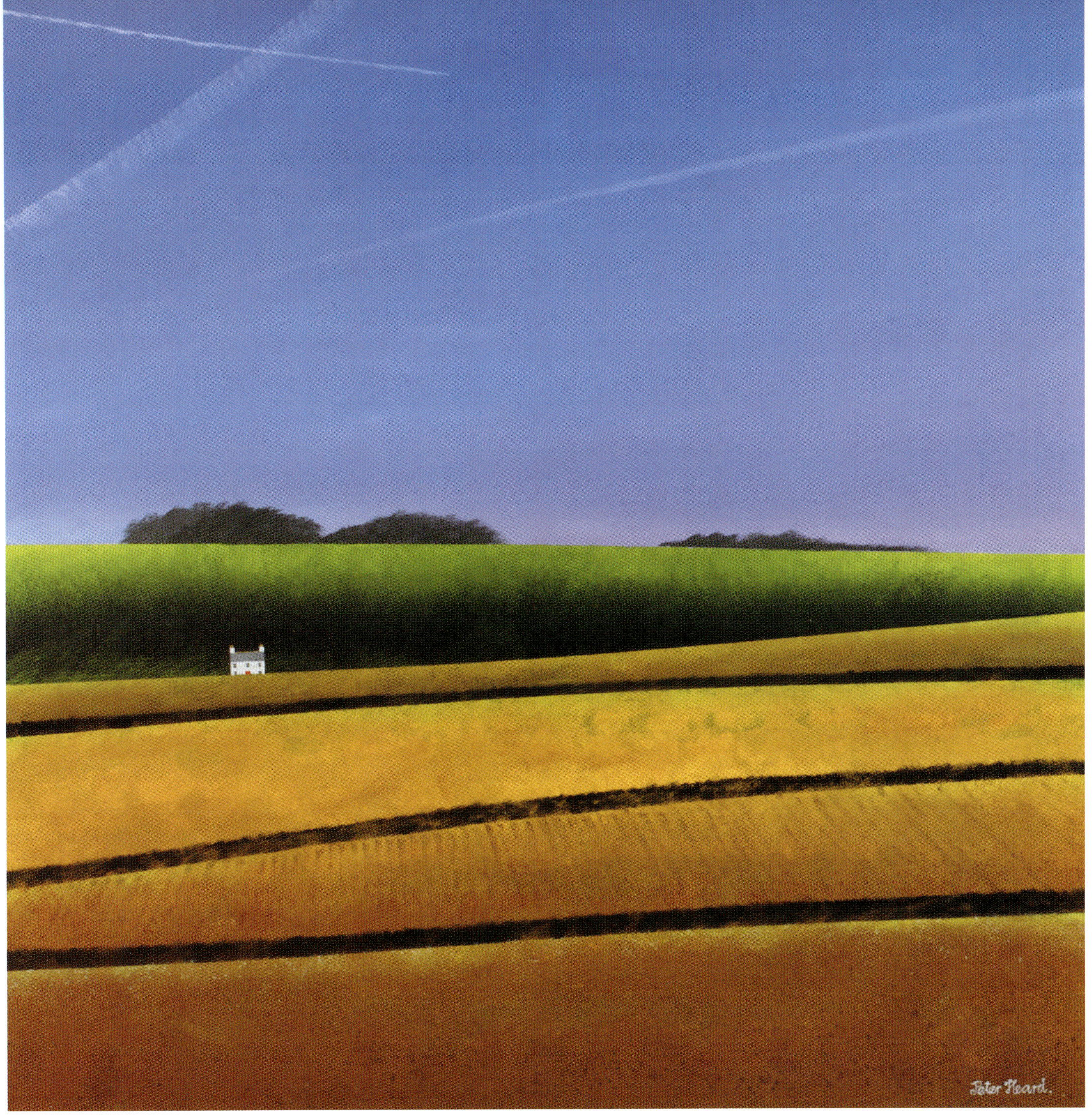
Peter Heard.

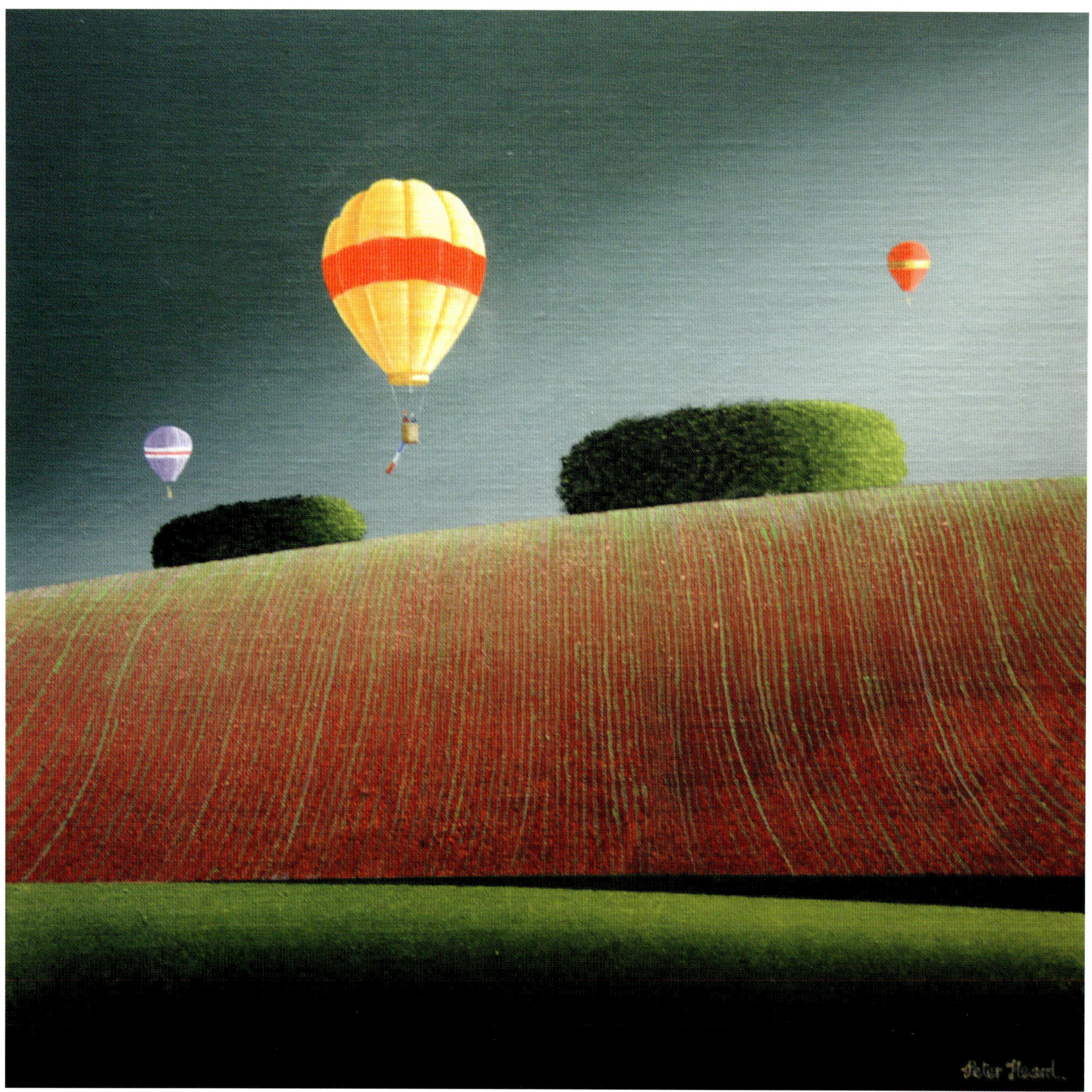

BALLOONS BY MONKSILVER

Most hot air balloon launches are made during the cooler hours of the day, at dawn or two to three hours before sunset when the winds are light, making taking-off and landing easier. The Bristol International Balloon Fiesta, held at Ashton Court each August, attracts crowds of more than 100,000. At times over 100 balloons take off together and a popular attraction is the night glow, when balloons are inflated and glow to music after dark. In 2003 the weight of crowds put such great strain on the Clifton Suspension Bridge it was decided to close the bridge to all traffic, including pedestrians, during the fiesta from 2004 onwards. Monksilver is a village on the boundary of Exmoor National Park. Peter was inspired by the fields of red earth with green stripes from the early stages of planting. Stillness in the air, stillness on the ground.

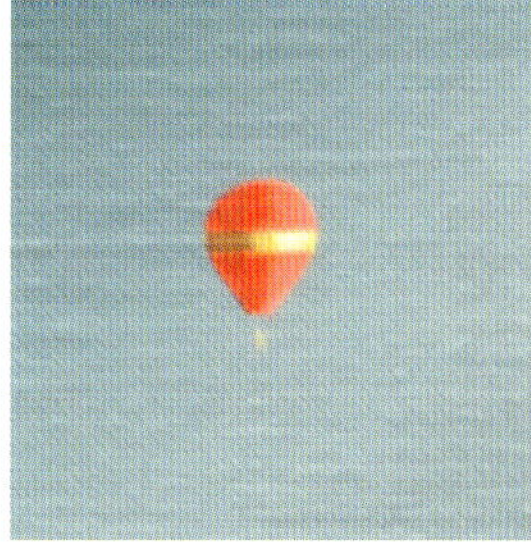

Balloons by Monksilver
Acrylic on Linen
40 x 40 cm

TRACTOR BY NETHER STOWEY

The poet Samuel Taylor Coleridge lived in the Somerset village of Nether Stowey from 1796 to 1798. William Wordsworth joined him there in 1797. Together the two friends wandered the Quantock Hills – and they didn't just talk about poetry. Both were fascinated by the emerging science of geology. The debate at the time was whether the formations of the land were created by fire or water. Certainly the landscape and the distinctive red earth inspired the two poets as it has countless artists including Peter. Coleridge wrote his two most famous poems 'The Rime Of The Ancient Mariner' and 'Kubla Khan' in Somerset and together the poets composed *The Lyrical Ballads*. And there was no sound of machinery to disturb their rambles. Here the tractor adds a touch of humanity to an almost abstract landscape. It is not a passive environment – the land is being worked and, possibly tired of following Cantona's trawler, the opportunist seagulls are now chasing the tractor looking for food as the earth is disturbed.

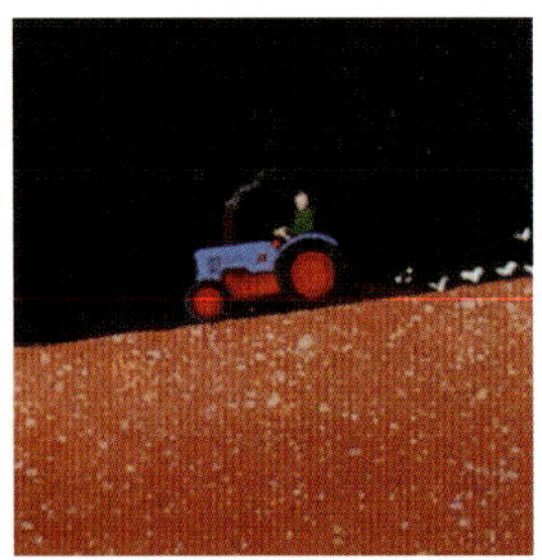

Tractor by Nether Stowey
Acrylic on Linen
50 x 50 cm

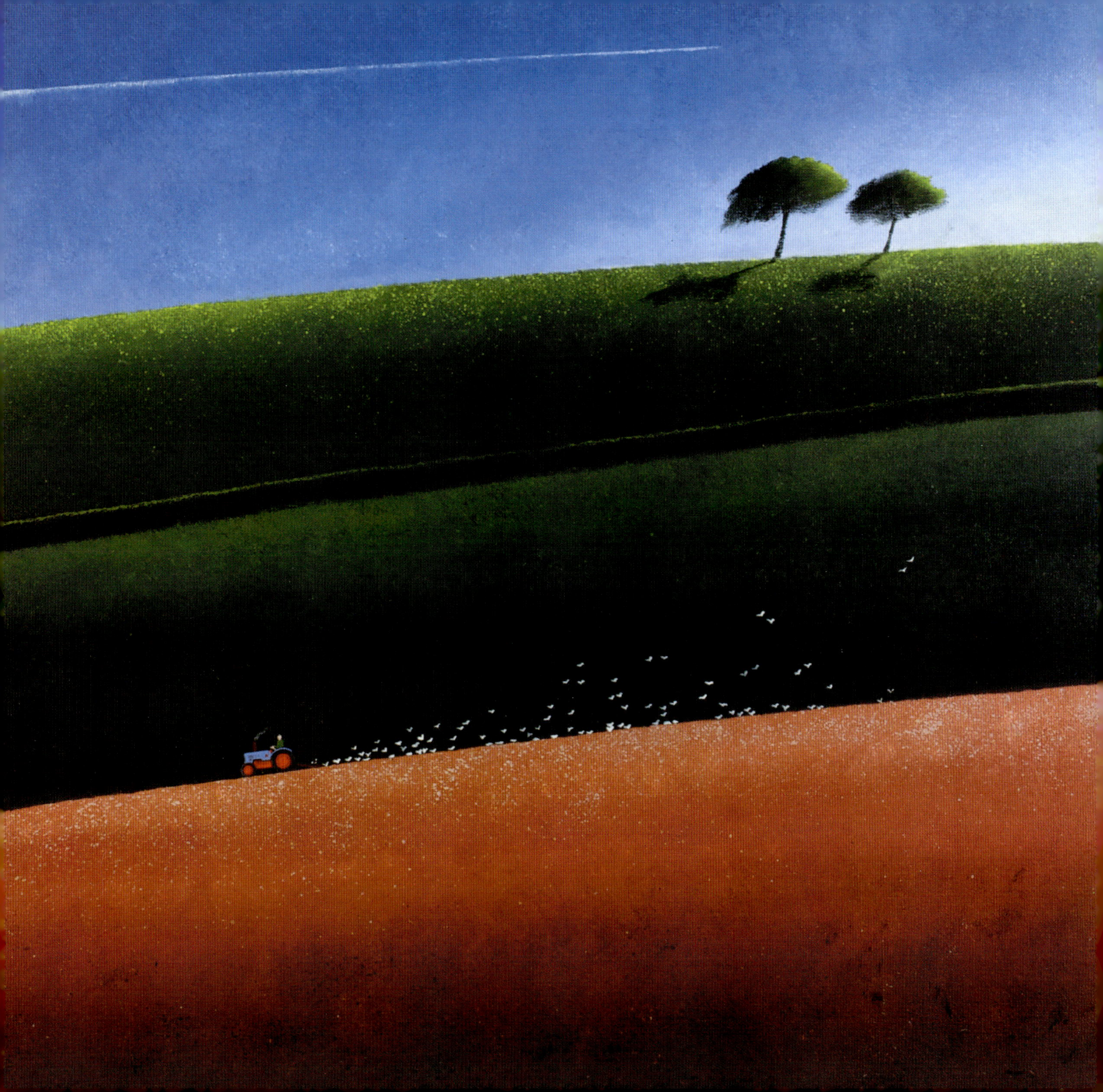

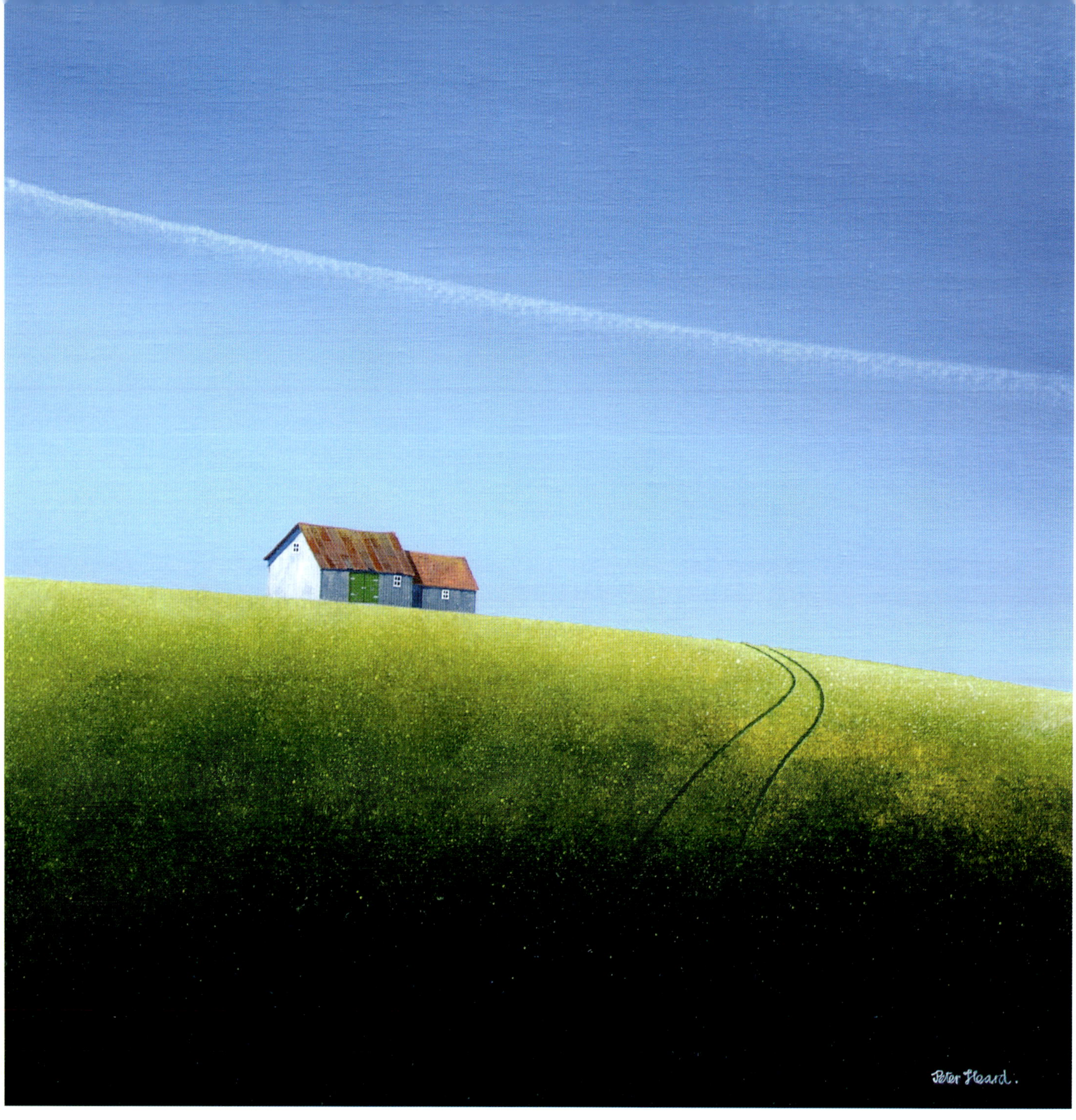
Peter Heard.

BARNS BY BLUE ANCHOR BAY

Barns are sometimes known as linhays in the West Country. Typically standing on their own in a field they had a dual purpose. The upstairs part – called the mow or hayloft – was used to store hay and grain to feed livestock. The lower part provided shelter for the animals in winter. Later it would also house farm machinery. From the Middle Ages onwards, most villages also had a tithe barn, which was for storing the tithes – a tenth of the farm's produce which had to be given to the church. Here again we have the combination of stillness and movement in the painting. The tractor lines and the vapour trail contrast with the stillness of the barns.

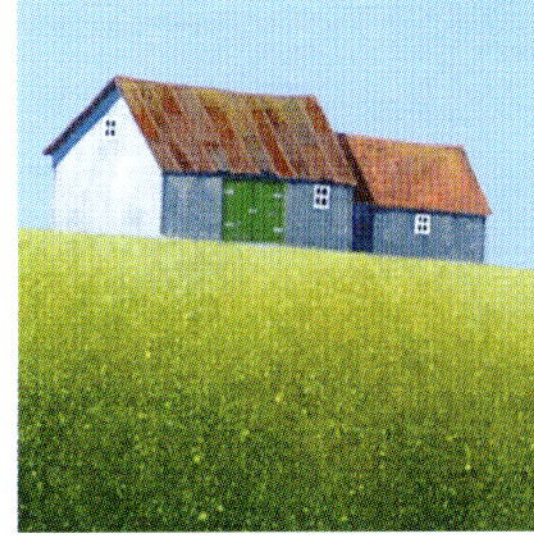

Barns by Blue Anchor Bay
Acrylic on Linen
50 x 50 cm

WIND PRUNED TREES ON EXMOOR

In 1954 Exmoor became one of the first National Parks. Several areas are Sites of Special Scientific Interest because of the abundant flora and fauna. The highest point is Dunkery Beacon at 1,704 feet. The Exmoor coast with its dramatic headlands and cliffs was also declared a Heritage Coast in 1991. The moor has 208 ancient monuments and 16 conservation areas. Yet despite all this it is still a working moor with farms and grazing animals particularly evident. Here Peter has created a graphic landscape reflecting the nature of Exmoor and the people who live and work there. The lines of fields, some cultivated, some still growing, hedges and tractor lines. And the chimney smoke – so some lucky soul is in front of a warm fire and out of the cold. A feeling of harmony and simplicity.

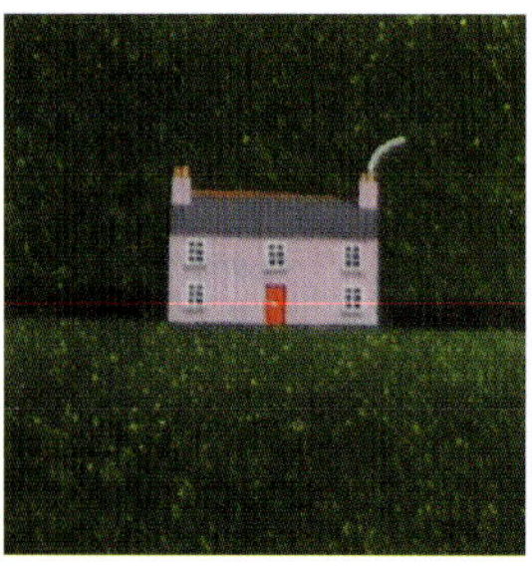

Wind Pruned Trees Trees on Exmoor
Acrylic on Linen
50 x 50 cm

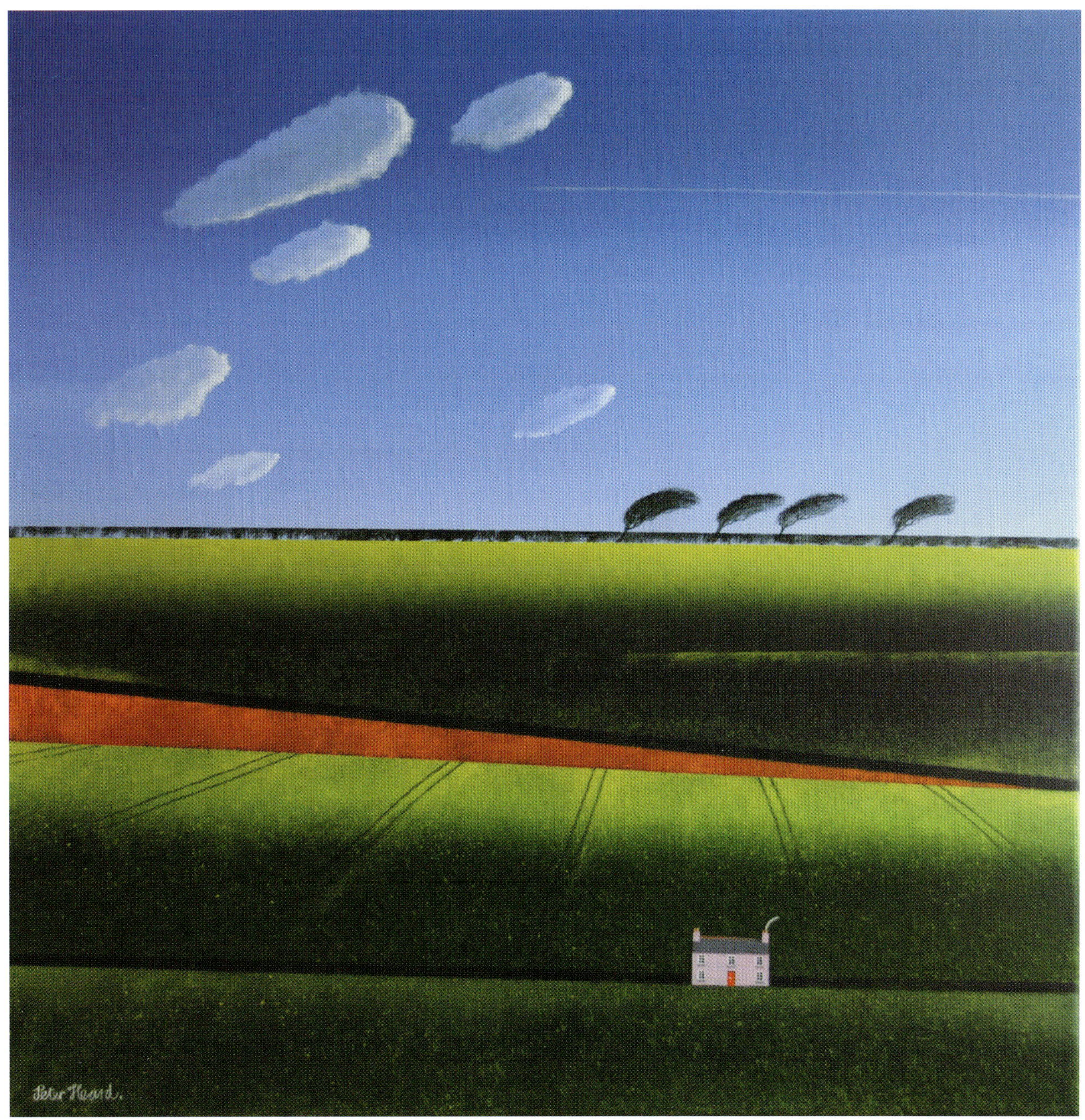

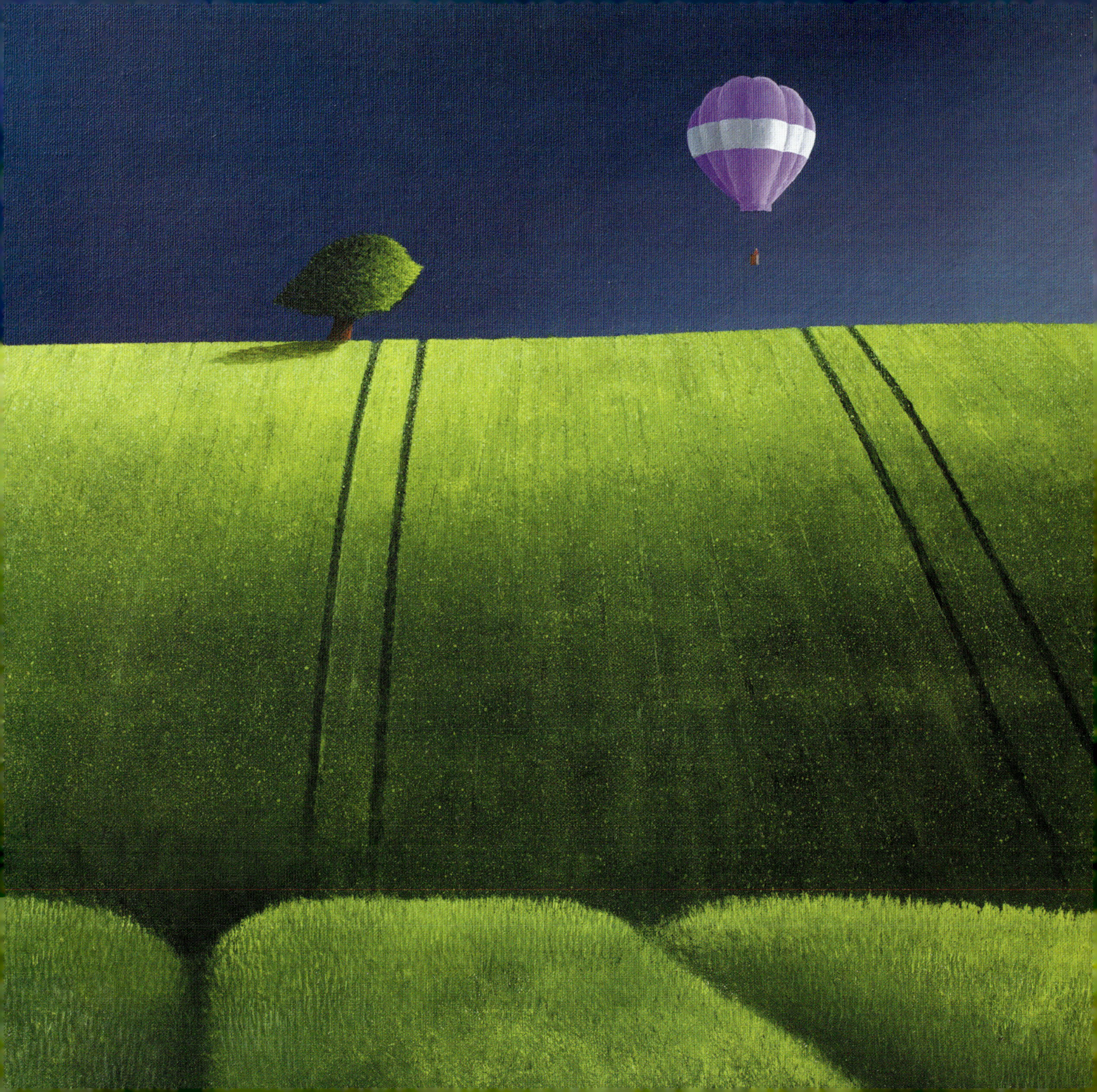

FIELD BY DAN'S FARM

Two French brothers, Joseph and Jacques Montgolfier pioneered hot air ballooning by discovering that heated air in a lightweight bag caused it to rise. In 1783, they demonstrated it for the first time in Annonay, France. A few months later they repeated the experiment before an amazed king and court at Versailles, this time sending up a sheep, a rooster, and a duck as passengers. Their first manned flight took place later that year in Paris. In the nineteenth century, sadly, the primary use of the balloon was in war, to spy behind enemy lines. For us, happily, Peter rediscovers the wonder of early flight. In this painting there is a constant feeling of movement – not just in the balloon perhaps running for home as the sky darkens but also in the tractor lines crossing the field of new growth.

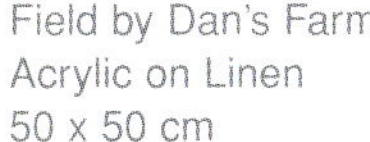

Field by Dan's Farm
Acrylic on Linen
50 x 50 cm

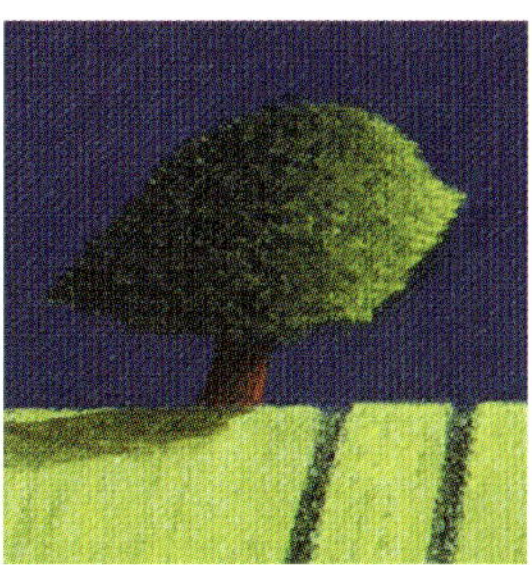

The West Country Farm

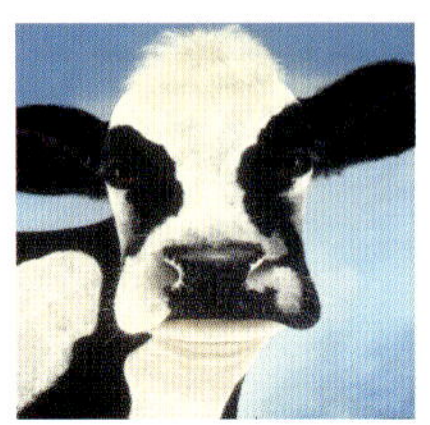

An interesting aspect of a town boy moving to the country is the realisation that the land never stands still. It is being worked – constantly – because it provides a livelihood for lots of people. So the fields change colour, the crops rotate and – suddenly – there are animals in a particular field that weren't there the day before. Also Peter loves the old traditions – hence the haymakers with their scythes and cider jug on the next page.

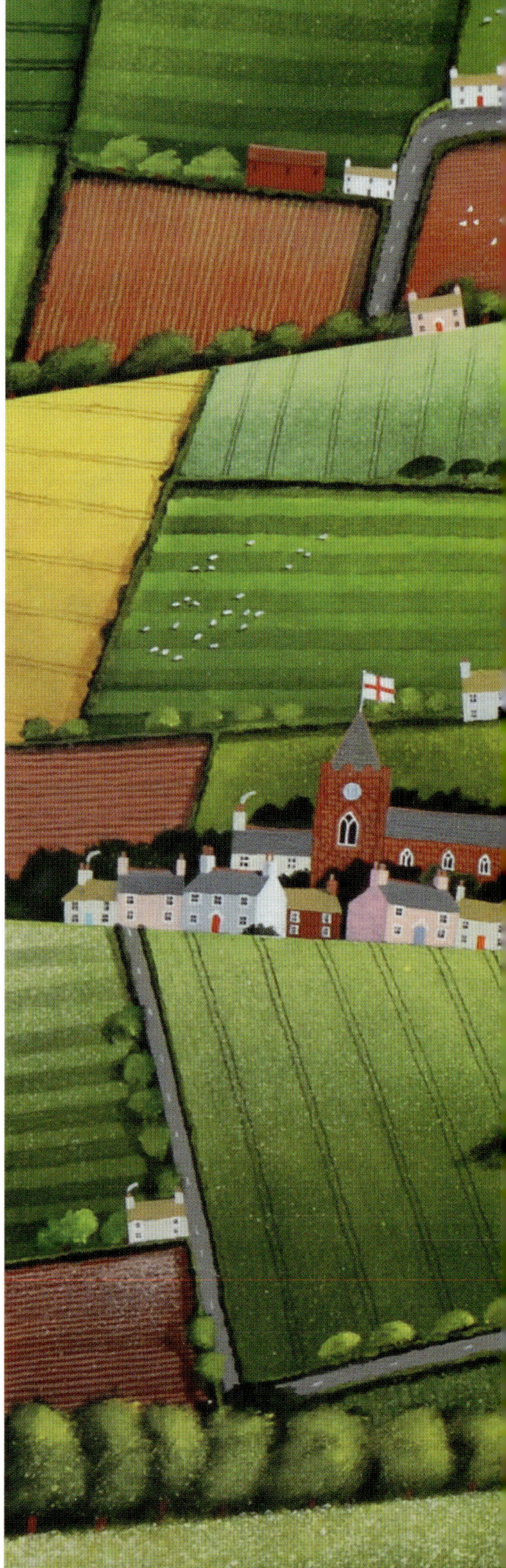

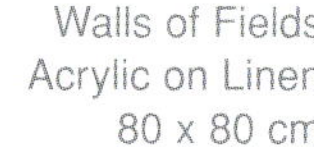

Walls of Fields
Acrylic on Linen
80 x 80 cm

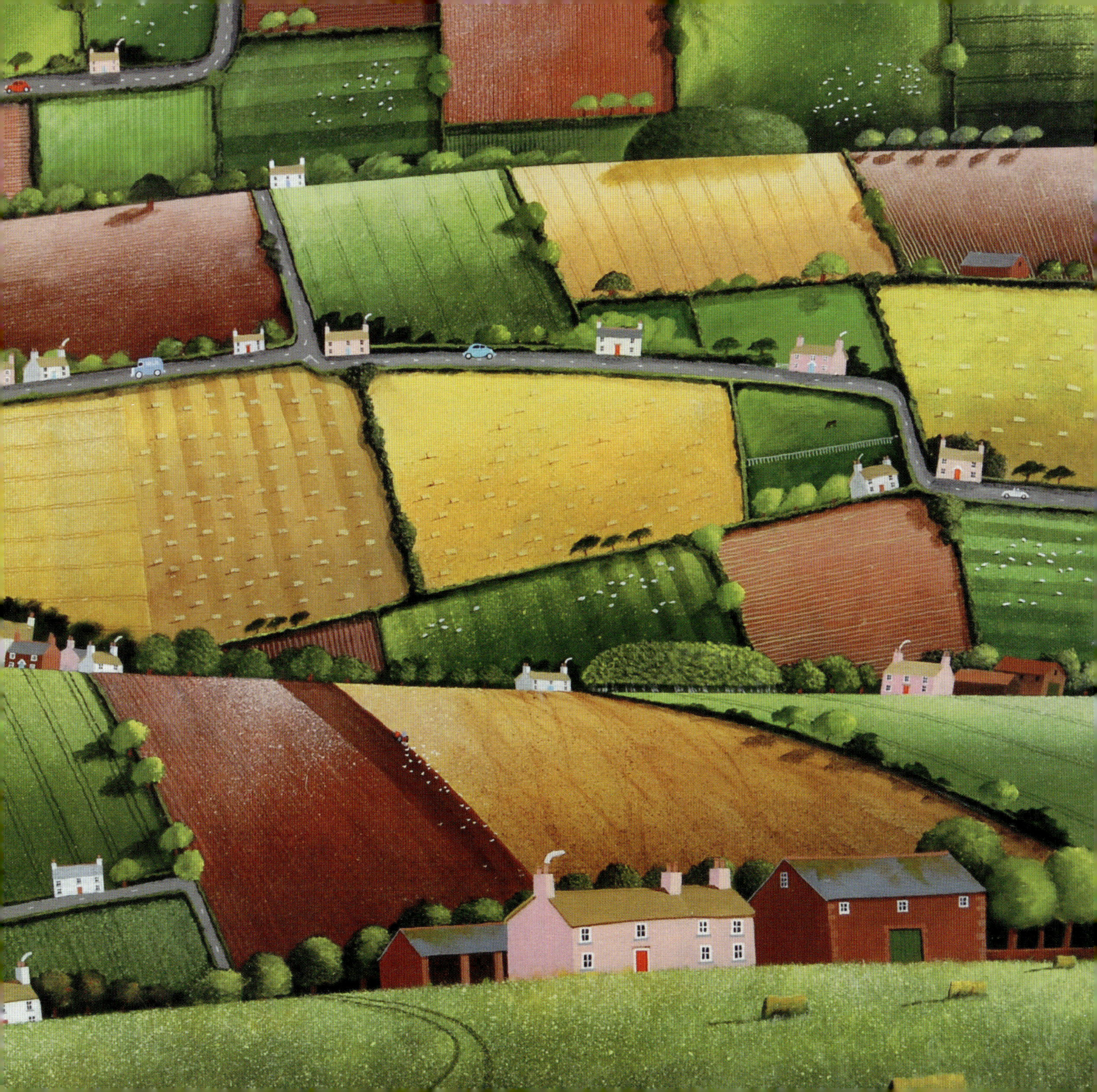

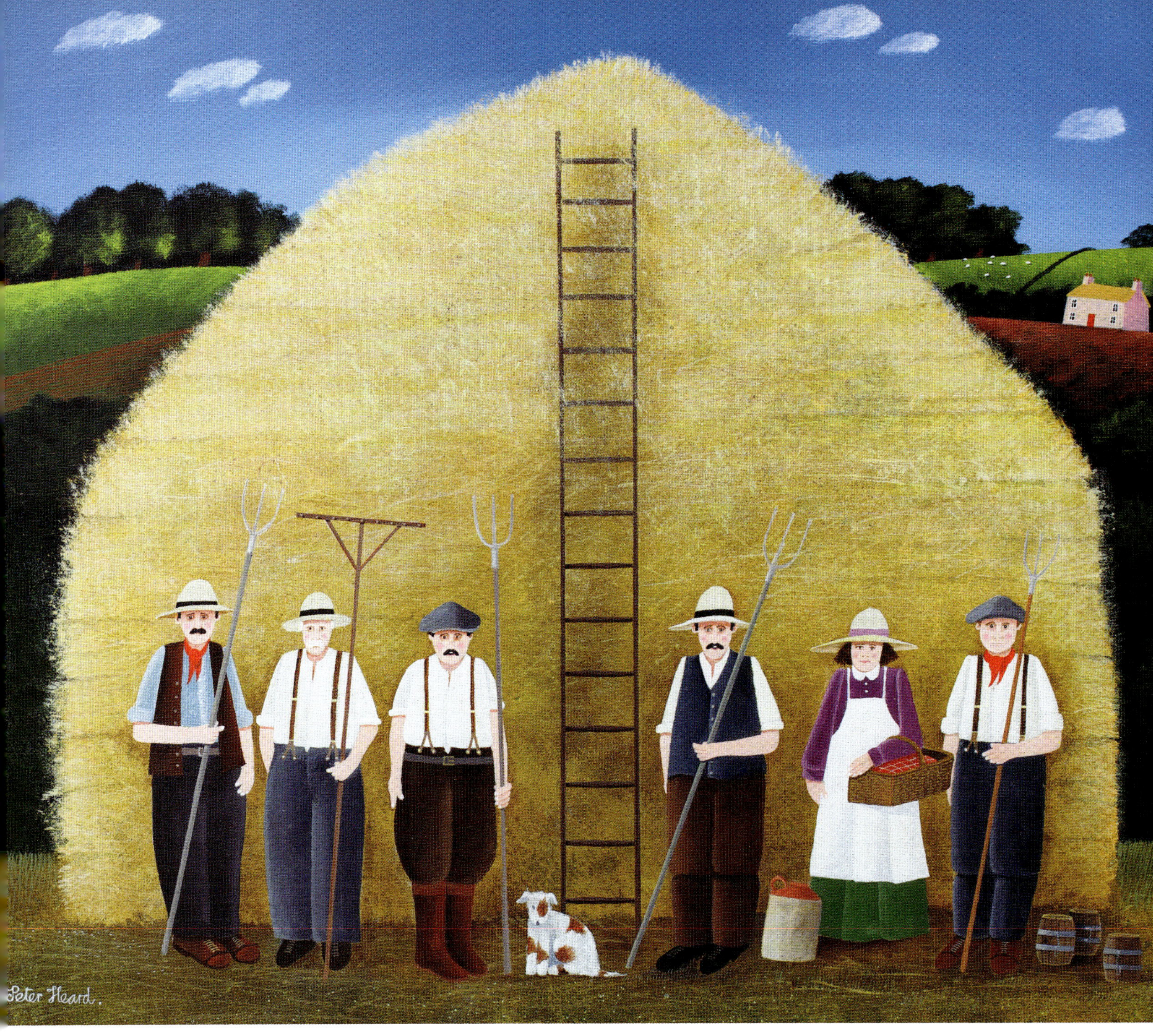
Peter Heard.

CIDER WITH ROSIE

Here we have the haymaking crew, sensibly wearing hats in the midday sun. In the days before animals were fed on root crops, cattle lived on hay and straw. Even sheep would eat it if they were hungry. A farmer needed to have enough for winter – and to feed the plough oxen or there would be no corn to make bread. Clever farmers had a year's supply in hand in case of a poor harvest. The hay had to be dry before it was baled or made into a rick. If not it could heat up and set fire to it. Great skill was needed to build the rick. The sides had to be upright and have an outward batter to shed water – this meant each layer had to be placed slightly overhanging and tied in so it would not slide off. In a badly made rick the corners fell out and it had to be built again. Rick-making is a lost art today – the only ones made are from stacked bales.

Opposite: Cider with Rosie
Acrylic on Linen
60 x 50 cm

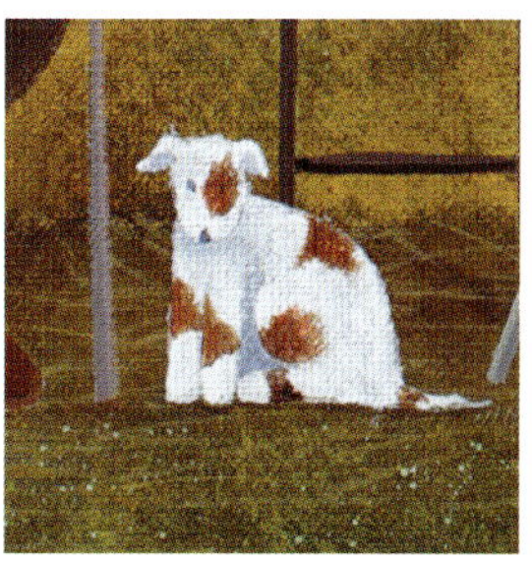

WELL EARNED REST

In *Far From The Madding Crowd*, Thomas Hardy writes of the "hiring fair" where up to 300 farm labourers from the surrounding villages would gather in a big town hoping to find work. They were instantly recognisable – shepherds carried sheep crooks, thatchers wore a fragment of woven straw, carters and waggoners had a piece of whip-cord twisted round their hats. And haymakers would carry their scythes. Part of their payment was in cider and these two haymakers are enjoying a flagon while taking a rest. They are also sensible and wearing hats. Many old photographs show farm workers without hats even in the height of summer. All that sun, all that cider, it's enough to boil the brains.

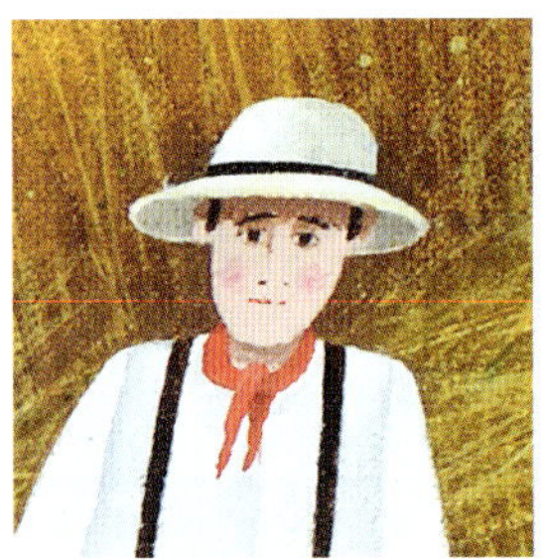

Opposite: Well Earned Rest
Acrylic on Linen
60 x 50 cm

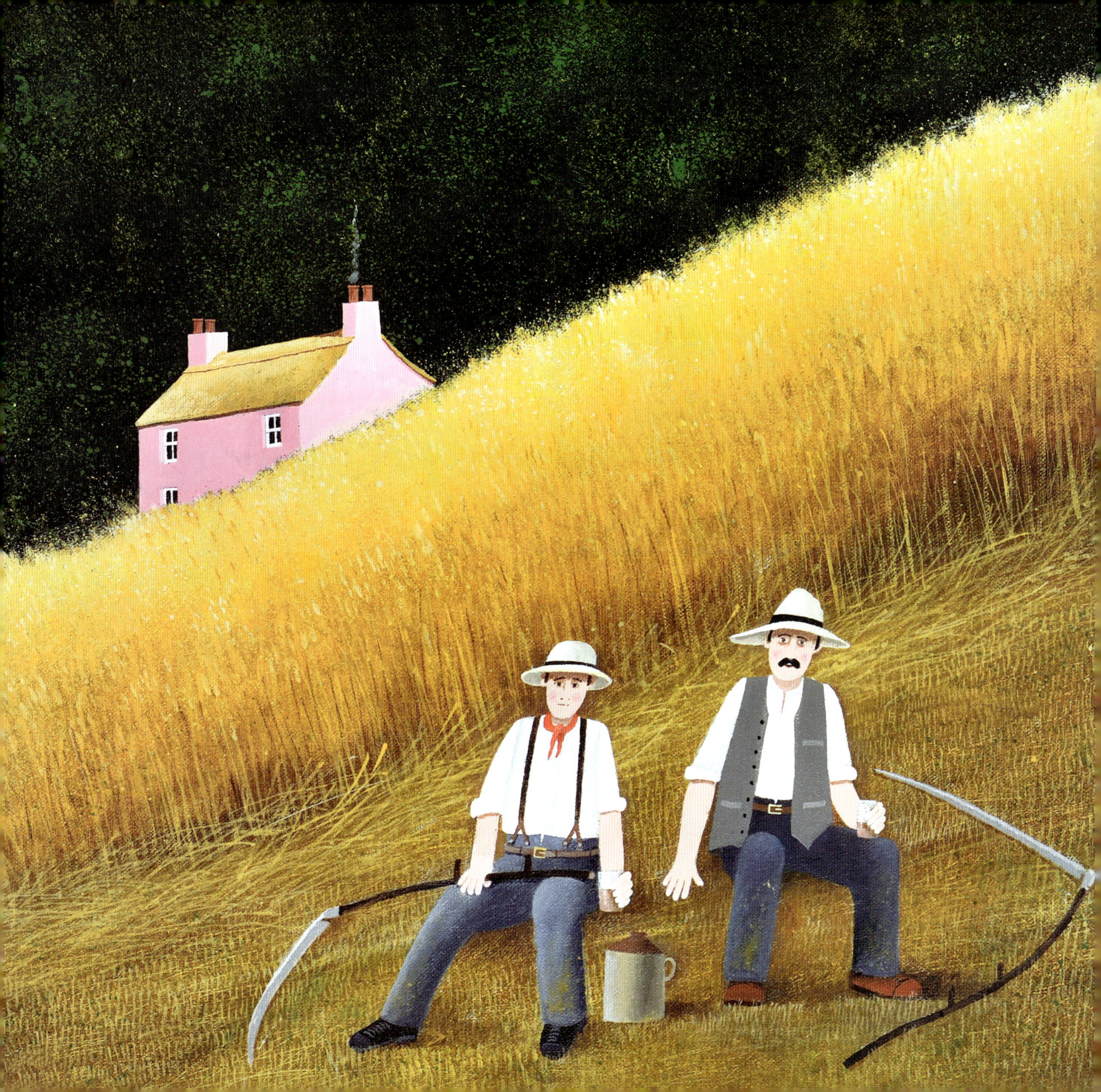

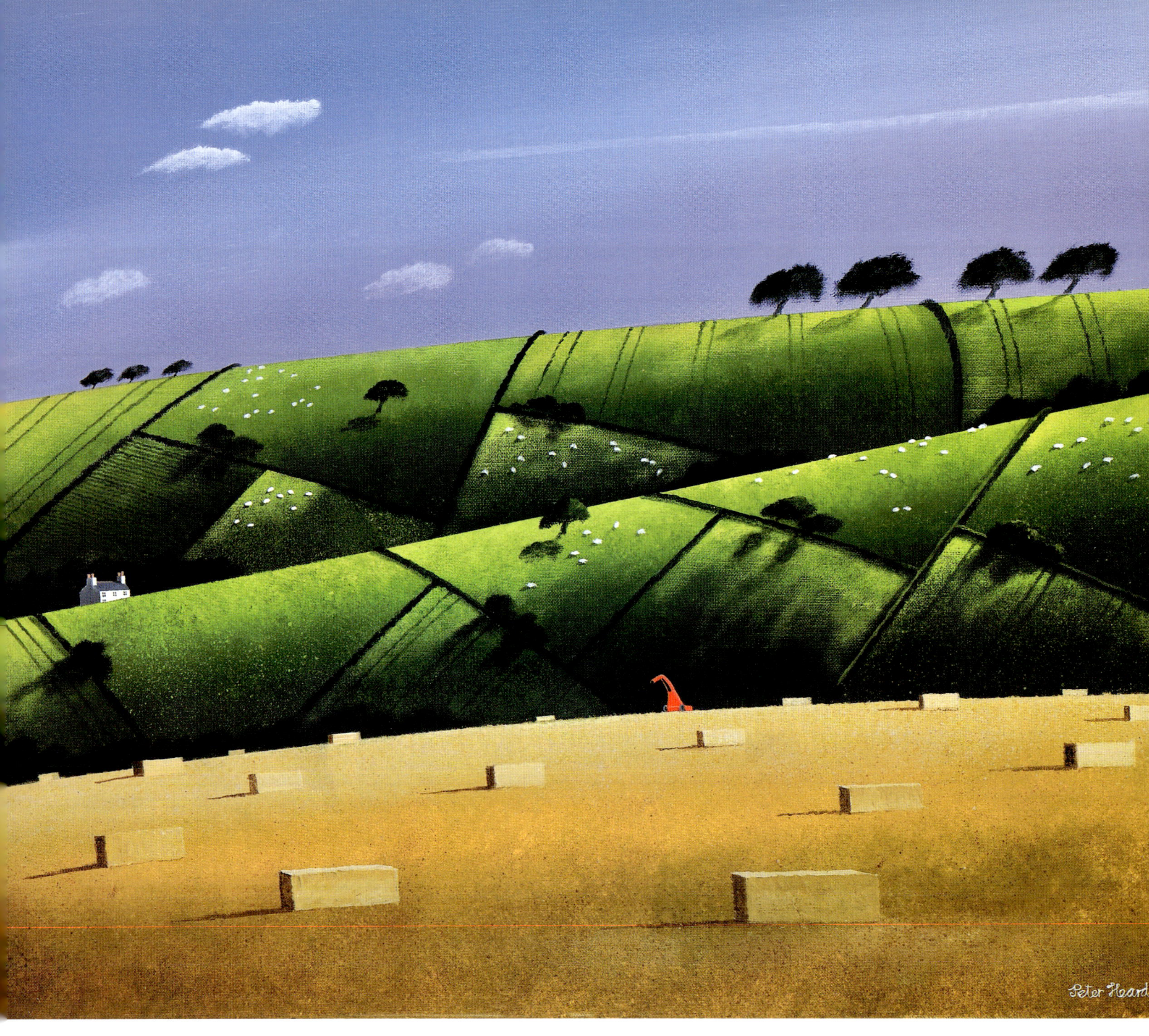
Peter Heard

EXMOOR FIELDS

Make hay while the sun shines goes the old proverb. First the grass crop is mown, just before flowering, then allowed to dry in the sun. Many crops are cut during flowering when pollen is being produced (hence hay fever). Once the crop is dry enough balers go into the fields and compress the hay into a block and tie twine round it. The bales that have been formed are left in the field until they are collected and taken away to be kept dry in a barn. Here again beyond the cut meadow we have Peter's wall of fields – a loosely painted background with windswept trees and a farmhouse. This contrasts with the tightly painted farm machine working in the field and used in the painting to provide a graphic burst of colour.

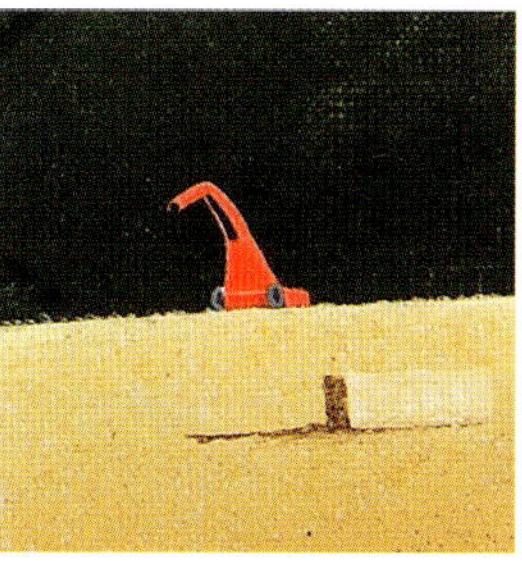

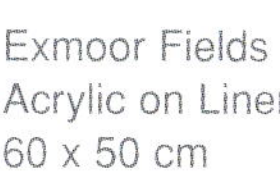

Exmoor Fields
Acrylic on Linen
60 x 50 cm

RUNS LIKE CLOCKWORK

No wonder this farmer looks fed-up. It's a cold early morning, he has got milk churns to deliver and his ageing tractor won't start, even though he has used the starting handle. The dogs are waiting patiently – they've seen it all before. The tractor is an Allis recognisable by its distinctive orange colour. Production of them stopped in 1985. The company Allis-Chalmers was based in Milwaukee, USA, and they started making farm equipment in 1914. They also built machinery for the Allied forces during the Great War. Allis-Chalmers started to struggle in the 1980s and the farm equipment division was sold to a German company. It closed its Milwaukee offices in 1999. But the farmer need not be too worried – there are still specialist garages and firms around that deal in parts for Allis tractors that won't start.

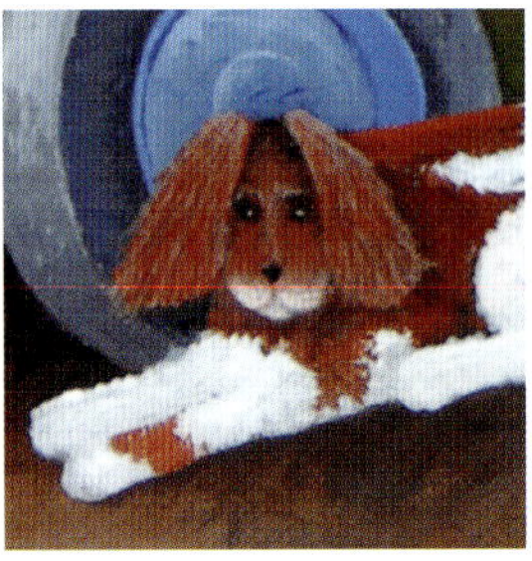

Runs Like Clockwork
Acrylic on Linen
40 x 40 cm

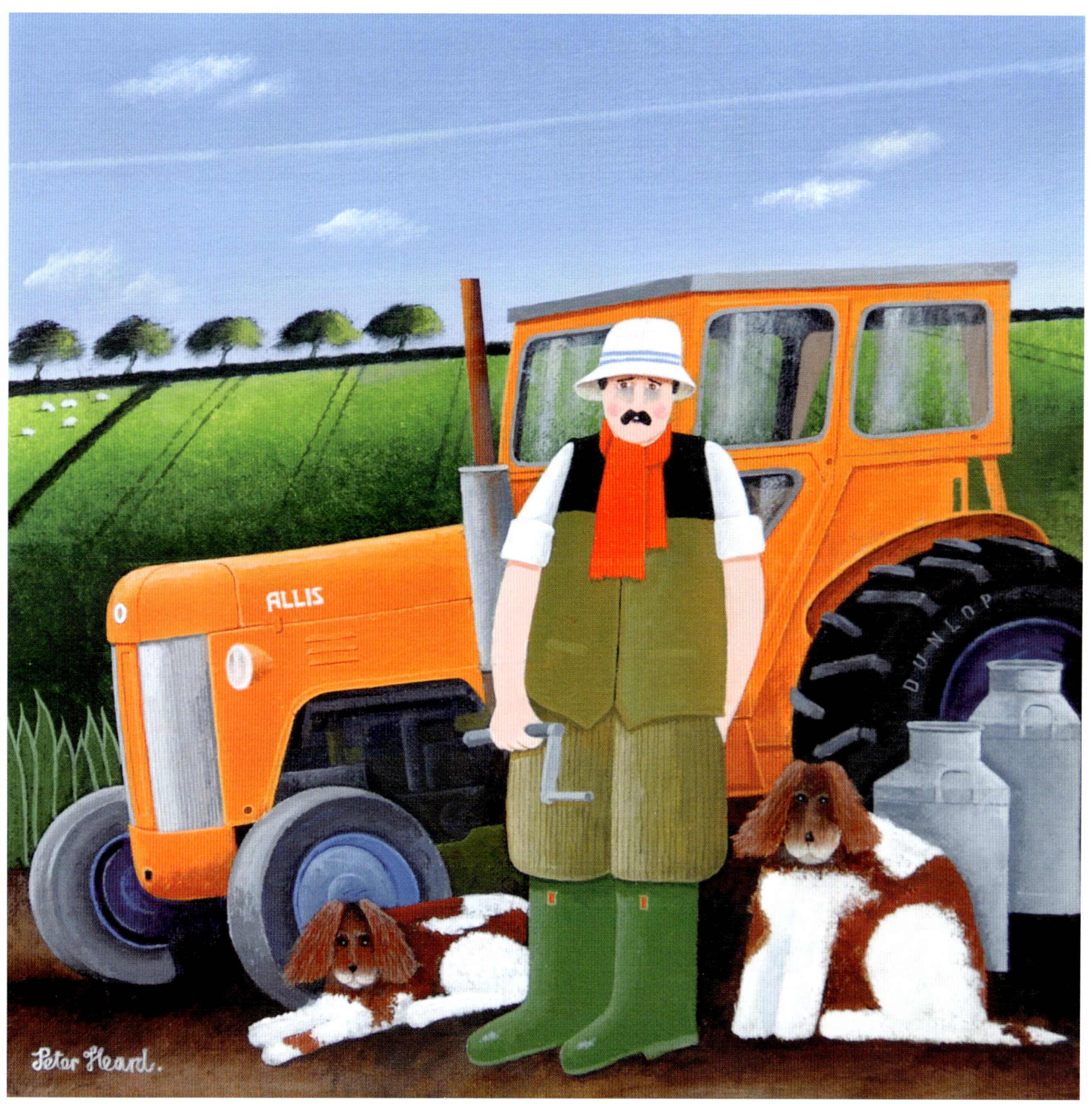
ALLIS
DUNLOP
Peter Heard.

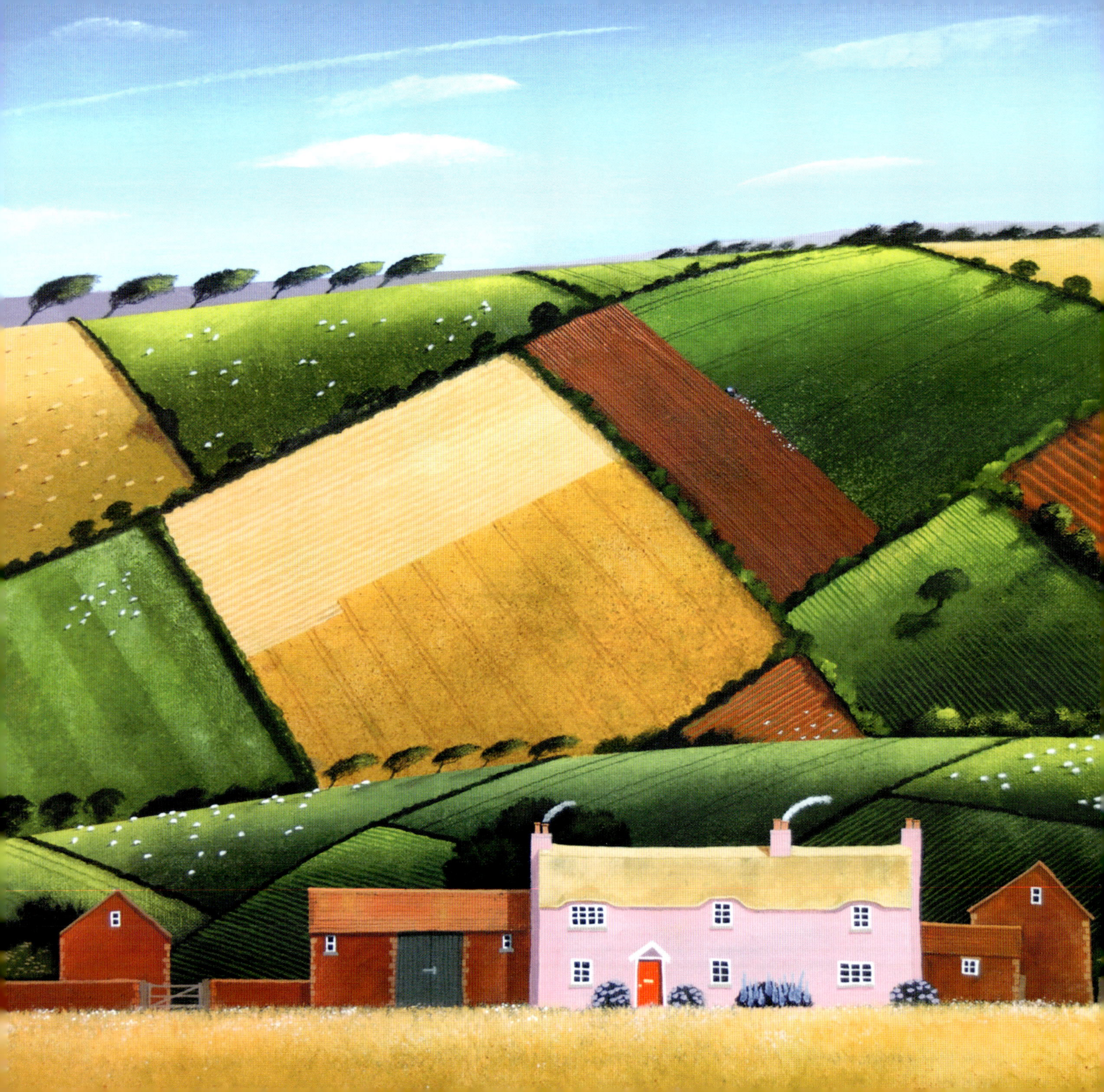

HILL FARM BY EXFORD

In the Middle Ages, people farmed on common land – a farmer would be allowed to farm strips of land in several open fields and the farmhouses as such were in the village. From the time of the Tudors came the Enclosure Laws which gathered pace in the eighteenth century when the common land became private property and was fenced or divided by hedges or stone walls. This benefited the church and the landed gentry who had money. The gentry then built their farmhouses and manor houses on their land. The house would be sited in the lee of the land on the southerly side of high ground, as in this picture. The hill, which is part of Exmoor, shows the patchwork of colour in the fields as they are planted and harvested at different times of the year.

Hill Farm by Exford
Acrylic on Linen
50 x 50 cm

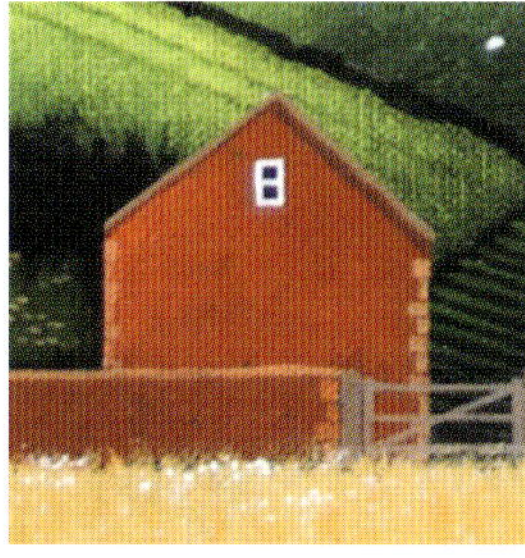

SPOT THE PORKER

In *Lark Rise To Candleford*, Flora Thompson writes of the importance of a pig to rural families. "Men callers on Sunday afternoons came, not to see the family, but the pig, and would lounge with its owner against the pigsty door for an hour, scratching piggy's back and praising his points or turning their noses up in criticism." A good pig could keep a family in bacon for a whole winter. And then there was the ceremony of its killing "some time during the first two quarters of the moon". If the pig was killed when the moon was waning the bacon would shrink in cooking! The porker in the painting may well be a Gloucestershire Old Spot, a famous West Country breed. The Old Spot is sometimes known as the "Orchard Pig" as it was traditionally pastured in an orchard where it gorged on windfall apples. It is also sometimes referred to as the "bacon pig" because, pound for pound, it can provide more English breakfasts than any other porker! There is a vintage tractor in the linhay which was built with circular stone columns so the animals would not mark their coats if they brushed against them.

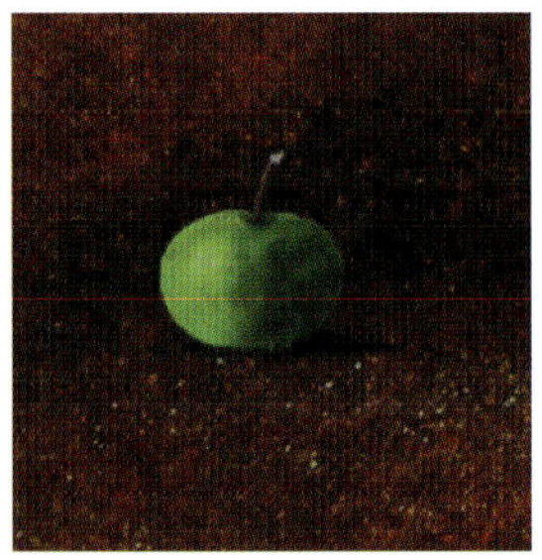

Opposite: Spot the Porker
Acrylic on Linen
65 x 50 cm

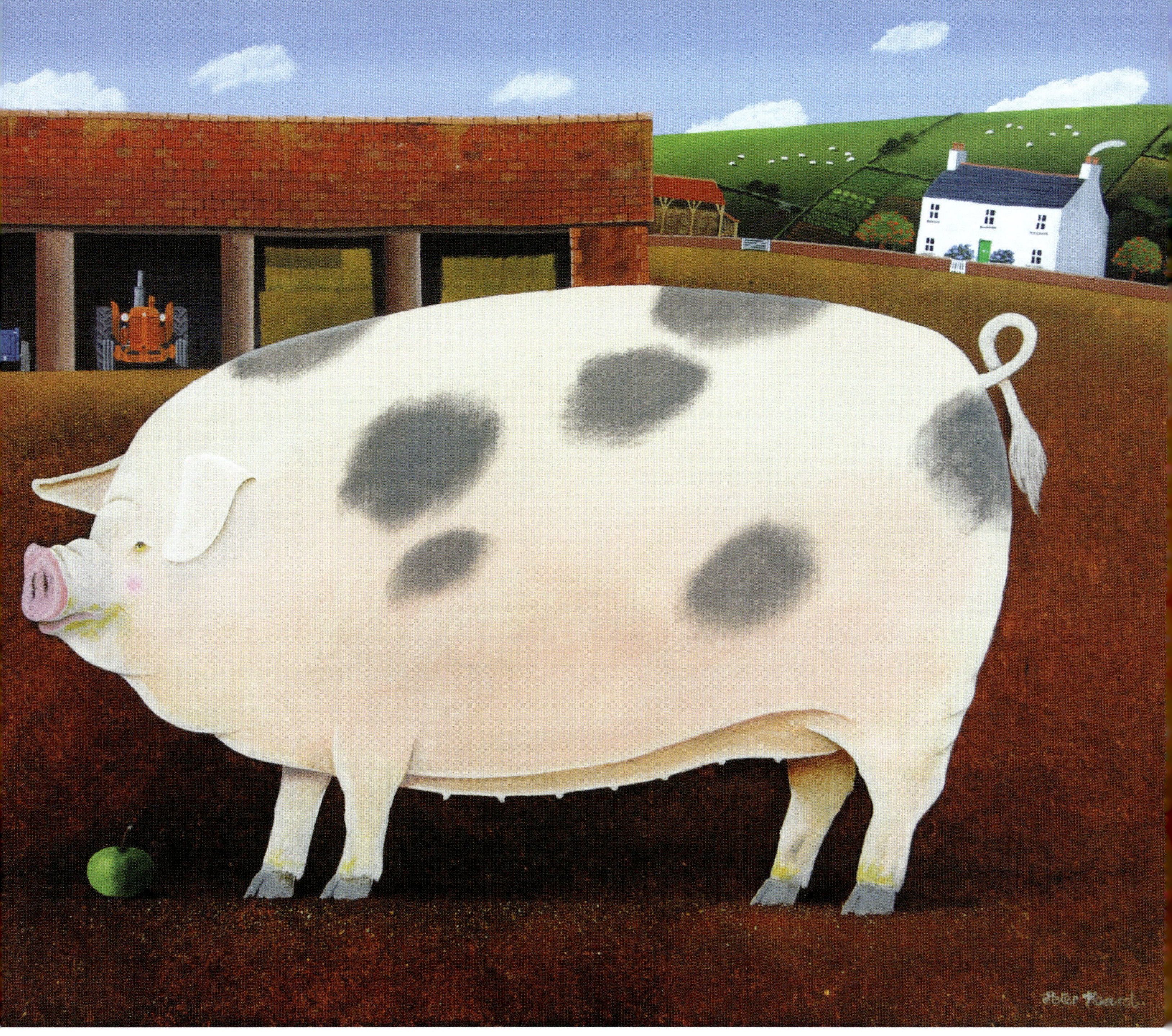

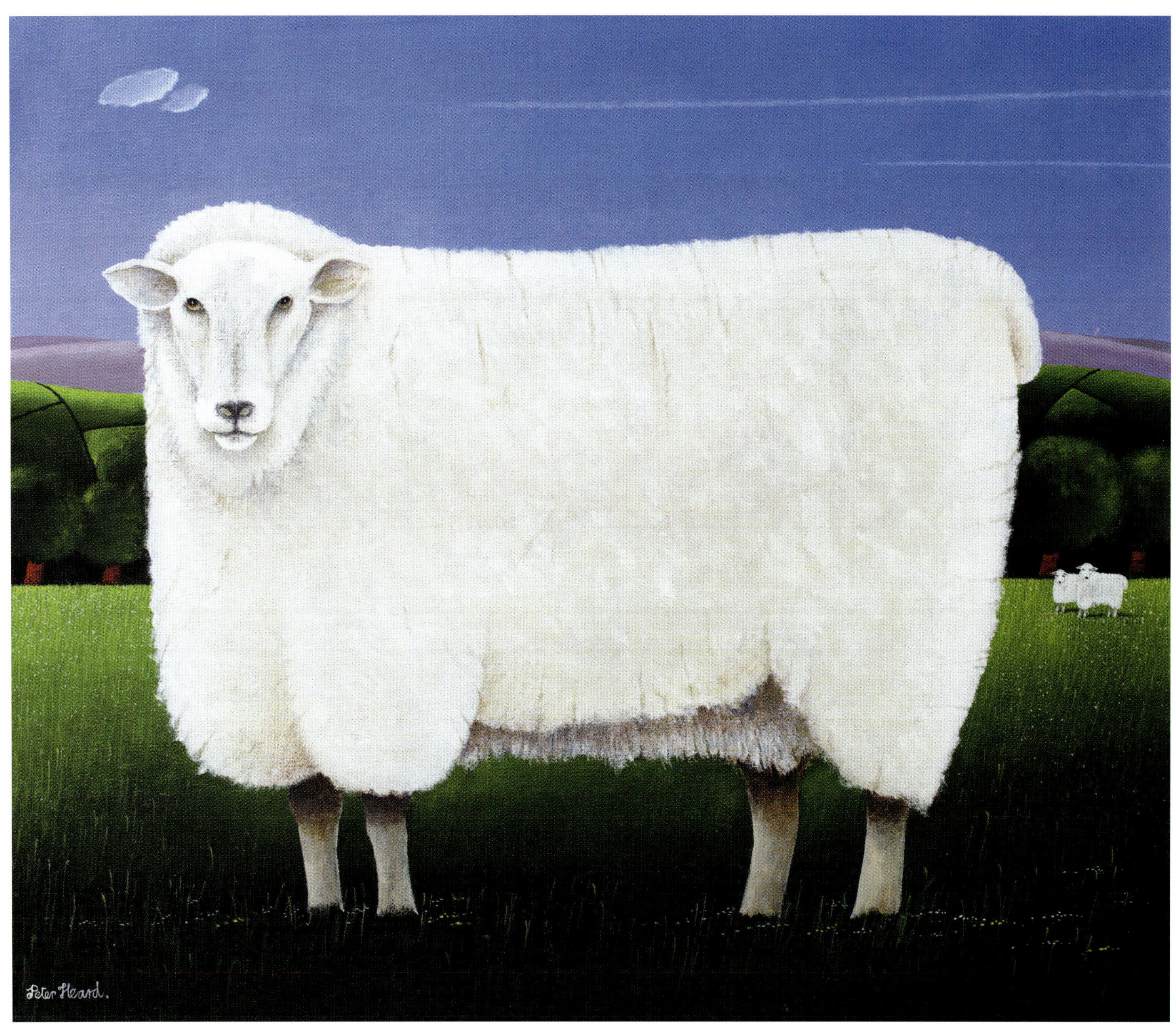
Peter Heard.

DOLLY

The title of this painting is a playful reference to Dolly, who in 1996 became the first animal to be cloned. She lived to the age of six and was known as "the world's most famous sheep". Sheep are part of the fabric of the West Country. The shape of Peter's sheep is rectangular, as many animals are in primitive art. And it is perfectly white and clean. That is the licence of the artist to sanitise paintings and edit out threatening reality. Also the sheep is set against an almost perfect blue sky apart from the odd cloud and some vapour trails. A pastoral idyll. Many of the sheep in Somerset have a pinkish tinge because they have picked up dust and traces of sandstone from the earth in their fleeces.

Dolly
Acrylic on Linen
60 x 50 cm

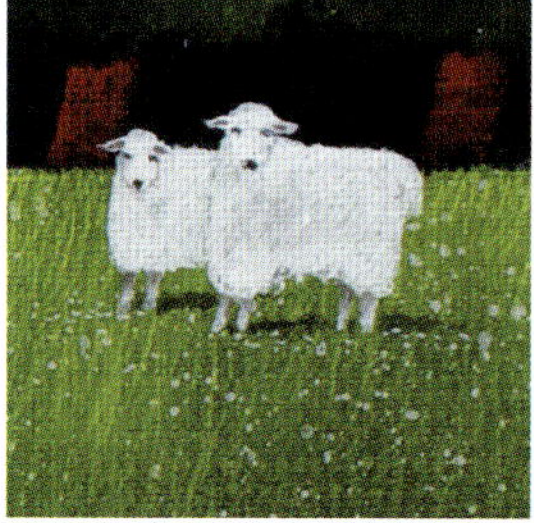

DAISY

Peter's cow could well be a rare breed – it has five teats instead of the usual four! The colouring suggests it is a Friesian although there are some breeds which are indigenous to the West Country like the North Devon which has a rich red colour. But many people think of cows as black and white. So much so that an initiative in Somerset in 2007 to encourage children to recycle used rubbish bins painted to look like Friesian cows. The bins were placed in a field next to the M5 near Weston-super-Mare. A three-month test "feeding the cows" showed that the amount recycled went up by more than 60% compared with using ordinary bins. Again Peter uses the device of rectangular shape to give the picture its naïvety.

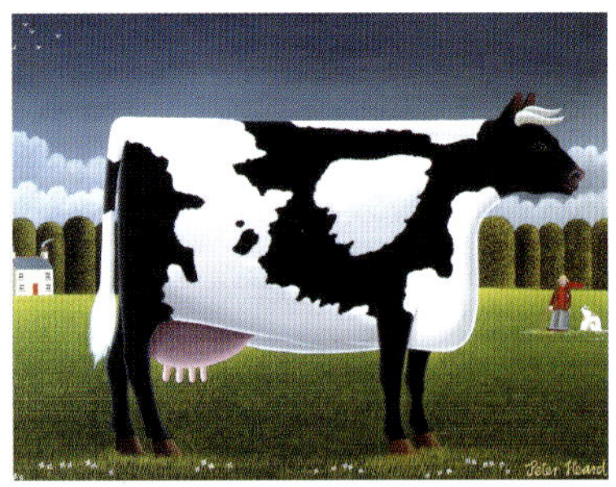

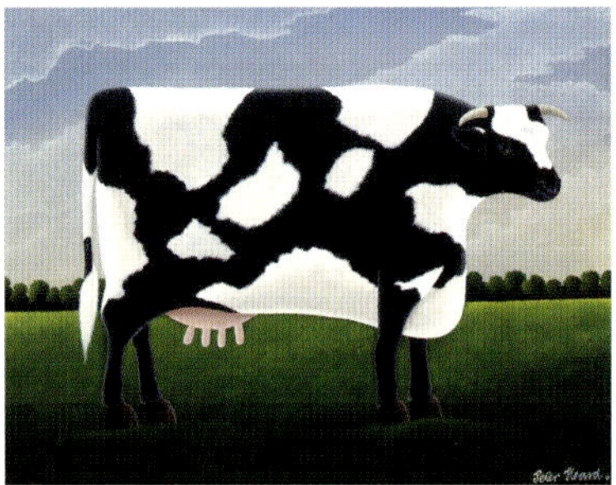

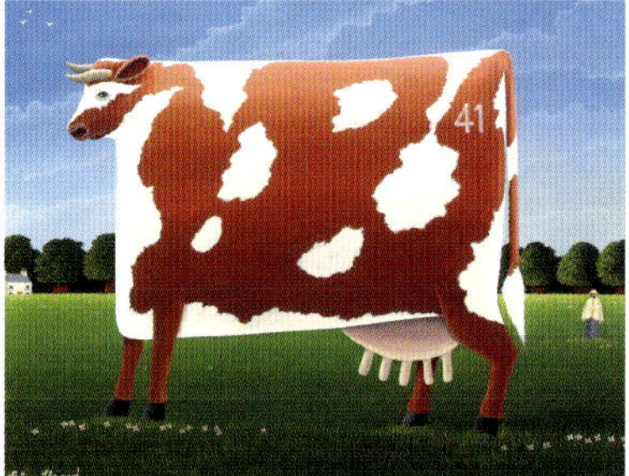

Daisy
Acrylic on Linen
80 x 60 cm

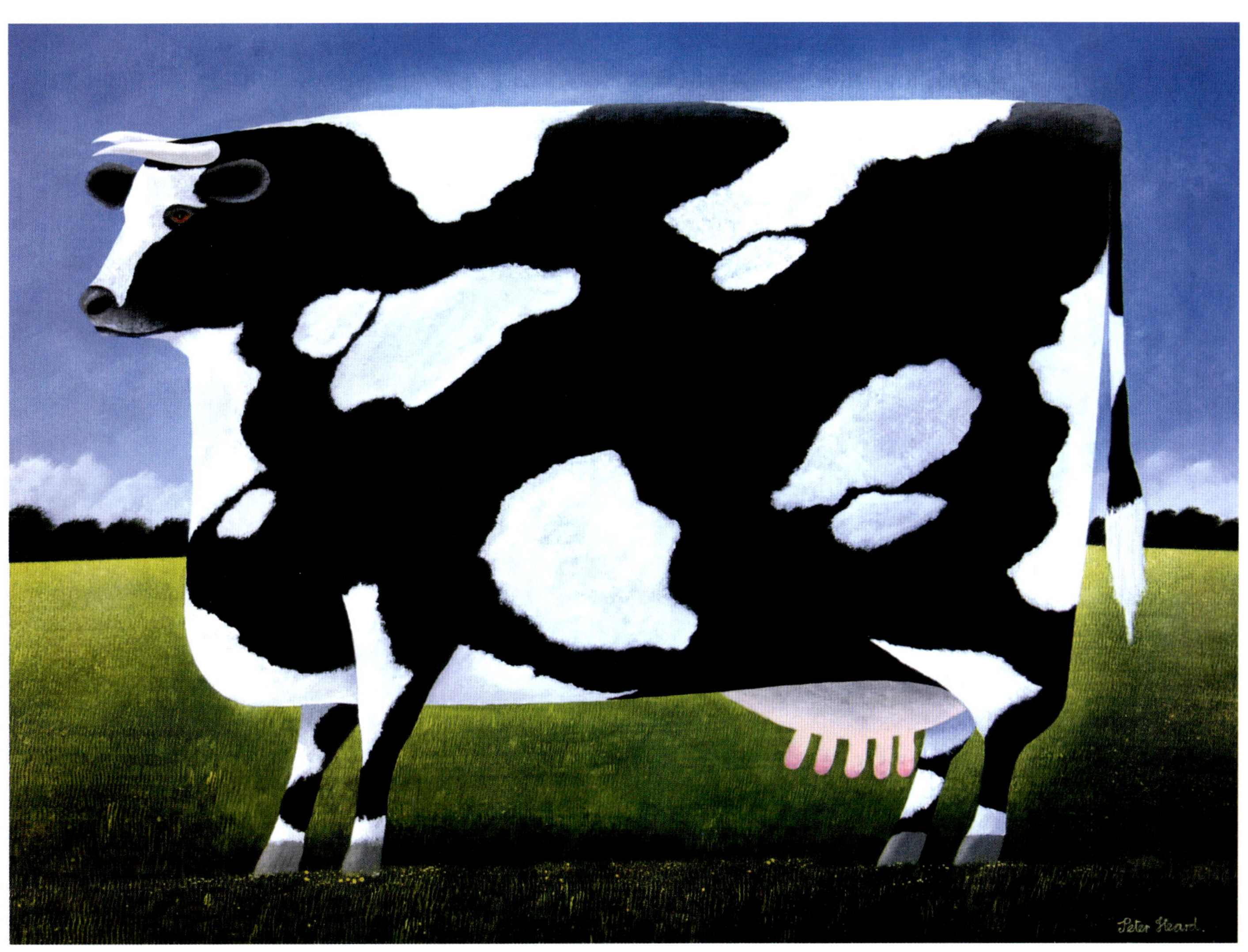
Peter Heard.

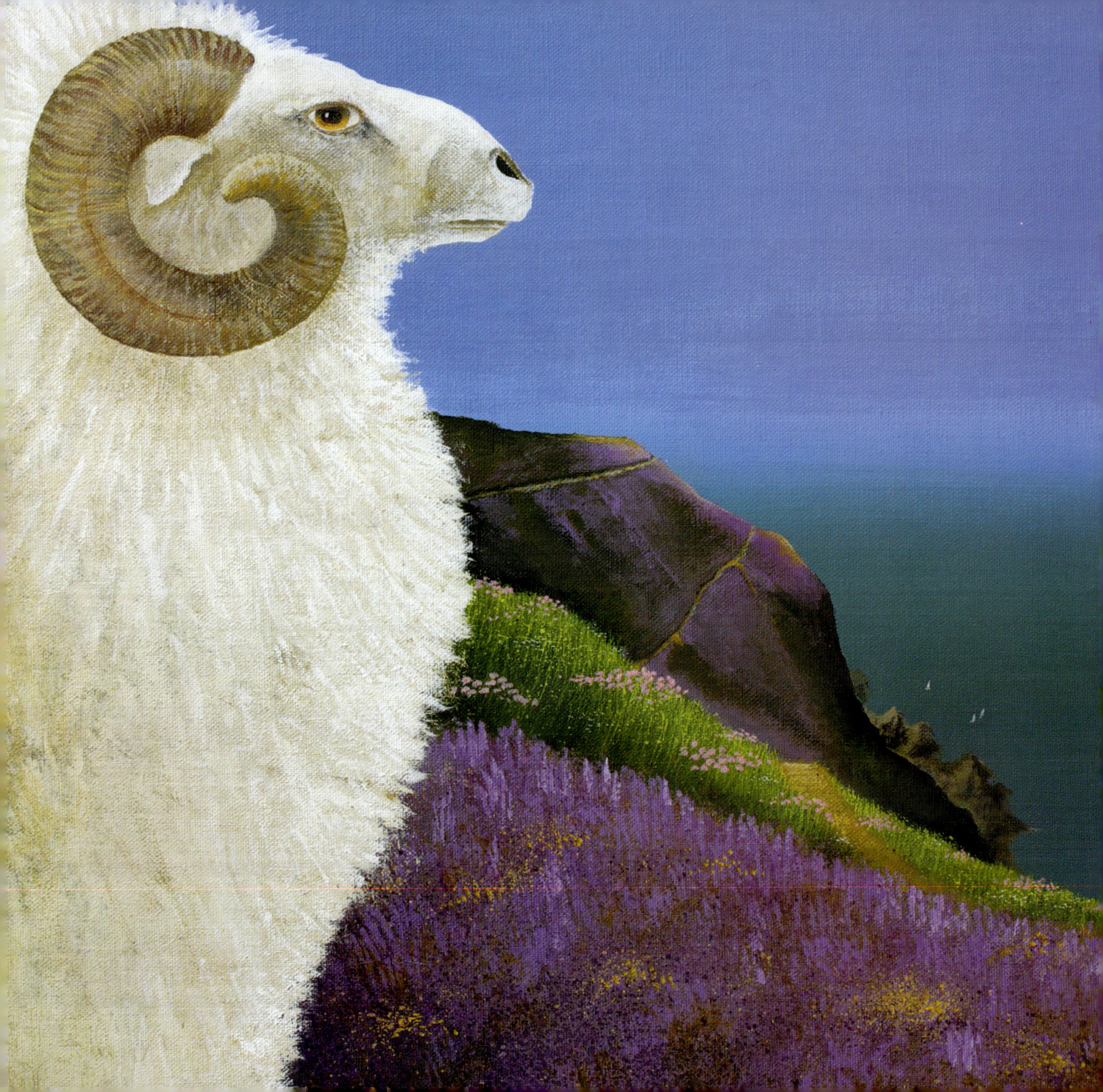

EXMOOR RAM

One of Peter's favourite artists and influences is the American Andrew Wyeth who died aged 91 in January 2009. He was classed as a realist painter and his favourite subjects were the people and the land around him in Pennsylvania where he lived. Hangman Cliffs are near Combe Martin in Devon where Exmoor meets the Bristol Channel. Great Hangman is 1,043 feet (318m) high with a cliff face of 800 feet (244m). It is the highest sea cliff in England. Its sister cliff is the 716 feet (218m) Little Hangman, which marks the edge of Exmoor. This picture has been composed of three elements – a ram in an Andrew Wyeth painting, a stuffed Exmoor Horn ram that Peter saw and photographed for reference in an Exmoor National Park shop and Hangman Cliffs. The Exmoor Horn is a hardy sheep and ideal for roaming on moorland. It has a white face with close forelock and black nostrils. Both male and female have horns.

Exmoor Ram
Acrylic on Linen
40 x 40 cm

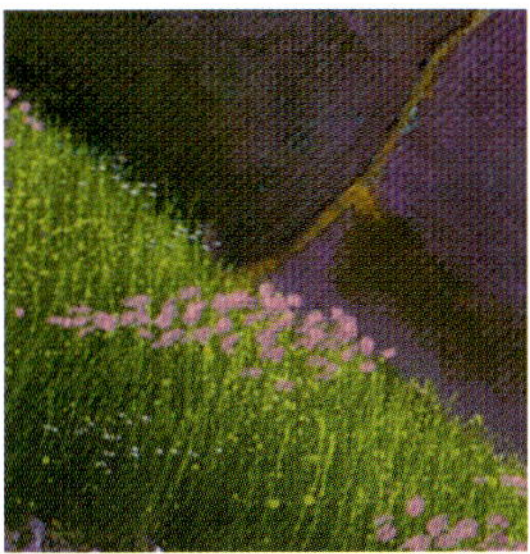

BASTARD BIRDS!

A major threat to crops comes from the air – in the shape of birds. To combat them farmers traditionally put a scarecrow in a field – often an effigy of a human – to frighten off the birds, especially crows. Hence the name. In Somerset it is called a mommet and in Devon murmet. And Shakespeare called it a Jack A Lent. Scarecrows are a rare sight today. But even with all the advances in technology, farmers still haven't found an answer to the bastard birds. The crow survives and still eats crops. So at times the frustrated farmer must resort to his gun to protect his precious fields! In parts of England villages have annual scarecrow festivals where there is a prize for the best dressed.

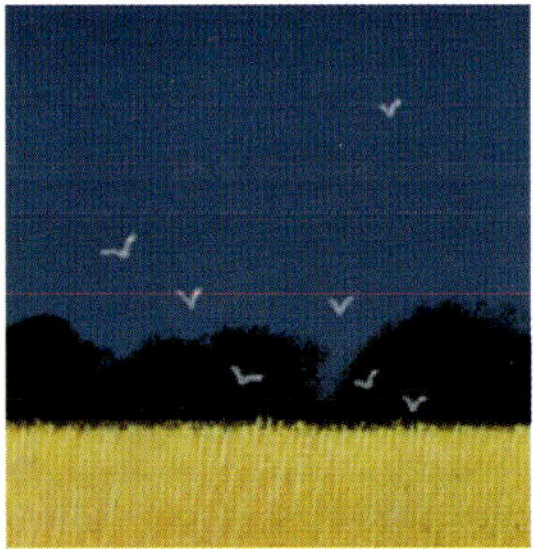

Bastard Birds!
Acrylic on Linen
40 x 40 cm

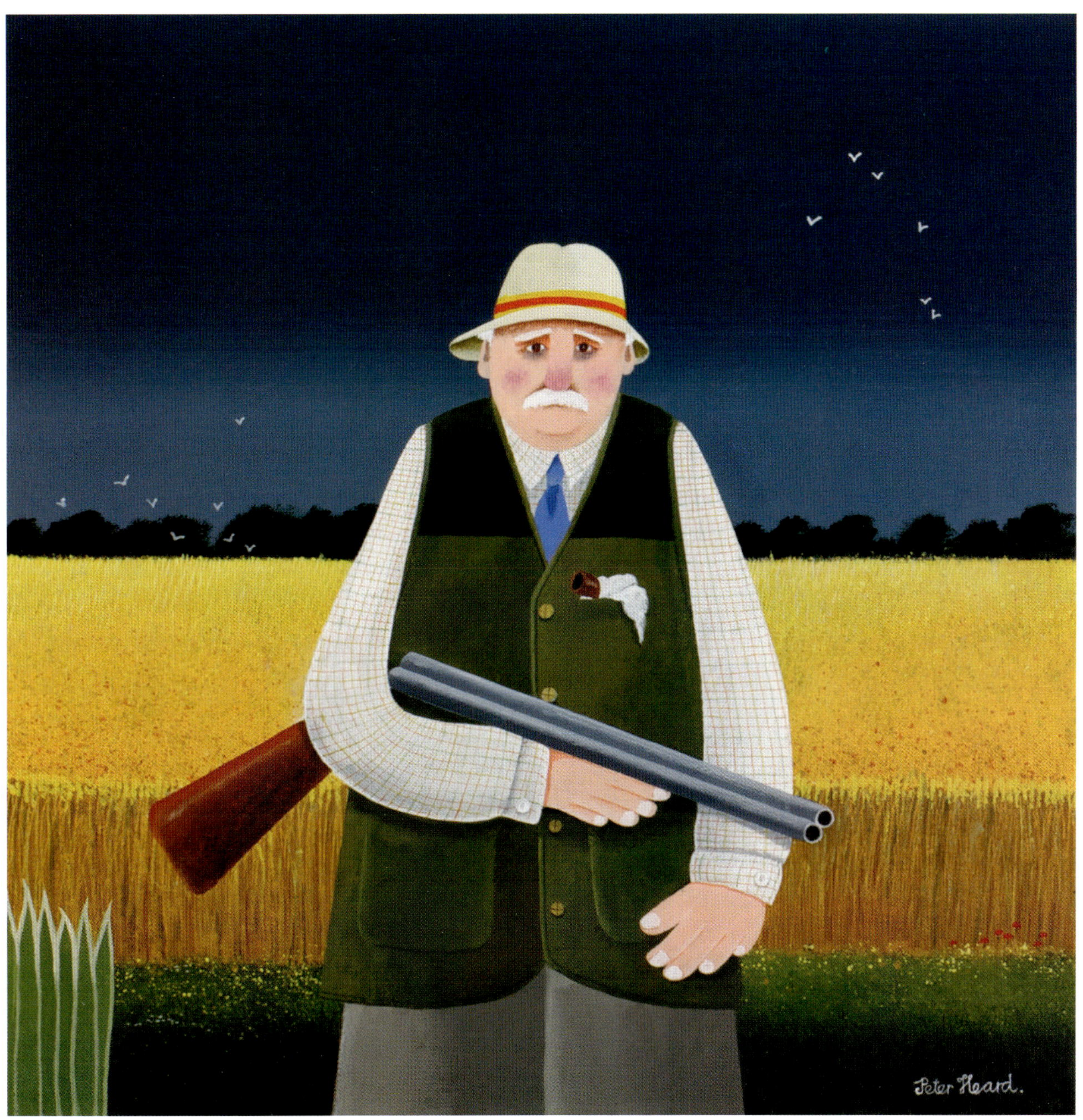
Peter Heard.

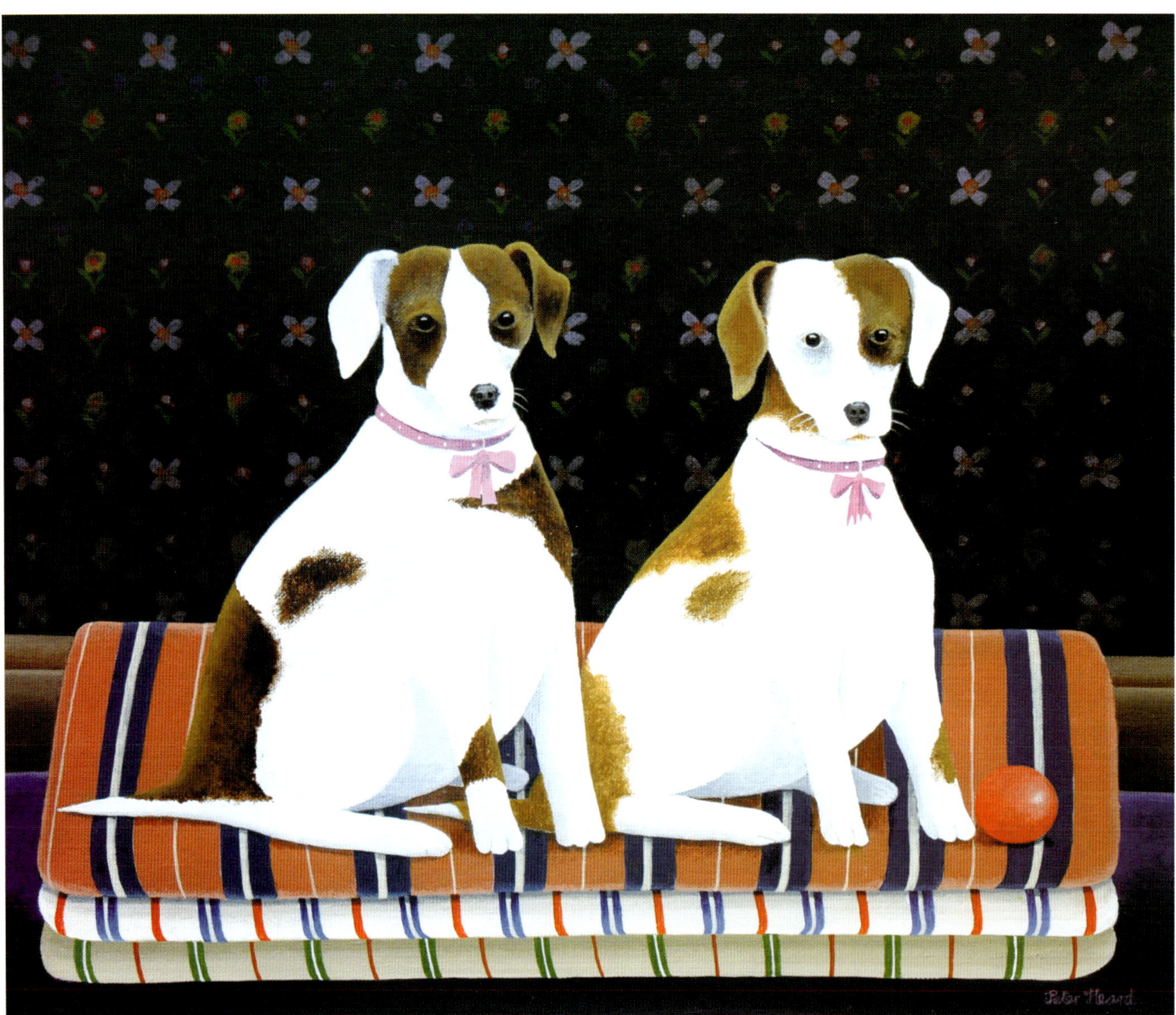
Peter Heard

JANE RUSSELLS

Peter loves Jack Russells – and had one called Bertie, named after the philosopher Bertrand Russell, as a pet when he lived in Epping. The terrier was bred in the nineteenth century by a Devon clergyman, the Reverend John (Parson Jack) Russell, for fox hunting – mainly because of its size and the fact that it looked similar to its prey. There are two varieties, the smooth and the wire-haired. The coat of the first is dense, short and flat, while that of the second is longer, harsh and wiry. The colouring is white with reddish brown, black or tan markings. It seemed to Peter that everyone in rural Somerset kept a pair of JRs plus a lurcher. A collection would not be complete without a portrait, so here we have two young ladies posing in their best pink collars, hoping for a Hollywood break.
Jane Russells indeed!

Jane Russells
Acrylic on Linen
46 x 38 cm

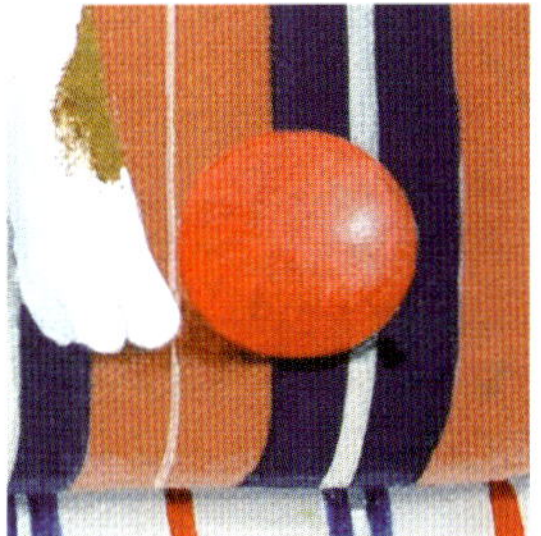

SPRING LAMB

One of the first signs of new life after winter is seeing spring lambs in the fields – even if they are destined for the dinner table. And research shows that more than 50% of lambing is now carried out by women. Still it is always a hazardous job keeping a watch on the flock – and ensuring the lambs survive. On the Quantocks dog owners have to keep their animals on a lead no longer than two metres between March 1 and July 31. This is to provide protection during the lambing season and to ensure the safety of ground nesting birds and calving deer. The penalty is a fine of £1,000 – and possibly having the dog destroyed. Peter once heard a farmer talking at a party about the price of lambs. He said they were worth £75 each but that would drop by £10 after Derby Day – because they were past their best. Fascinating! In this painting Exmoor is in the background and the sheep have been raddled – which means that they have been marked with a coloured pigment to show ownership or even to show which lambs belong to which ewe or that the ram has done his job. The copse is there because Peter wants it to be.

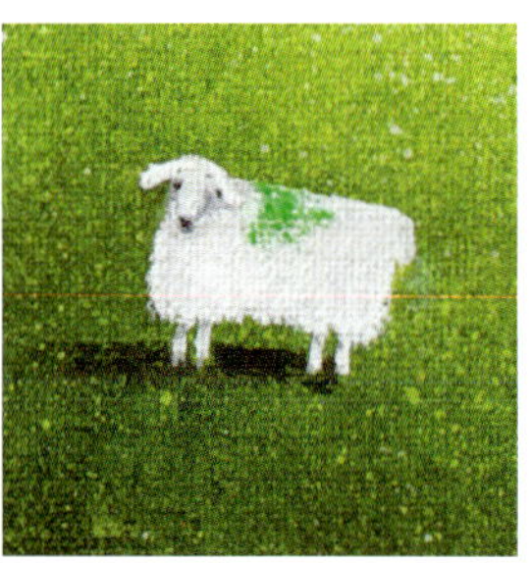

Spring Lamb
Acrylic on Linen
40 x 40 cm

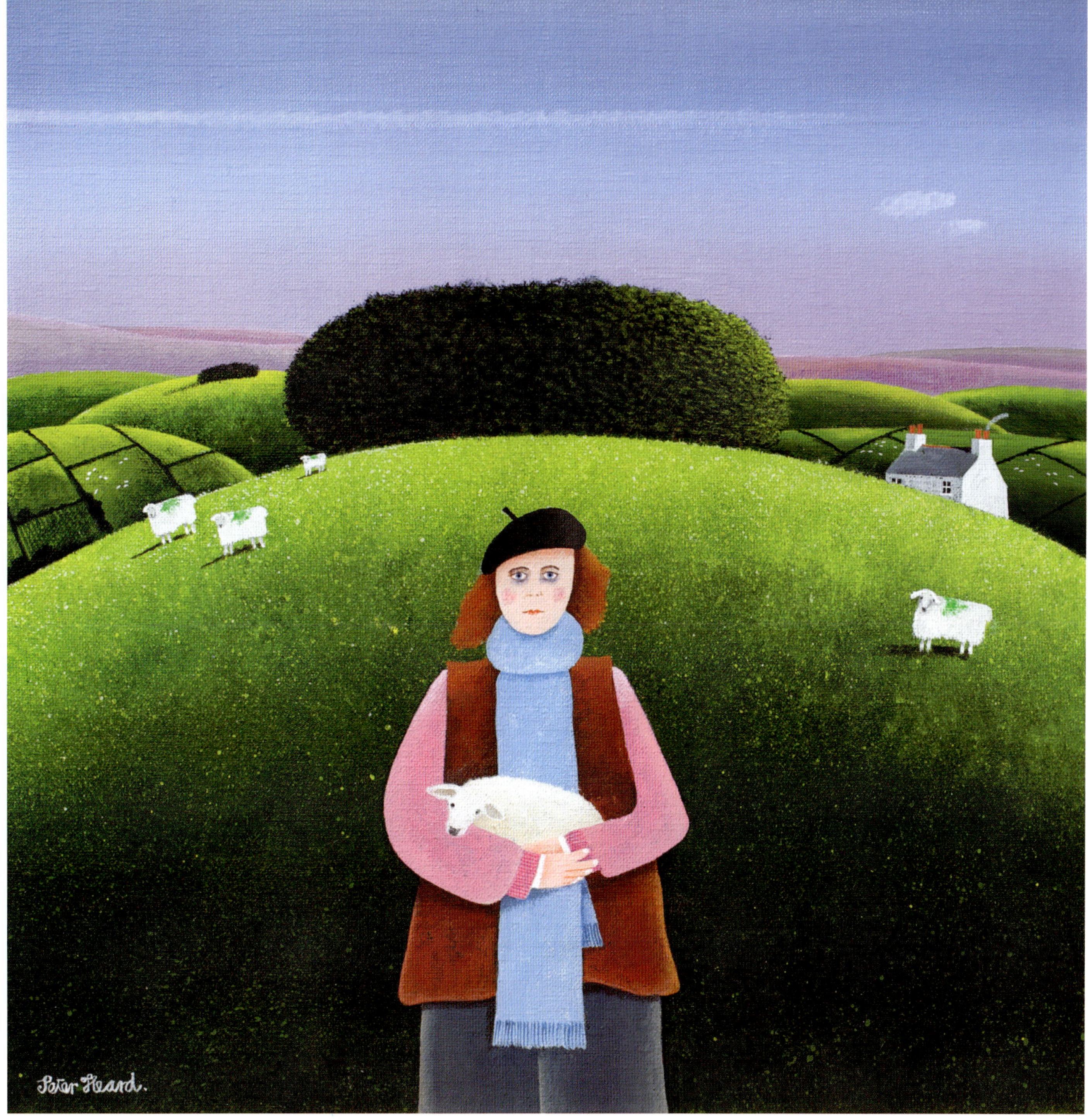
Peter Heard.

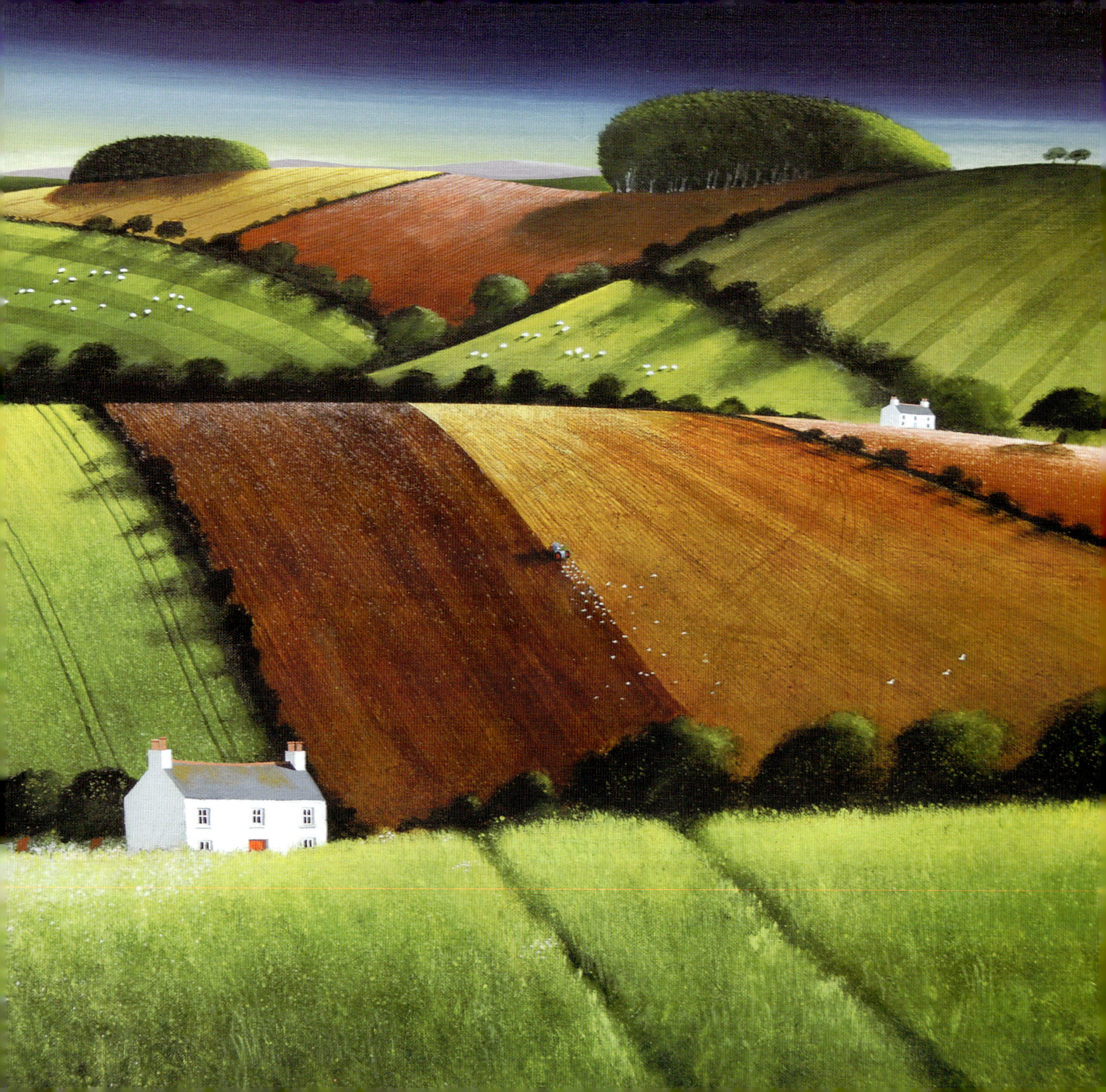

PLOUGHING THE SET ASIDE FIELD

Crop rotation has been a feature of farming since Roman times. From the Middle Ages to the twentieth century the system practised in Europe meant the rotation of a winter crop of rye or wheat, followed by spring oats or barley, then leaving the field fallow for a time. In 1988 the European Union introduced Setaside to help reduce the "grain mountain" caused by the guaranteed price system of the Common Agricultural Policy. Farmers were forced to set aside so much land each year. It was also hoped it would help the environment and wildlife. The policy has now been abolished. Here the farmer is ploughing his setaside field in a painting that seems a bit like a telephoto version. Peter is getting in tighter to the landscape. Setaside fields are orangey yellow and criss-crossed by lots of wheel marks. The light and shadows are accentuated, which works well with the vertical fields, hedges and trees.

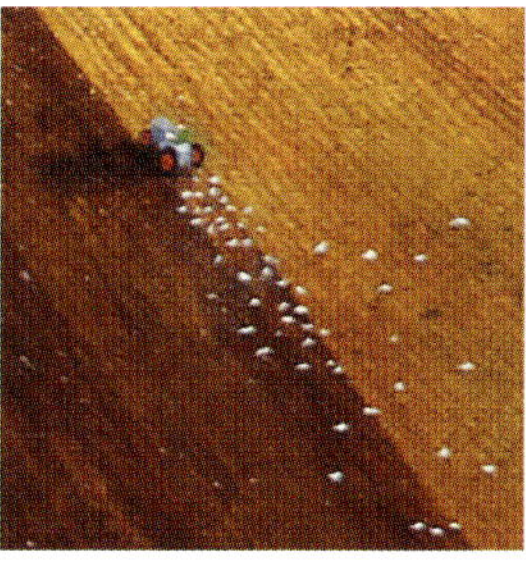

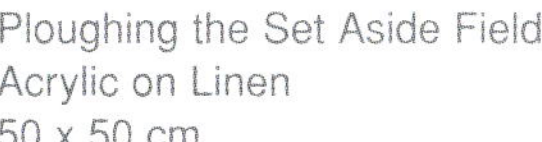
Ploughing the Set Aside Field
Acrylic on Linen
50 x 50 cm

Village Life

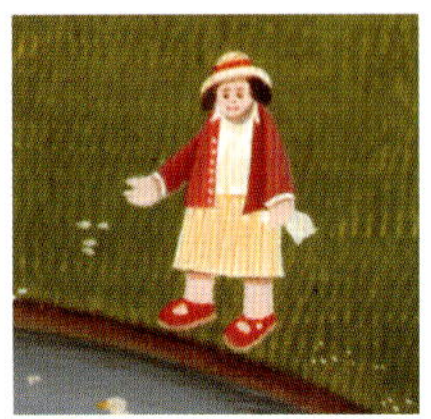

Ah yes, this is where the fun starts as anyone who has listened to *The Archers* will understand. Here Peter has given us a snapshot of some of the staples of life in a village. There are essential services like the postman and the mobile library, then some of the regular events in the village calendar – like the open gardens, the local hunt and a game of darts in the pub against the village down the road. And in the snug you will find Mr Grumpy from Bastard Birds regaling everyone with tales of taking pot shots at the birds stealing his crops.

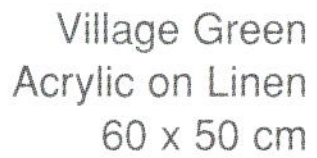

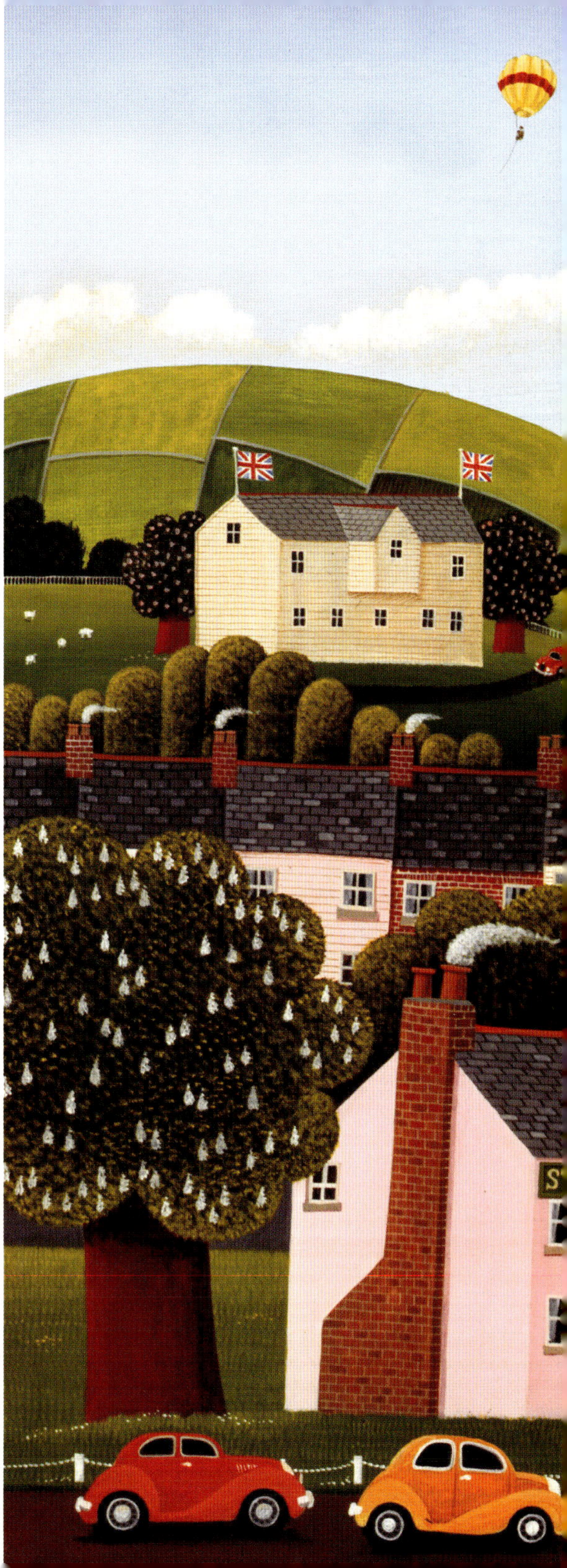

Village Green
Acrylic on Linen
60 x 50 cm

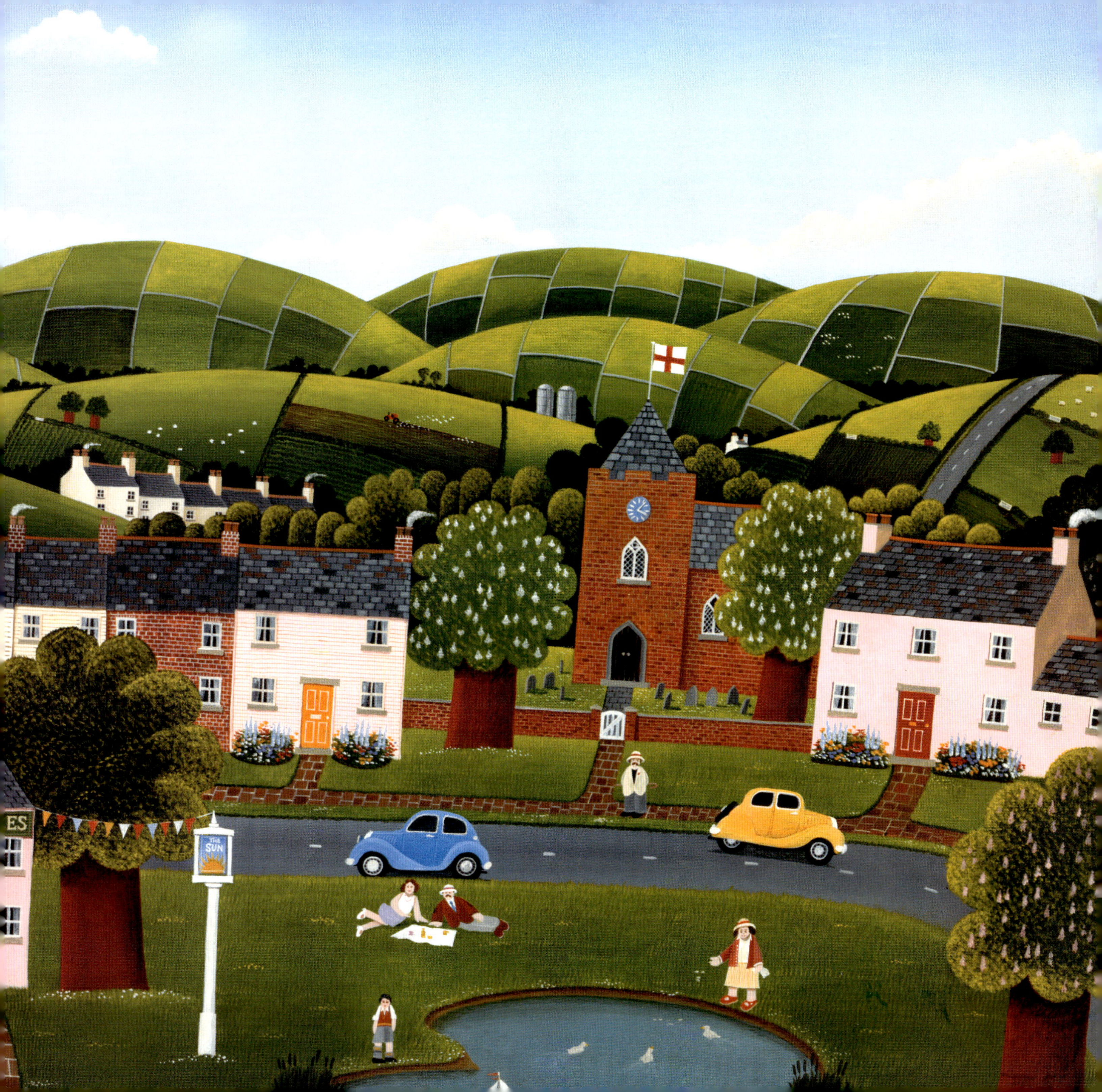
The SUN

VILLAGE RUSH HOUR

From spare, minimalist and surreal landscapes to a village teeming with life – this is where Peter shows the other side of his craft. The precise draughtsmanship, the minute detail. And yet there is still room for his other elements – the walls of fields in contrasting colours, some with grazing sheep, and the moorland beyond, flaked with heather on the horizon. There is a post office, antiques shop, brewery, church flying the flag of St George, two pubs and the farmer coming to town on his tractor transporting bales of hay. Mr and Mrs Somerset are also about to go into the antiques shop to buy some stripped pine furniture. With paintings like this Peter also loves to add a personal or humorous touch. The flower shop – Kitty's – is named after one of his granddaughters!

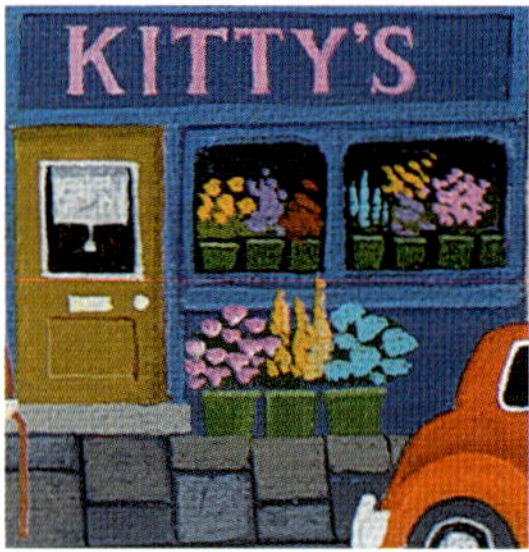

Village Rush Hour
Acrylic on Linen
60 x 50 cm

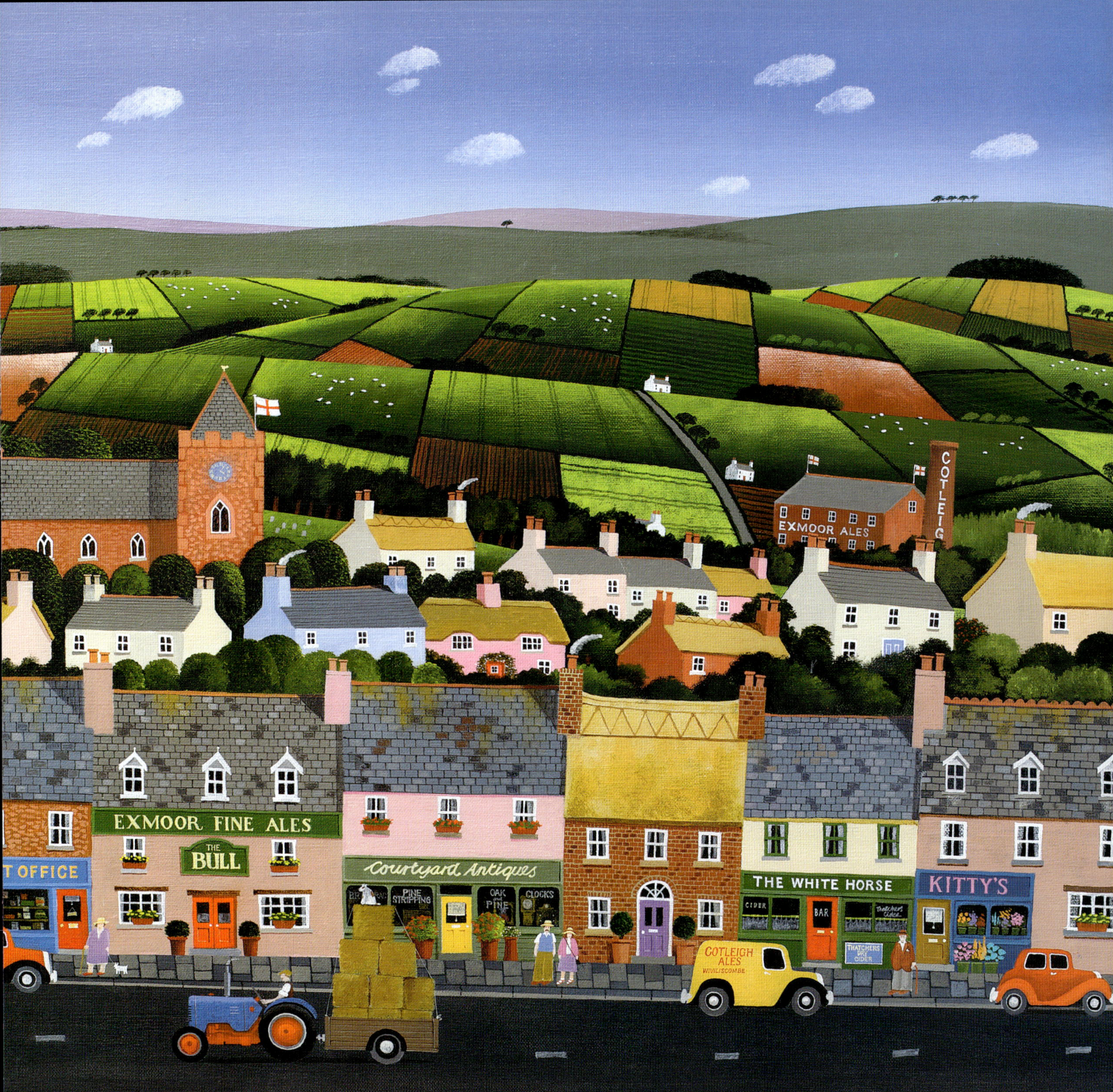
COTLEIG
EXMOOR ALES
EXMOOR FINE ALES
THE BULL
T OFFICE
Courtyard Antiques
PINE STRIPPING
OAK and PINE
CLOCKS
THE WHITE HORSE
CIDER
BAR
Thatchers Cider
THATCHERS DRY CIDER
KITTY'S
COTLEIGH ALES
WIVILISCOMBE

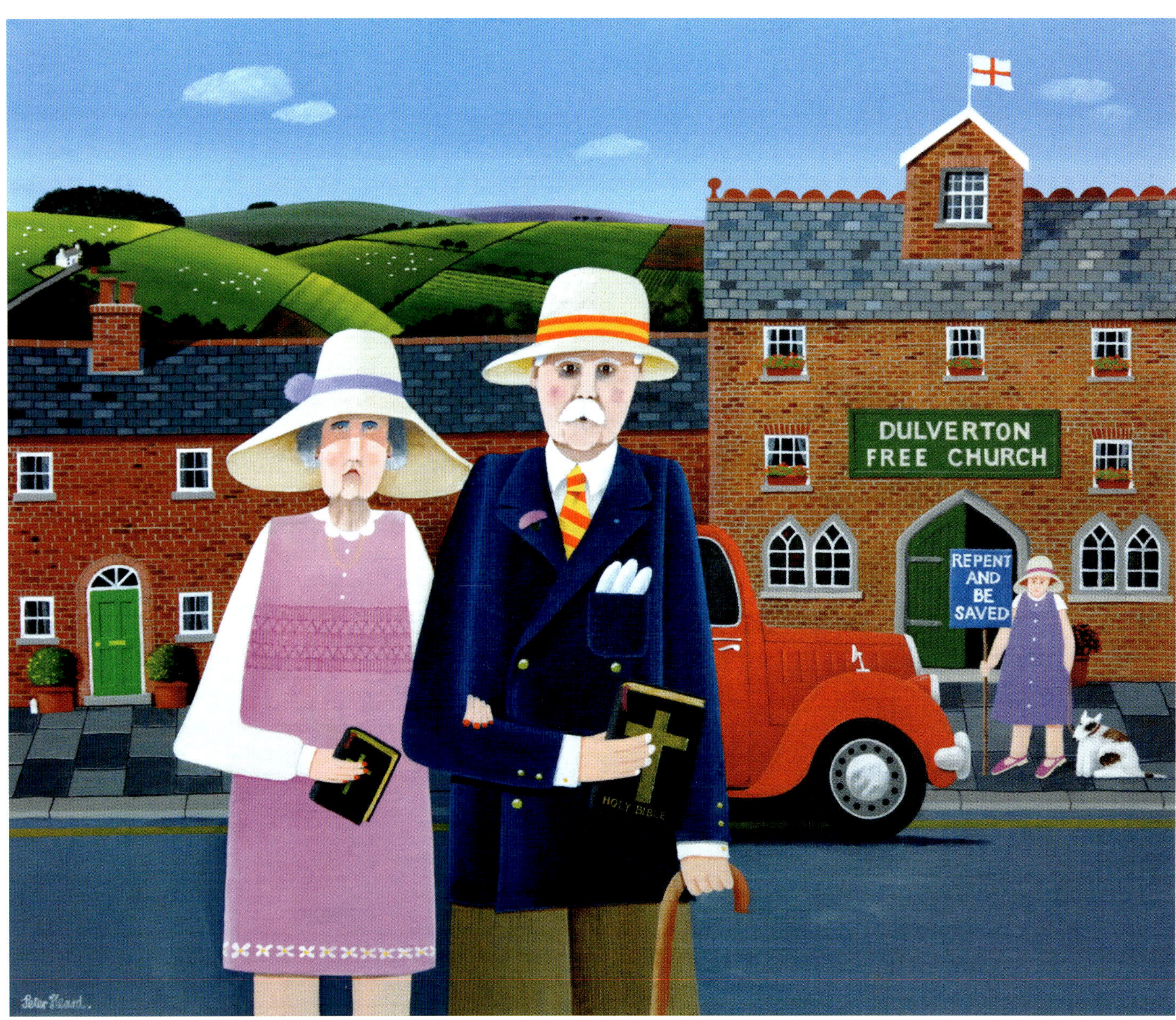
DULVERTON
FREE CHURCH
REPENT
AND
BE
SAVED
HOLY BIBLE
Peter Heard.

DULVERTON SUNDAY

Peter was looking through a 1977 copy of *Art & Artists*, a long gone arts magazine, that he had kept. There was an article on an exhibition of British Primitive Art at the Ikon Gallery in Birmingham that he was part of. One of his paintings was used in black and white for the article. Peter thought he would repaint it and see where it led him. Thirty-odd years ago church on Sunday was more of a bastion of English life. And the sight of people, generally out-of-work men, walking round with sandwich boards warning that the end of the world is nigh. Here the woman outside the church is holding a board that says "Repent and be Saved". Anyway our church goers are a very serious and devout looking couple, dressed in their Sunday best and carrying their own Bibles. The Free Church in the West Country was started in the 1840s after a falling-out between a minister in Totnes and the Bishop of Exeter. The rebels wanted less pomp and ceremony and less interference from both Canterbury and Westminster. How different things are today. Religion has been replaced by supermarket shopping in many people's Sunday rituals.

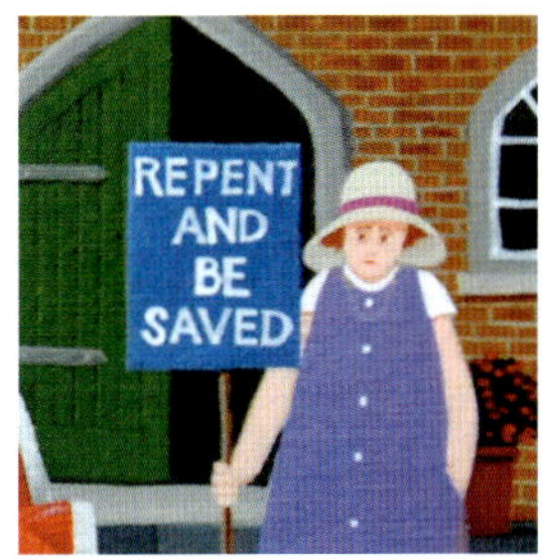

Dulverton Sunday
Acrylic on Linen
60 x 50 cm

NERDY! ME?

Peter went into his local newsagent's to find FOUR different magazines about vintage tractors. It transpired there is huge interest in boys' toys – vintage cars and motorbikes, steam engines and machinery. And, yes, vintage tractors. Type vintage tractors into Google and you get 190,000 results. There are rallies and shows and specialist firms that restore tractors. Somerset has its vintage tractor shows and vintage tractor and engine clubs, reflecting the importance of the vehicle in the farming life of the county. For instance, more than 20,000 attended the North Somerset Show in May 2009, when there was a display of 76 restored machines belonging to members of the North Somerset branch of the Vintage Tractor and Engine Club. They dated from 1945 to the mid-1970s and included vehicles made in Britain, America and Australia. Here Mr Somerset is getting his vintage International machine ready for a show, washing it as he would his car!

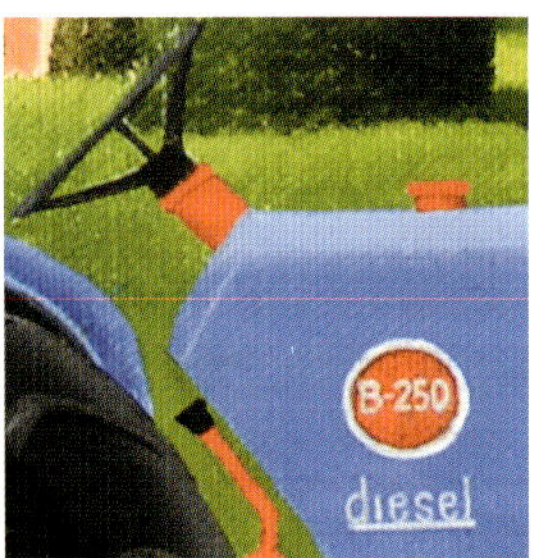

Nerdy! Me?
Acrylic on Linen
40 x 40 cm

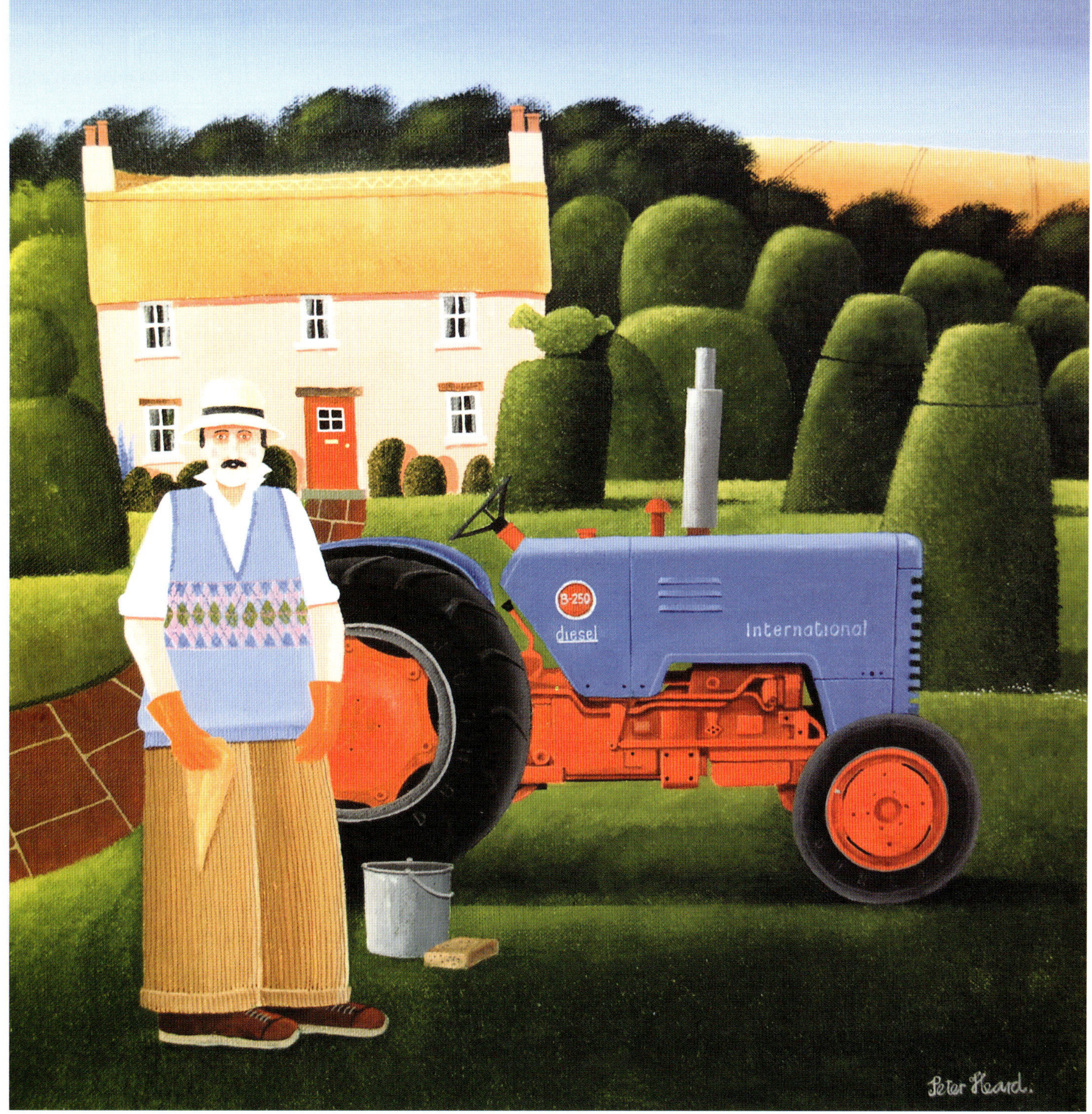
B-250
diesel
International
Peter Heard.

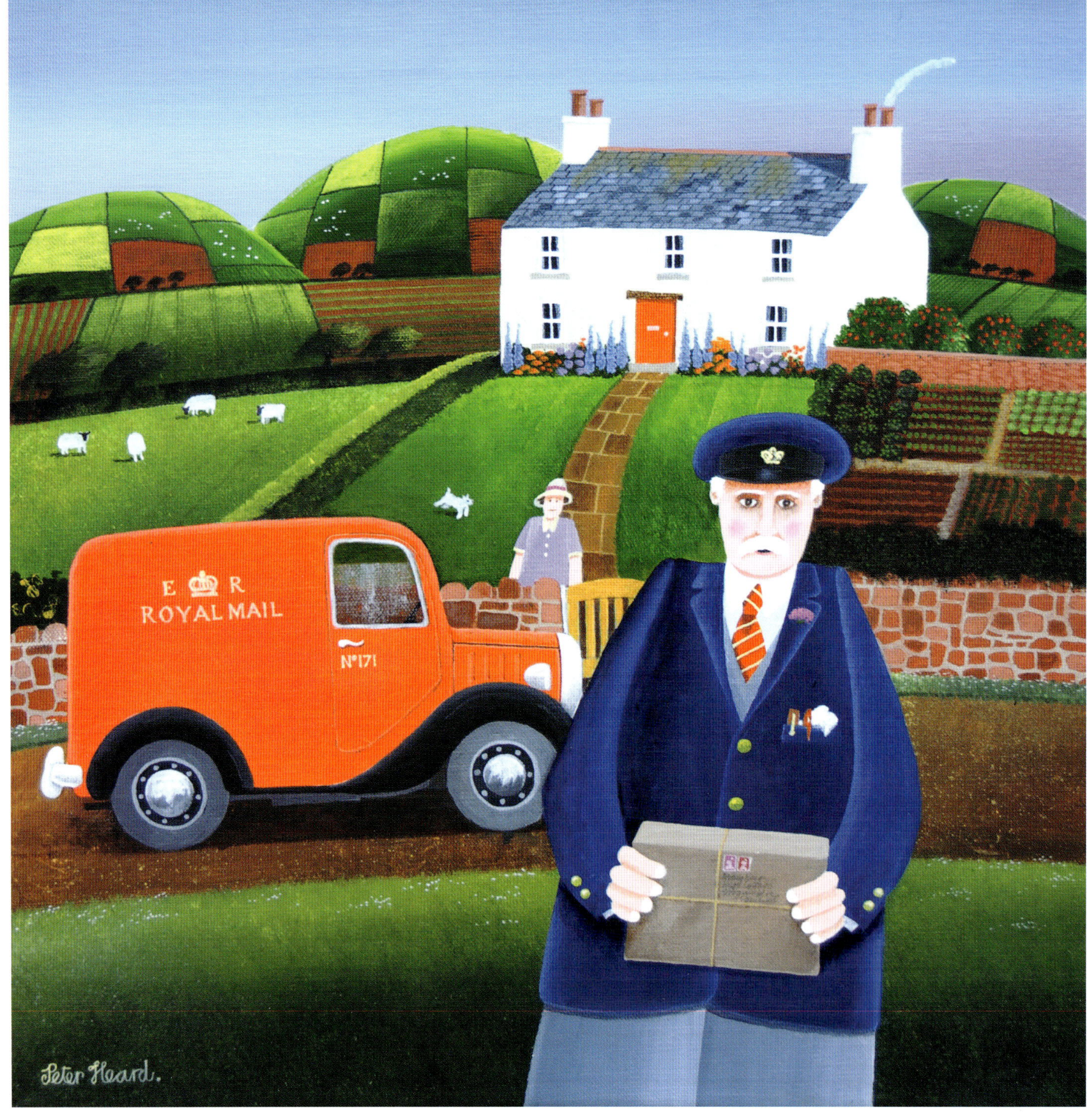
E R
ROYAL MAIL
Nº171
Peter Heard.

VILLAGE POSTIE

The village shop is the lifeblood of many villages and in many cases its economic viability relies on a post office. Thousands of them have been under threat for several years because the Post Office says they do not make money as more and more people switch to the internet for banking and paying bills. Yet the post office is often a place where people meet and chat, especially where the village does not have a pub. In summer 2008 a coach party of residents from the Somerset village of Hinton St George re-enacted their annual Punkie Night Parade in Westminster to protest at the closure of their post office, which has been there since the 1840s. They carried mangelwurzel lanterns and jars of home-made cider. And the leader, in traditional white overcoat and black top hat, rang a bell as he sang the age-old Punkie Night song with the words changed to:

It's Punkie Night tonight
It's Punkie Night tonight
So Mr Brown we've come to town,
for Hinton's going to fight.

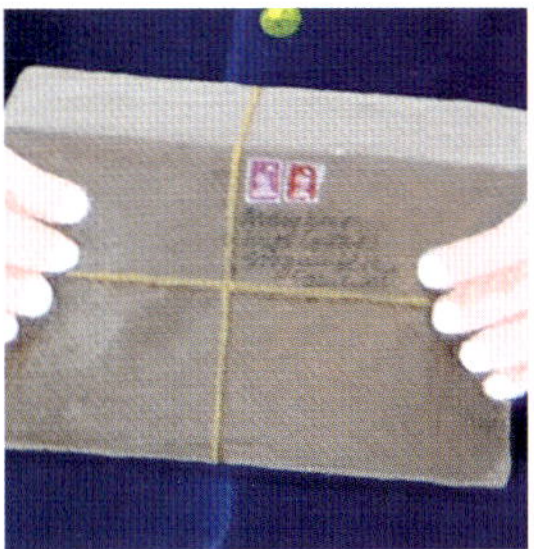

Village Postie
Acrylic on Linen
40 x 40 cm

DOUBLE TOP

Of all the games associated with public houses – pool, snooker, skittles – darts is perhaps the most famous because it is believed to have been started in old inns and taverns during medieval times. One theory is that archery teachers shortened arrows and got their students to throw them at the bottom of an empty wine barrel. In parts of England darts are still referred to as arrows. Archers then took their shortened arrows with them to the local drinking house to show off their skill and have a bit of fun. Henry VIII is believed to have instructed his archers to play darts to keep their skills honed all year round. The bar-room here shows how a village pub can transcend the social classes. The darts player could be described as working class – he is wearing a flat hat and drinking a pint of Exmoor ale. Yet on the wall are photographs of huntsmen, suggesting it also the setting-off point for the local hunt.

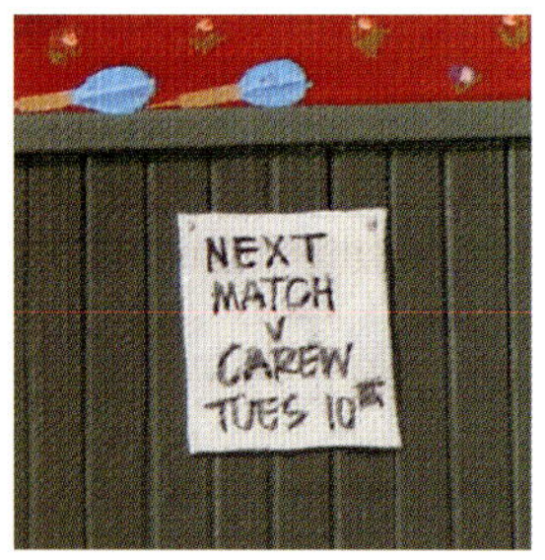

Double Top
Acrylic on Linen
40 x 40 cm

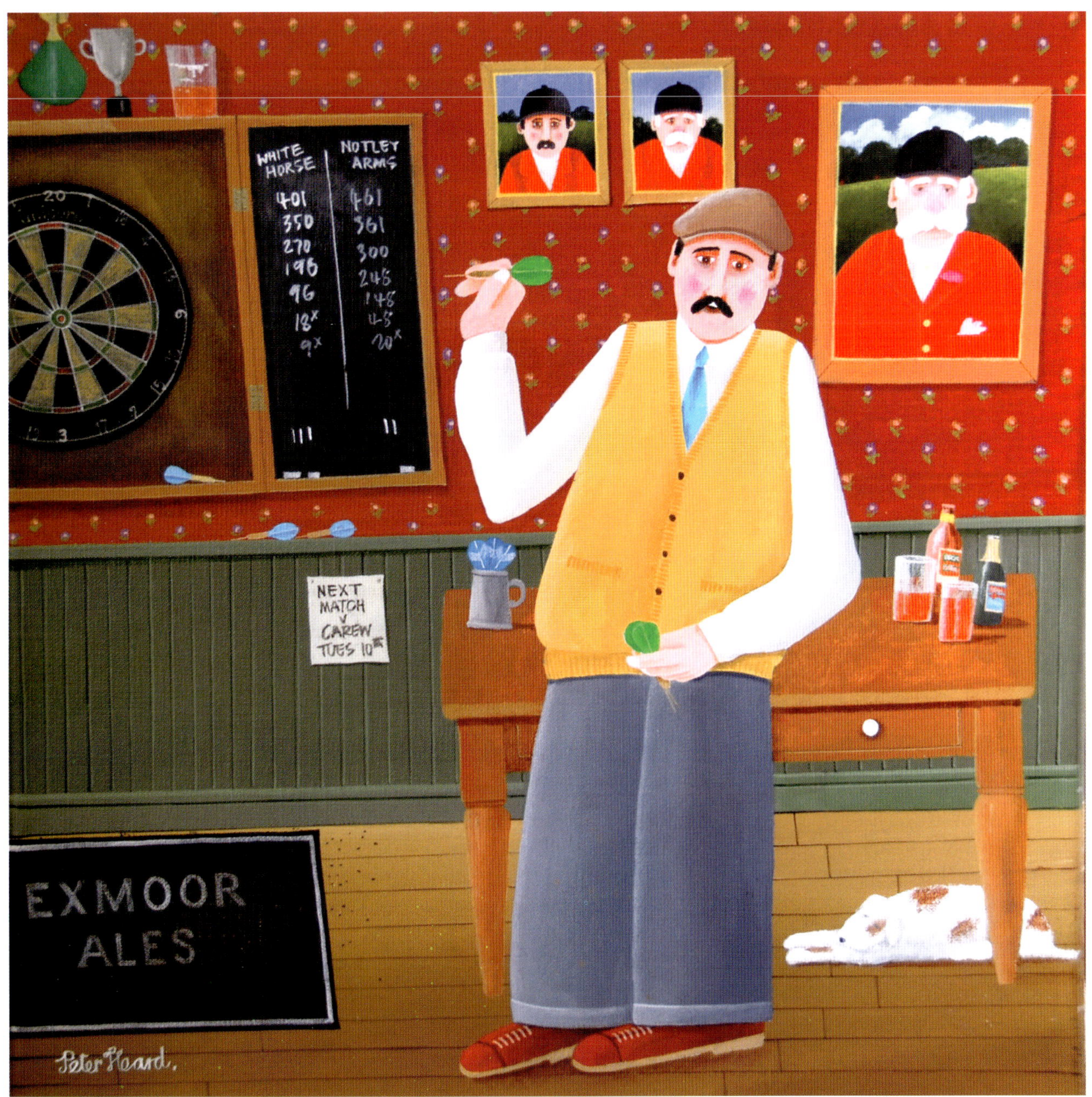
WHITE HORSE
NOTLEY ARMS
NEXT MATCH v CAREW TUES 10th
EXMOOR ALES
Peter Heard.

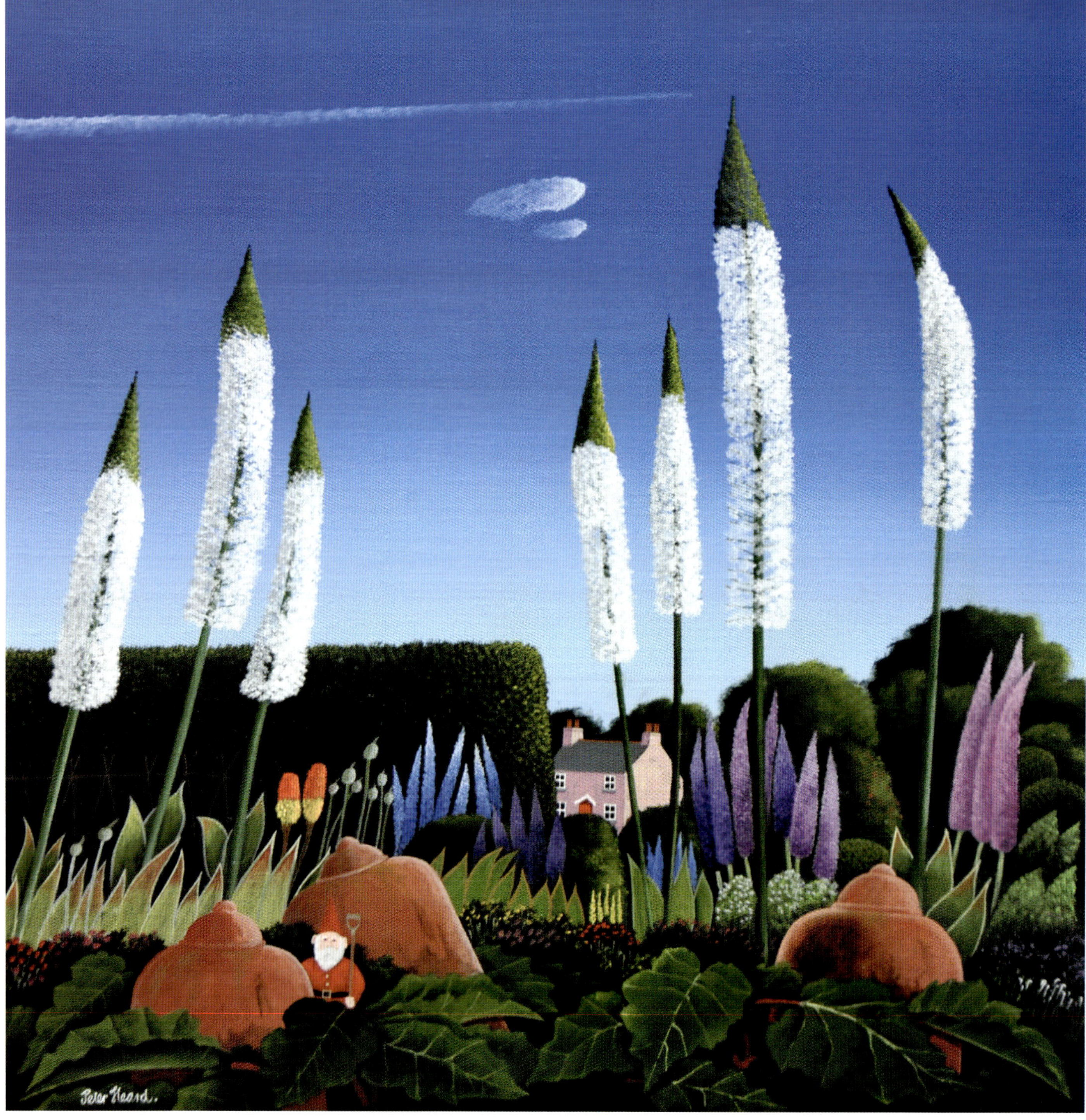
Peter Heard.

GIANT FOXTAIL LILIES

These spectacular lilies rocketing into the air can grow from six to ten feet high and have up to 700 flowers which blossom in June. Much too tall for our garden gnome. He, of course, is quite real, living in his forcing pot and tending some early sprouting rhubarb. Ornamental garden gnomes, on the other hand, were first made in Germany in the mid-1800s. Stories and myths told of how gnomes were willing to help in the garden at night when everyone else was asleep. They arrived in Britain in 1847 when Sir Charles Isham brought 21 terracotta gnomes back from Germany and put them in his garden at Lamport Hall in Northamptonshire. Only one, called Lampy has survived and he is insured for £1million. Our little gnome is still working away, quietly and out of sight. We've known him for nearly 30 years now. And there's many a tale we could tell about him...

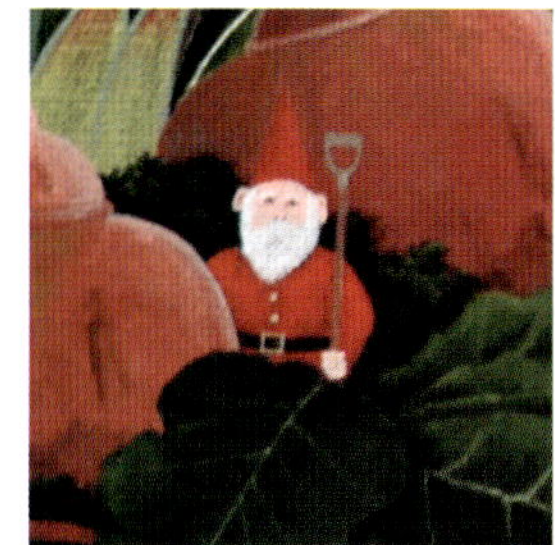

Giant Foxtail Lilies
Acrylic on Linen
50 x 50 cm

STOGUMBER GARDENS OPEN

Here are Mr and Mrs Somerset in the garden of their vermillion cottage. Lots of villages open their gardens to visitors once a year. It is a chance for people to admire the hard work gardeners have put in, get ideas, cuttings and sometimes buy produce like ripe summer fruit. Stogumber, for instance, has about 20 gardens open with visitors piling into the village. It is part of the tradition of Englishness that fascinates Peter. The couple are well-hatted in a well-ordered world in the shadow of the Quantocks. They are also possibly refugees from London as Mr Somerset is wearing an MCC hat. Once again there is topiary in the background, illustrating the hard work done in these gardens in anticipation of visitors.

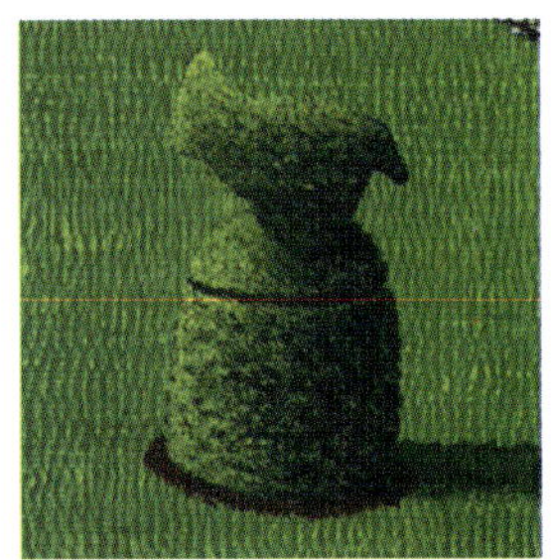

Stogumber Gardens Open
Acrylic on Linen
50 x 50 cm

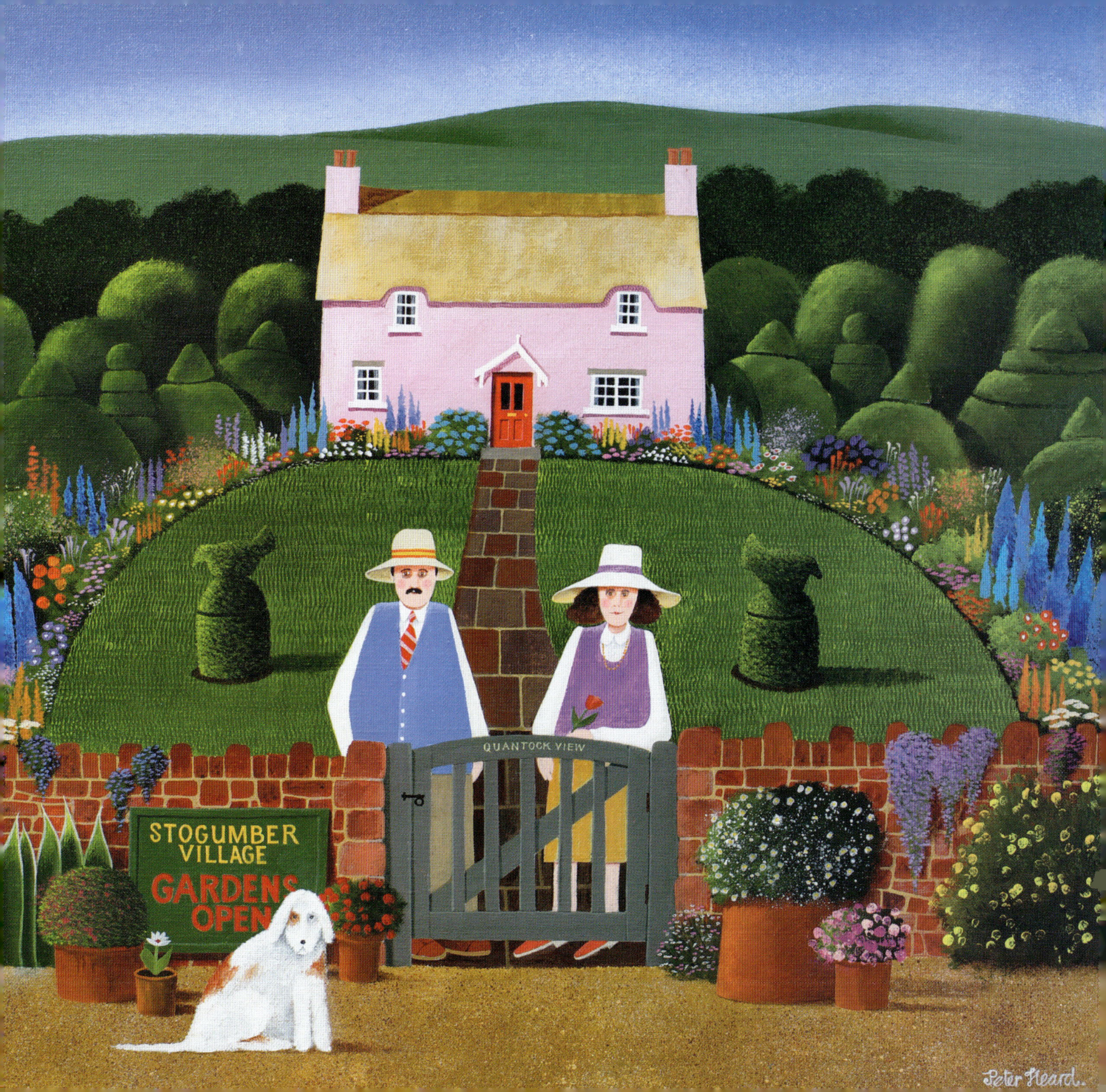
QUANTOCK VIEW
STOGUMBER
VILLAGE
GARDENS
OPEN
Peter Heard.

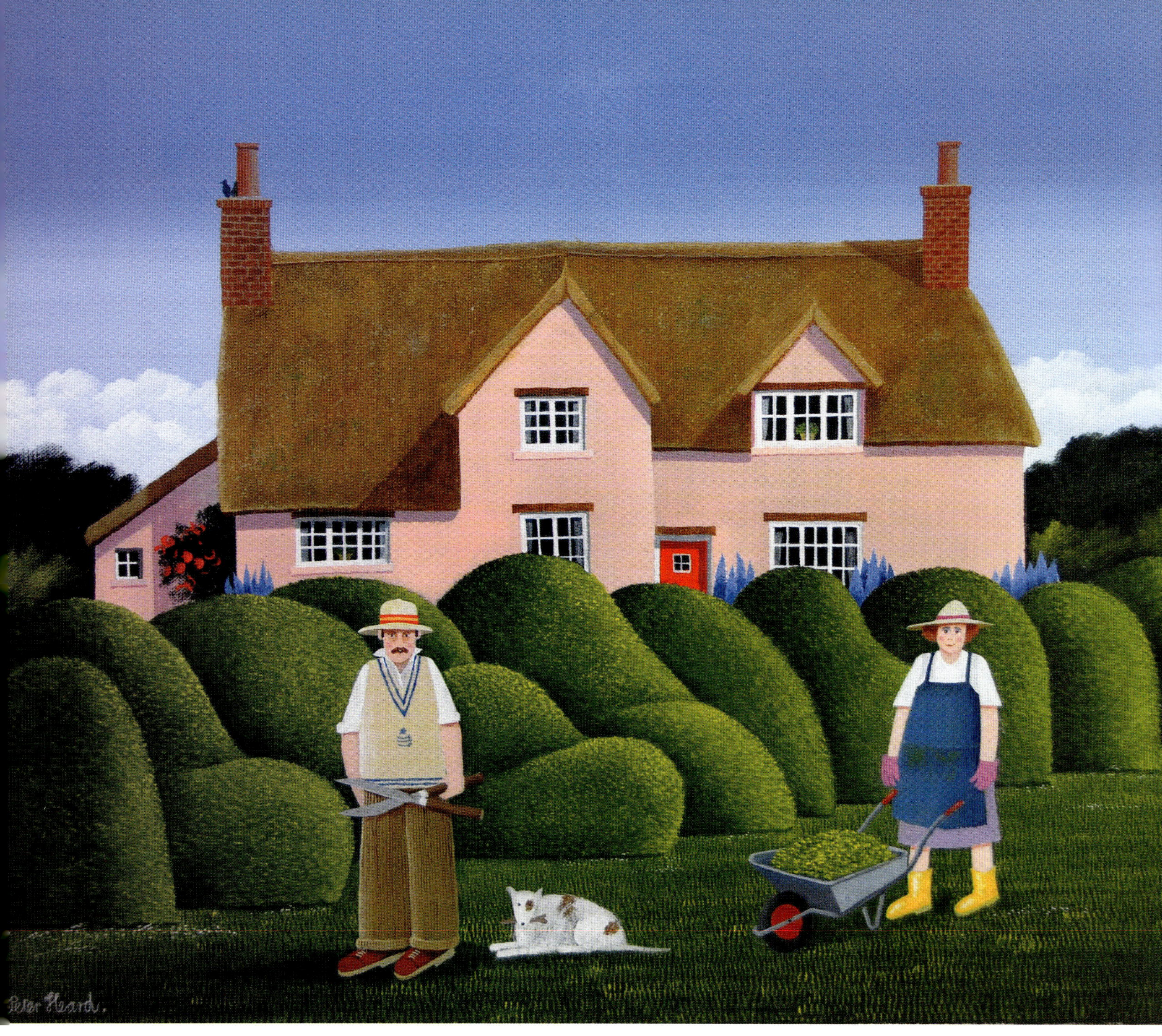
Peter Heard.

TOPIARY COTTAGE BY HALSE

Is this confirmation that Mr and Mrs Somerset have retired to the West Country from London? This painting is the country idyll many city dwellers dream of – a vision of England's green and pleasant land. Everything is in perfect order – the house with its pink walls, thatched roof and white-painted windows. The garden is just so – immaculate topiary hedges and bowling green lawn. And Mr and Mrs Somerset are perfect too – he with his Middlesex county cricket club 2nd XI sweater with three scimitars and she in her yellow wellies and pink gardening gloves. Bet you wish they could give us a smile just for once!

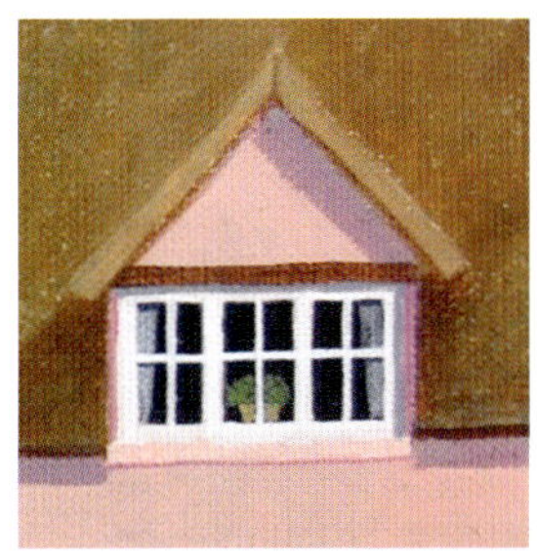

Topiary Cottage by Halse
Acrylic on Linen
60 x 50 cm

OFF RABBITING

Hunting, shooting and fishing are all major aspects of life in the country. And when it comes to hunting, rabbits are high on the list. Children may view them as cuddly pets to be nurtured and loved. But farmers see them as a pest that ravages their crops and costs them a lot of money. Many take matters into their own hands – as the gentlemen in the painting is doing as he sets off with his gun and his dog to do some rabbiting. Again the painting has many of the devices Peter uses in his rural compositions – patchwork fields, a linhay, a pink cottage and cider apple trees in the garden. The hunter himself is wearing an MCC tie and a blue cornflower in his button hole – which is a Masonic emblem.

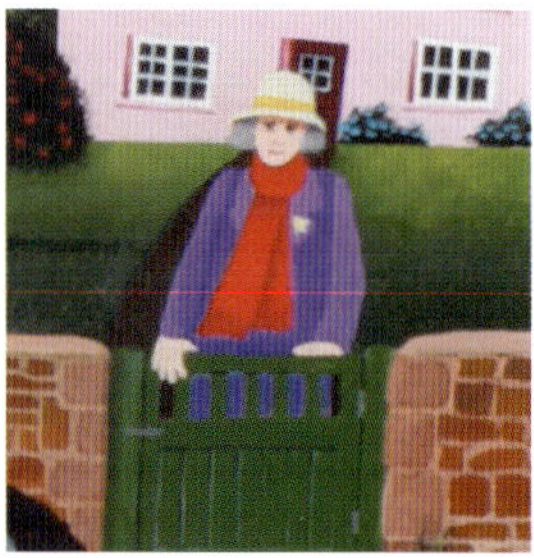

Off Rabbiting
Acrylic on Linen
50 x 50 cm

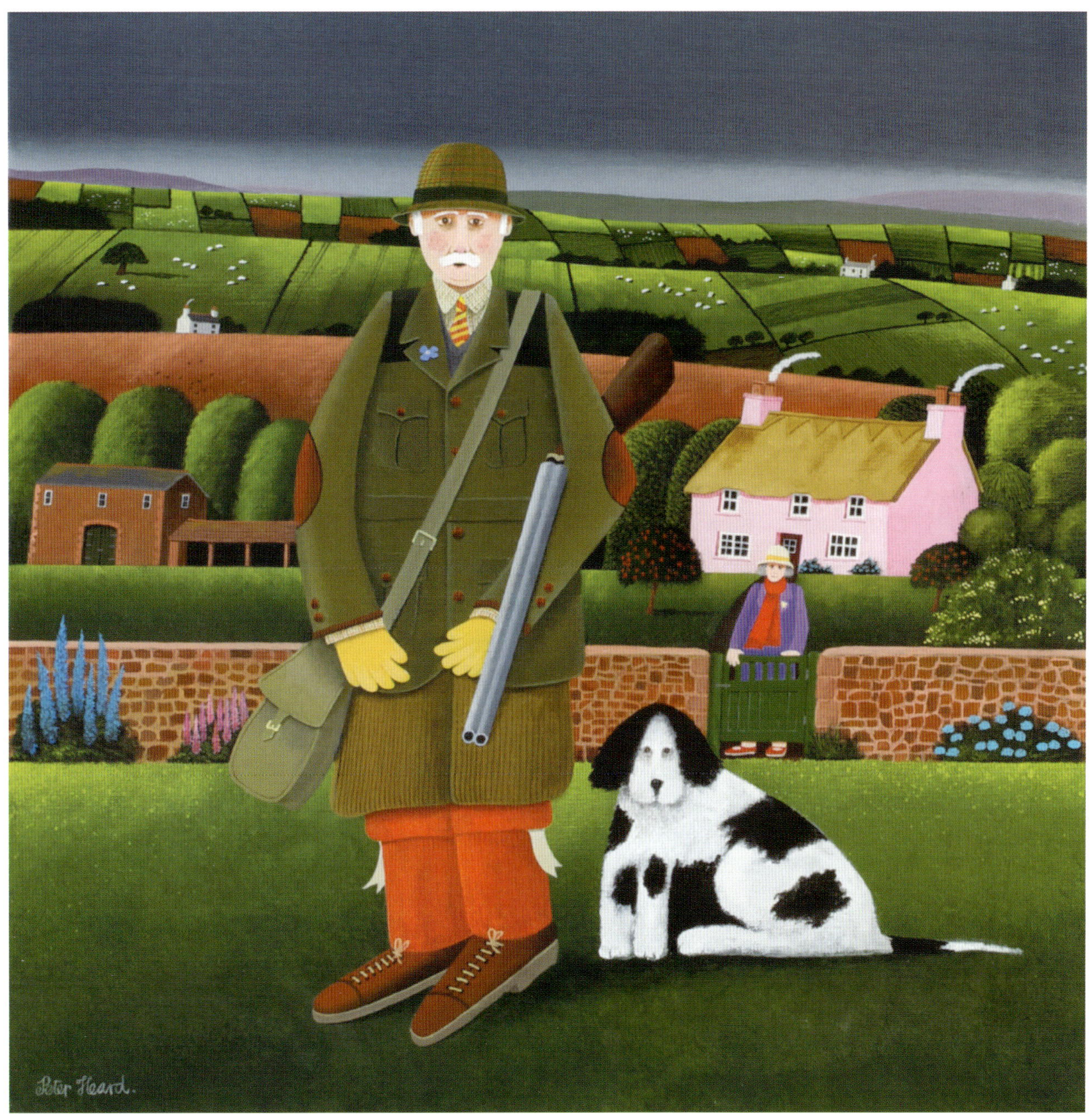
Peter Heard.

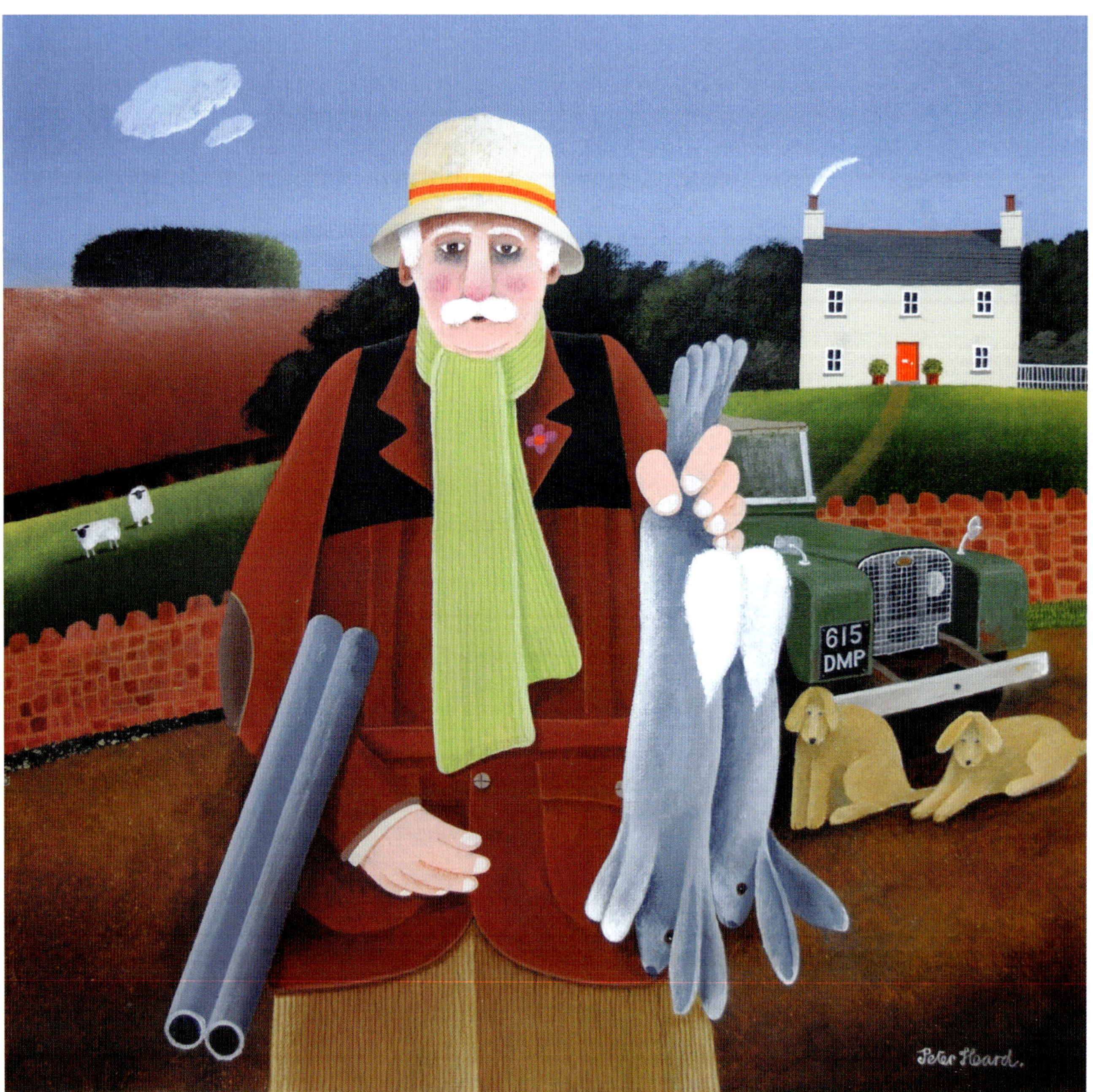
615
DMP
Peter Heard.

TWO FOR THE POT

Once you have caught and skinned your rabbit, here's how to cook it. This recipe is called Somerset Rabbit:

Ingredients:

1 Rabbit

2 Tablespoons flour, seasoned with salt and pepper

2oz Lard or oil

1 Onion, chopped

1lb Mixed root vegetables, scrubbed and cut into chunks

1 Tablespoon tomato puree

1 Teaspoon yeast extract, such as Marmite

1/2 Teaspoon mixed herbs

1/2 pint Cider

1/2 pint Chicken stock

Salt and pepper

Method:

Keep rabbit whole or, if it will not fit in casserole, cut in two between hind legs and rib cage and dust over with seasoned flour. Heat lard or oil in a pan and turn rabbit in it until brown. Lift out of fat on to plate. Fry onion gently to soften. Put rabbit in pan or casserole. Put veg on top and add other ingredients. Cover with a lid or foil. Either bring to the boil and simmer until tender, about 1.5 hours, or put casserole into a warm oven, gas 3, 325F, 160C, for about 2 hours or until tender. Lift out rabbit, remove all meat from bones and return to pan and re-heat. Serve as a stew with potatoes and green vegetables or with pasta shells. Serves 4. Goes well under a pie crust or with dumplings. Freezes very well.

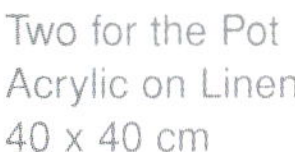

Two for the Pot
Acrylic on Linen
40 x 40 cm

BEATER'S BOOTS

And here are a hunt couple, enjoying a small libation after the excitement of the chase. There is something of the British stiff upper lip about them – him with his moustache and her with a patrician gaze. There are several hunts in the West Country – and the beaters are the people who flush out the animals for the hunters. Fox hunting was banned in England in 2004. Incidentally, a member of the Exmoor Foxhounds became the first person in England to be convicted of breaking the ban. He was fined £500 and ordered to pay £250 costs in 2006 – but had the verdict overturned on appeal. The inspiration for this painting was Peter visiting his village pub to find dozens of pairs of muddy wellies outside. They belonged to the beaters of the morning's hunt who were enjoying a pint and a sandwich.

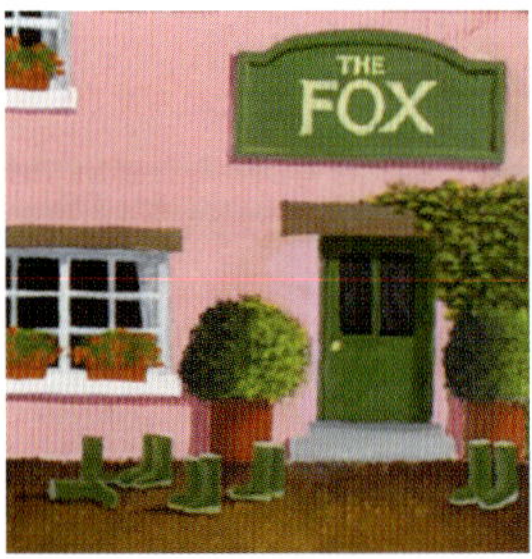

Beater's Boots
Acrylic on Linen
50 x 50 cm

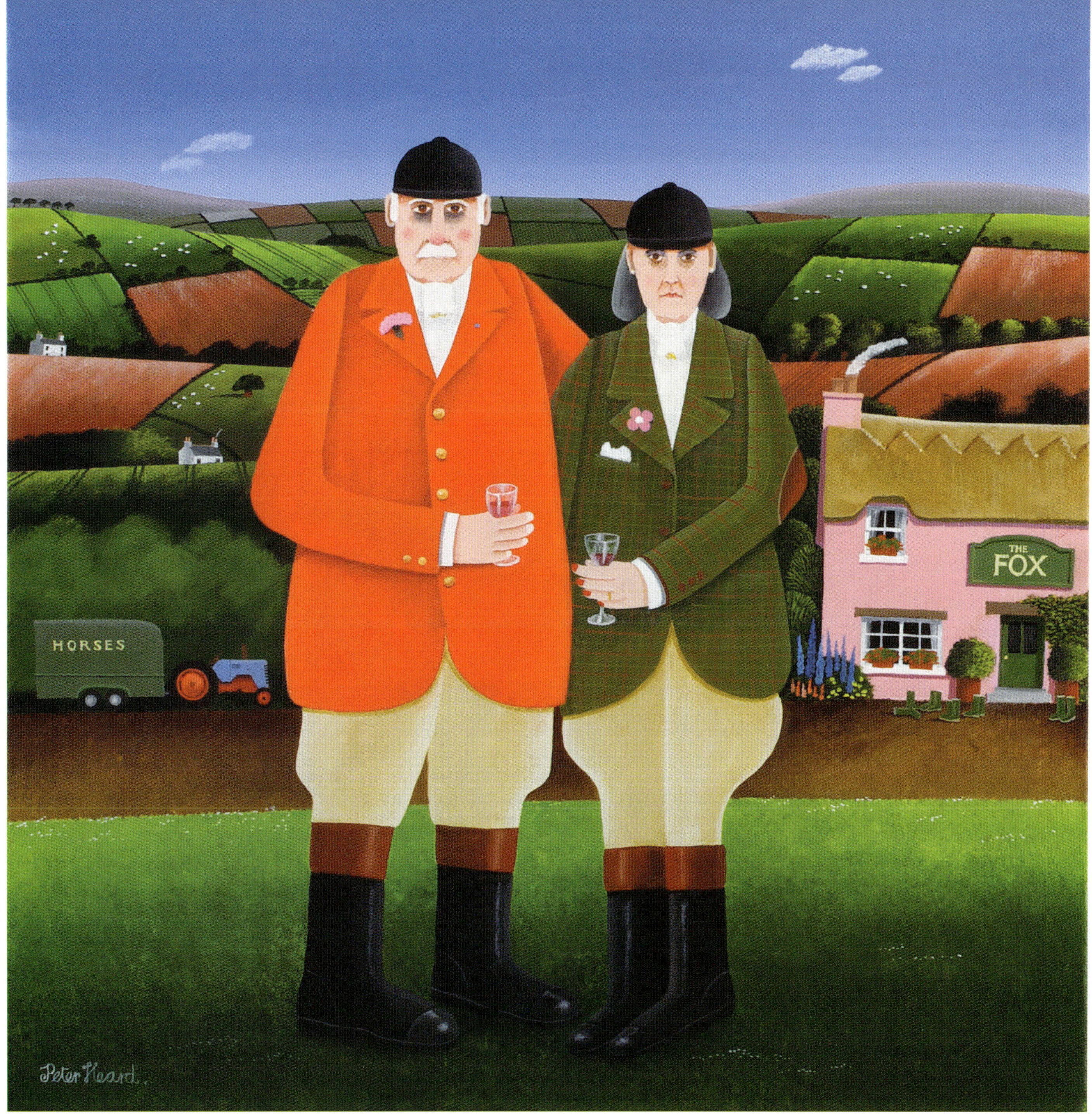
HORSES
THE
FOX
Peter Heard.

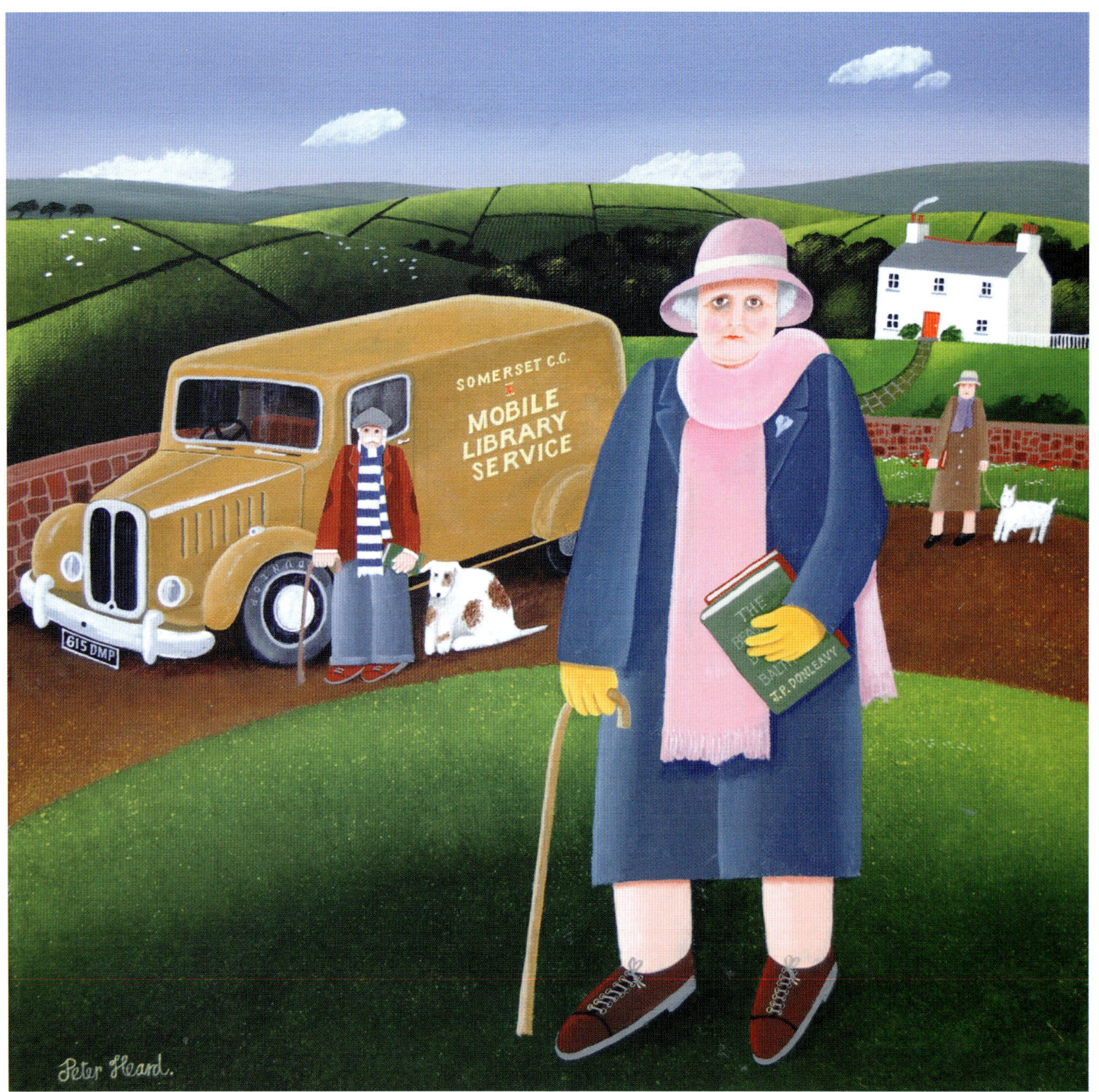
SOMERSET C.C.
MOBILE
LIBRARY
SERVICE
615 DMP
J.P. DONLEAVY
Peter Heard.

MUCH LOVED SERVICE

Mobile libraries are a lifeline in rural villages where public transport is scarce – for instance Stogumber has two buses a week. As a Londoner Peter was used to having everything on his doorstep – including a library within walking distance. But villagers have to rely on a service that visits possibly once a fortnight. Although mobile libraries are becoming more sophisticated – you can now borrow CDs and DVDs as well as books and you can also access the internet. In a typical Peter Heard quirk, the book that the painting's staid-looking lady has in her hand is *The Beastly Beatitudes Of Balthazar B* by JP Donleavy – an author whose early work caused outrage in the austere 1950s. The book holds a very special meaning to Peter and Mary that will remain a secret.

Much Loved Service
Acrylic on Linen
40 x 40 cm

BEST IN SHOW

Many of Peter's paintings have a summertime feel to them, along with the continuing traditions of rural life in England. Of these, the agricultural show, village show, country fair are a once-a-year festival bringing together many of the elements – and people – that make up life in a village. Here we have the WI tent, flower show, the flags of St George flying – and the dog show. The first dog show in England was held in 1859 – a social event organised by aristocrats to raise money for charity. The first dog society was formed in Birmingham the following year and the Kennel Club was founded in 1873. It held its first show the same year at Crystal Palace with 975 entrants. The dogs here wouldn't win any prizes at Cruft's. And the poor little Jack Russell terrier at the far right of the painting looks a little fed-up – he wasn't considered smart enough to enter the show!

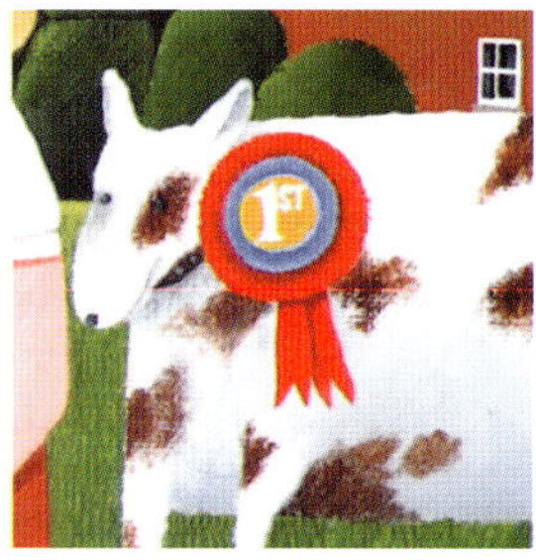

Best in Show
Acrylic on Linen
70 x 50 cm

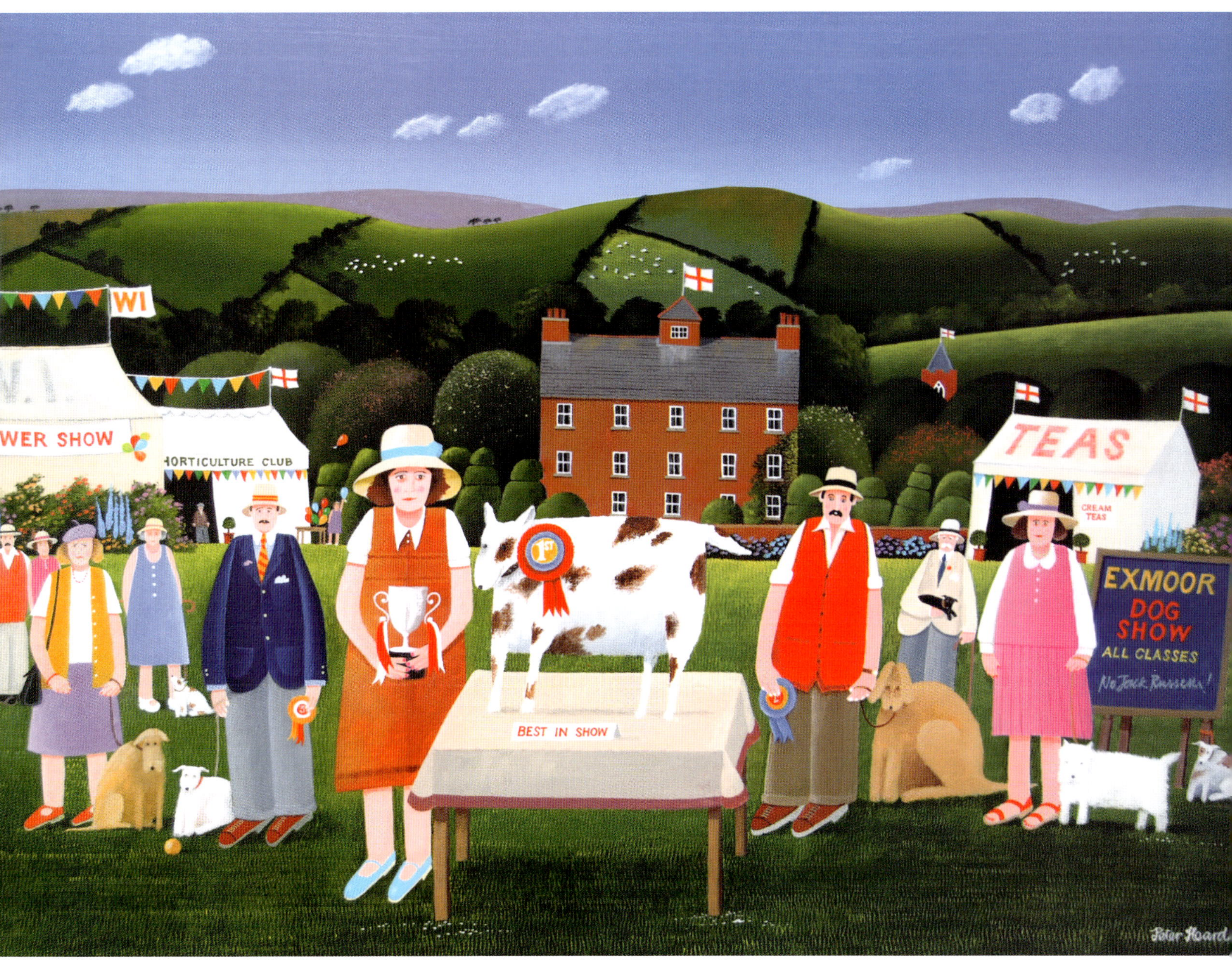
WI
WER SHOW
HORTICULTURE CLUB
TEAS
CREAM TEAS
1st
BEST IN SHOW
EXMOOR
DOG SHOW
ALL CLASSES
No Jack Russells!
Peter Heard

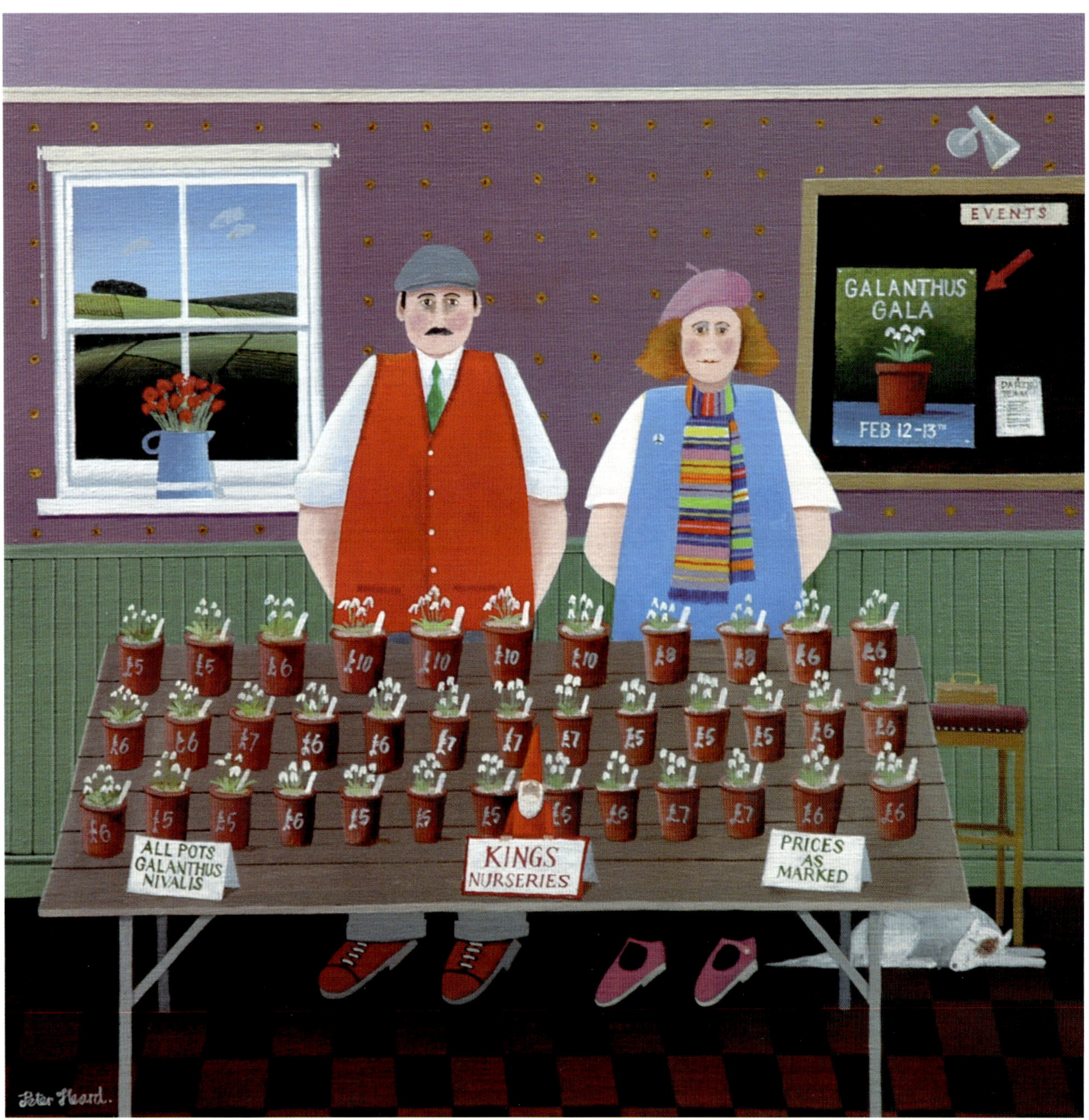
EVENTS
GALANTHUS GALA
FEB 12-13TH
ALL POTS GALANTHUS NIVALIS
KINGS NURSERIES
PRICES AS MARKED
Peter Heard.

GALANTHUS GALA

Peter entered the strange world of the Galanthophiles after a visit to Snowdrop Valley on the tourist trail of Exmoor National Park. Visitors are ferried by bus down a narrow Somerset lane to see the spectacular white display. Dot Rouge, Peter's family fine art print company, publishes a wonderful artist called John Morley who not only paints snowdrops and auriculas but grows and sells them as well! Research for this painting revealed a world of snowdrop enthusiasts who love and nurture the "Fair Maids of February". A national Galanthus Gala is held each February where collectors flock to buy new and rare specimens which can cost £150! Our couple have set up their stall early to await the pandemonium when the doors open. At that time their garden gnome will beat a hasty retreat...

Galanthus Gala
Acrylic on Linen
40 x 40 cm

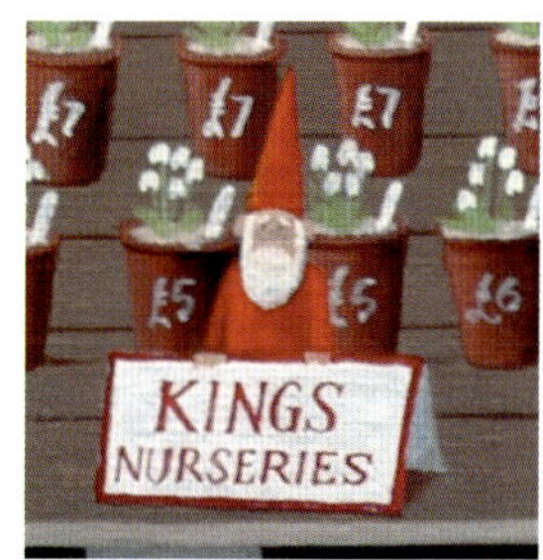

AURICULAS

Peter became fascinated by snowdrops and started a painting featuring them. But halfway through he realised high summer was not their season. The snowdrops rapidly became auriculas and, guess what, it transpired that all manner of auricula societies, collectors, growers and aficionados are out there! Here we meet Mr and Mrs Somerset again safe in their walled garden trying to raise money for the church bell appeal. Suitably and immaculately hatted for the sun they await the rush to buy the auriculas they have lovingly grown in the greenhouse. They may not realise but the health and quality of their flowers has been guaranteed by their garden gnome. He has kept an eye on things from start to finish and has fashioned a red auricula for himself!

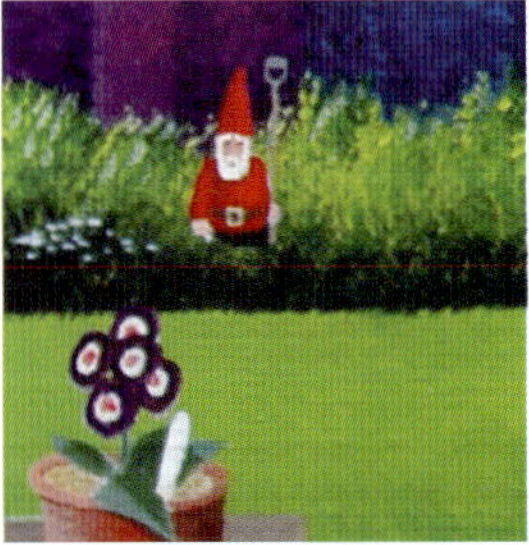

Auriculas
Acrylic on Linen
40 x 40 cm

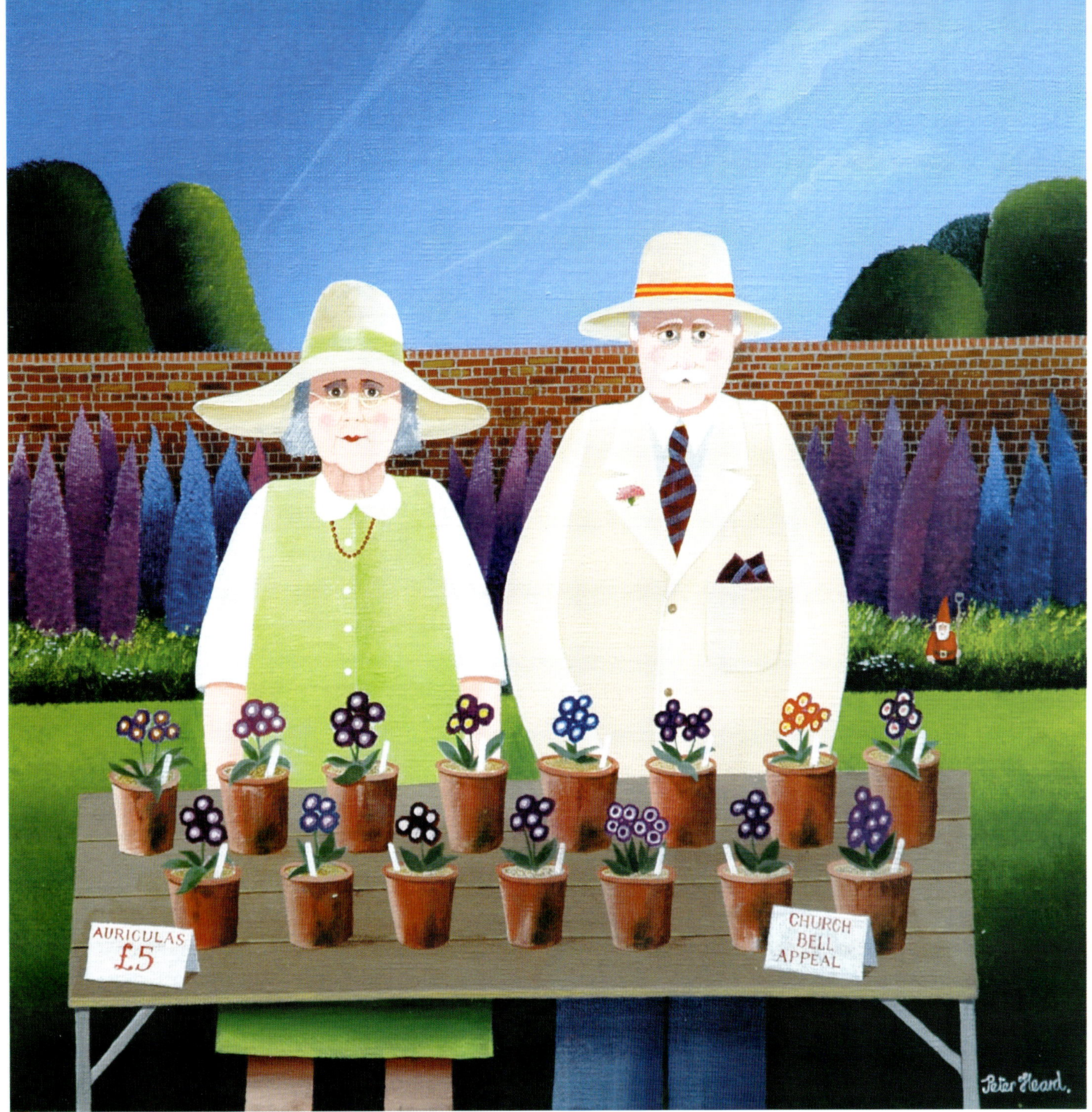
AURICULAS
£5
CHURCH
BELL
APPEAL
Peter Heard.

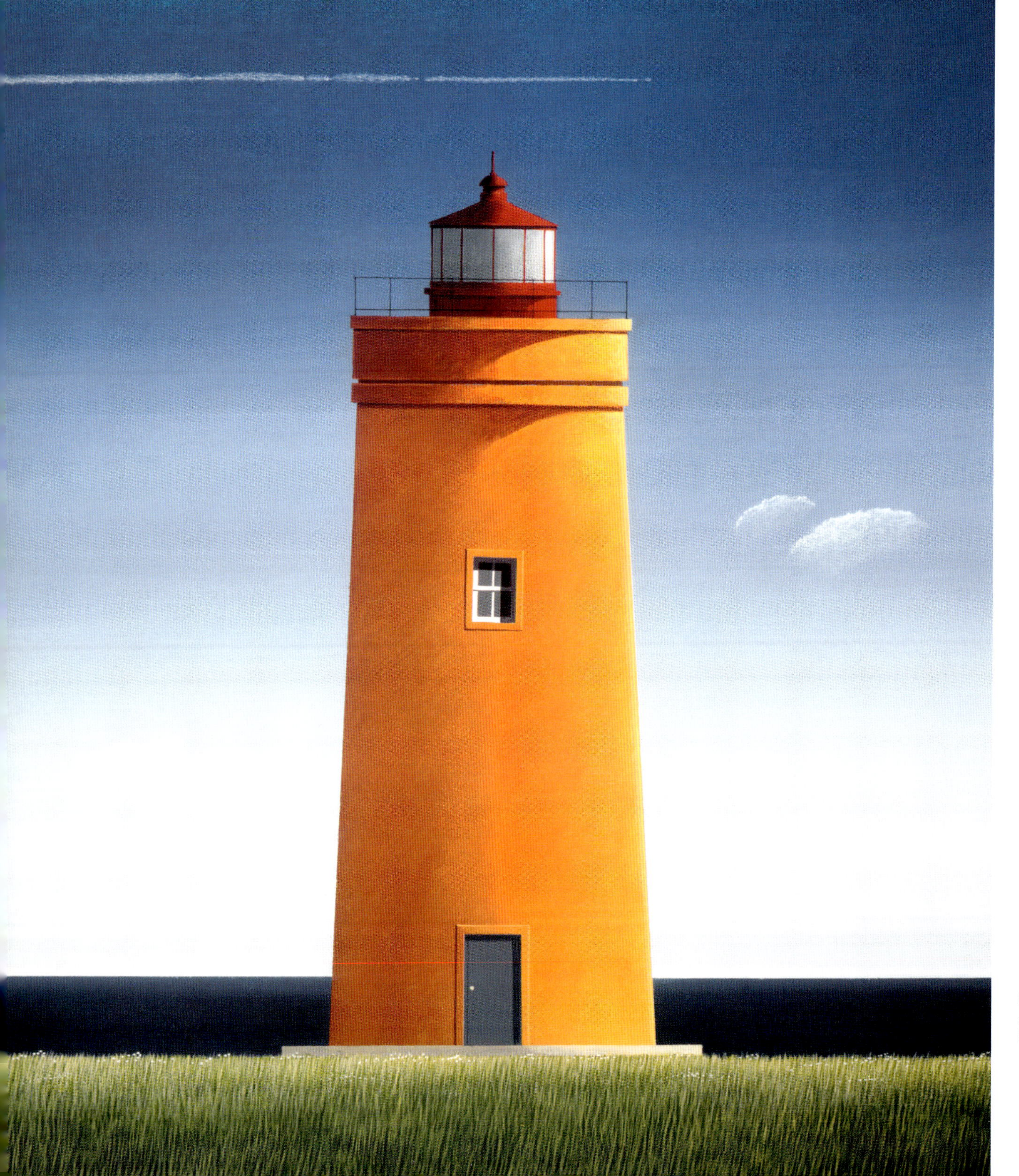

Keflavik
Acrylic on Linen
50 x 60 cm

CURRICULUM VITAE

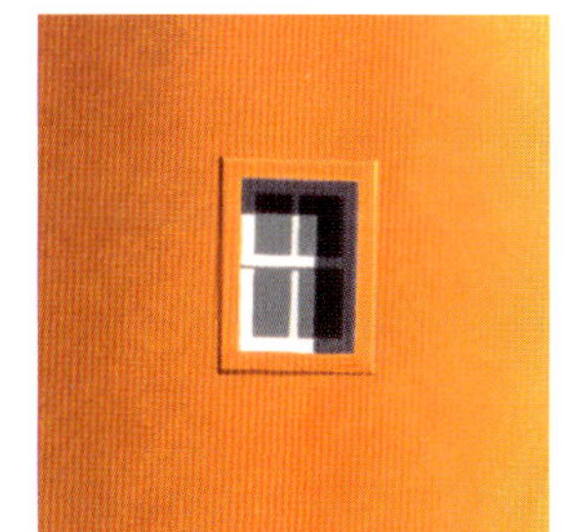

Born in London in 1939, lived in or around London for 67 years and now lives and works in Somerset.

SOLO EXHIBITIONS

1978 Portal Gallery London In England's Green and Pleasant Land.

1980 Portal Gallery London The English at their Sports and Pastimes.

1982 Portal Gallery London Dear Old England.

1986 Portal Gallery London Forever England.

1989 Portal Gallery London The English Difference.

1990 Central Square Gallery New Jersey USA.

2004 Artist's Harbour Gallery Portsmouth.

2006 Artist's Harbour Gallery Portsmouth.

2007 John Noott Gallery Worcestershire.

2009 John Noott Gallery Worcestershire - West Country Life

2011 John Noott Gallery Worcestershire - Loose Ends

GROUP EXHIBITIONS AND FAIRS

1977 British Primitive and Naïve Art IKON Gallery Birmingham.

1977 Naivii 77 International Exhibition of Naïve Art Zagreb.

1978 London Naïve Art Festival Hall London.

1985 Bath Festival of Naïve Art.

1989 Art Expo New York USA.

1990 Art Expo New York USA.

1991 Art Expo New York USA.

2004 On The Wall Olympia London.

2007 Affordable Art Fair London.

2008 Affordable Art Fair Bristol.

2008 Floren Gallery Poole Dorset.

2009 Affordable Art Fair London

2009 Affordable Art Fair Amsterdam

2010 John Noott Gallery Spring Exhibition

2012 The Hunter Gallery Long Melford

INDEX OF PAINTINGS

Sky
Acrylic on Linen
50 x 50 cm

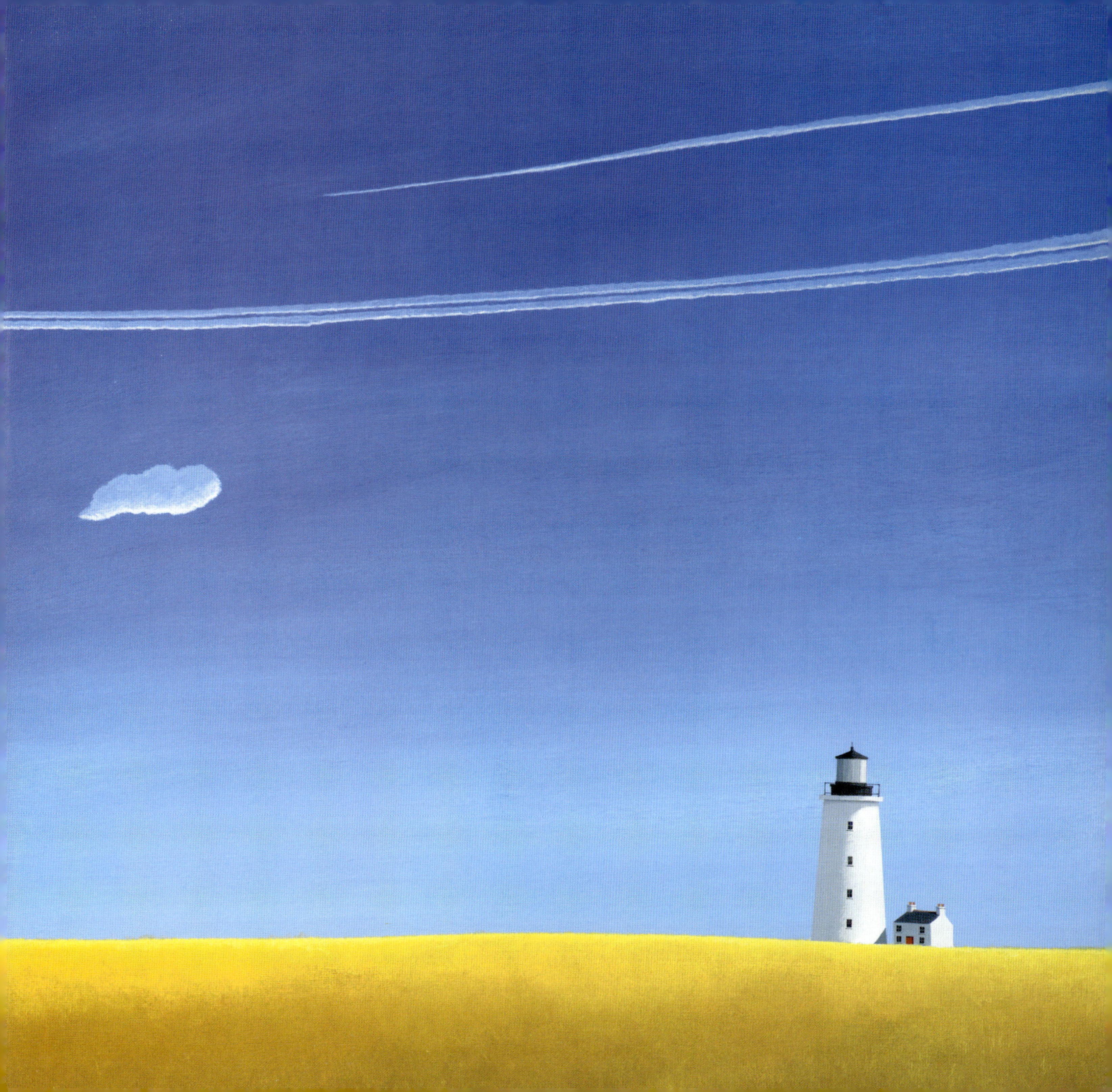

Peter Heard

Peter lives in Somerset where he moved a few years ago following a lifetime in London.
He shares his life with Mary and two cats, Foxglove and Bluebell.

Michael Woods

Mike is a journalist.
He is married with two children and lives with his wife Lesley in Lancashire.

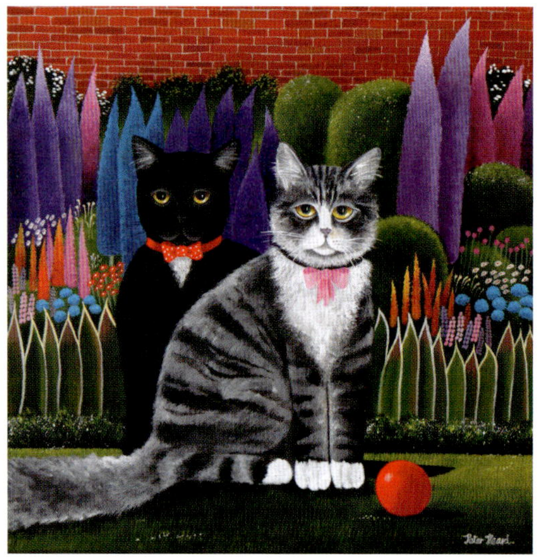

Website

peterheard.com

Original Paintings

John Noott Gallery
Bell Fine Art
The Hunter Gallery
Store Street Gallery

Limited Editions

dotrouge.co.uk

Cards

The Robertson Collection.